THIERRY
THE BIOGRAPHY
HENRY

OLIVER DERBYSHIRE

JB
JOHN BLAKE

Published by John Blake Publishing Ltd,
3 Bramber Court, 2 Bramber Road,
London W14 9PB, England

www.blake.co.uk

First published in paperback in 2006

ISBN 1 84454 281 5

British Library Cataloguing-in-Publication Data:

A catalogue record for this book is available from the British Library.

Design by www.envydesign.co.uk

Printed in Great Britain by Bookmarque

1 3 5 7 9 10 8 6 4 2

Papers used by John Blake Publishing are natural, recyclable products made
from wood grown in sustainable forests. The manufacturing processes conform
to the environmental regulations of the country of origin.

Photographs © Federation Francaise de Football, Cleva Media; Corbis; Empics;
Getty and Sporting Images.

Every attempt has been made to contact the relevant copyright-holders,
but some were unobtainable. We would be grateful if the appropriate people
could contact us.

Contents

Chapter one
The Boy from Paris

When the first film of the record-breaking *Star Wars* saga opened in 1977, another less-publicised but still earth-shattering event was taking place in a small community in southwest Paris: the world was welcoming the birth of a footballer blessed with talents from 'a galaxy far, far away'. Thierry Daniel Henry was born in the Les Ulis maternity clinic, on 17 August of that year, the first son of two immigrants from the French Antilles, Antoine Henry and his wife Maryse Sandia.

The young Caribbean couple had left their homes and families across the Atlantic and moved to France in search of a better life. Gone were the empty beaches, golden sand, clear water and blue skies of tropical Guadeloupe, replaced instead by the concrete jungle of suburban Paris. When Antoine, who likes to be known as 'Toni', and Maryse arrived in the mid-1970s, Les Ulis had a population of about

26,000, with a 40 per cent ethnic make-up, many of whom lived in state-subsidised, high-rise tower blocks. A grey canvas for the young footballer to illuminate with his skills, it was an area that had more abandoned supermarket trolleys than jumpers for goalposts. Thierry Henry will never forget the grim, concrete-rich surroundings. 'When I was growing up, all I saw was cement,' he says. 'Tall buildings, long buildings, walls we played football against.'

Turning adversity to advantage in developing skills for the future – in a style reminiscent of the Williams sisters, superstar siblings who grew up playing tennis together in the slums of LA – the young Thierry Henry and his brother Willy, two years his junior, played football with the local children in streets which most Parisians considered too dangerous to walk through at night. Willy was a gifted goalkeeper for Les Ulis junior and senior teams, but not a world-class talent like his big brother. Showing his passion for football, Thierry refused to let the surroundings dampen his ambitions. 'I'd occasionally notice the arrival of a police car,' Henry says today, 'but in the middle of a street football game, it meant nothing.'

Despite the rough neighbourhood in which they lived, the Henrys found solace in the flourishing community of other families from the Antilles. Toni came from Guadeloupe, and Maryse was originally from neighbouring Martinique. These were two Eden-esque French-governed islands in the Caribbean, both covered in dense tropical forest, beautiful banana and pineapple plantations and fields full of sugar cane, alongside rum distilleries, fishing villages and golden beaches. It is hard to imagine anyone wanting to give up such surroundings for the Paris ghetto, but the Henrys were prepared to sacrifice everything for their children.

'Everything I have, I got from my parents,' says Henry. 'They didn't have much, but whatever they had they were prepared to give up so that my brother Willy and I had a chance.'

Toni Henry was the kind of male role model supposedly missing in so much of today's society, a man who valued discipline and respect – he was also a good footballer. According to his old friend Tapha, Toni Henry was an aggressive and highly vocal forward, a real leader of the line. Tapha, a tall, wiry middle-aged greengrocer, came to Les Ulis from Senegal in the mid-1970s, at roughly the same time as Henry's parents, and he used to play football with Thierry's papa. He told the *Daily Telegraph* how they played day after day in the local park. 'Henry [senior] was a lively man on a football pitch,' he explains. 'He was a colourful man, aggressive, and passionate about the game. He loved his football. "Henry", as we all used to call him, was always shouting on the park and was a strong forward. He was always urging the boys on.

'We would all gather at the Pampre Stadium after work. You didn't have to call anyone or organise anything. A game would get started and we'd play until the sun went down. Girlfriends used to come and watch and, once he was big enough, Thierry was always on the sidelines watching his father play. Occasionally, his mother would come by, but she would watch from a distance.'

As far as football was concerned, this seemed to be the way of things in the Henry household: Toni at the centre of the action shouting encouragement, Maryse always in the background watching from afar. It was Toni Henry who declared that his son Thierry would be a footballer almost from the second he was born, as Henry himself later confessed to *GQ* magazine. 'It's strange but he always knew. People thought he was over the top to keep saying it when I was so young, but it didn't stop him… he just kept saying it louder.'

Toni Henry was dedicated to the belief that his son, whom he calls 'Titi', would make it as a footballer, going to all sorts of lengths to give his son every chance. He recalls one particular incident where the budding footballer came first. 'I was so determined he should get the best chance I actually lost a job over it once. I missed the start of a shift as a security guard after driving Titi to a game and was fired when I turned up two hours late.'

It was typical of Toni's commitment to his son's youthful promise – there were other jobs, but there was only one Thierry Henry. Toni's dedication in putting his son ahead of his work was all the more incredible in view of the family finances. 'There was not much money around and Titi had to wear the same boots as me when he was 12. Fortunately, our feet were about the same size at the time.'

Henry Senior is still effusive about his son's embryonic skills. 'He was such a gifted player. Even as a kid, he could cushion the ball, perform bicycle-kicks and do all the tricks. His pace was truly exceptional. Just as well because his game invites people to kick him…

'Speed actually runs in the family. I was quick myself, and my older brother was even quicker,' Toni continues. 'He was a champion of France at the 400 metres hurdles.'

These 'hurdler genes' make Thierry Henry a natural sportsman; he was always faster than his buddies and more than one of them said he should follow his uncle into athletics. But Thierry did not hear the call of the track, and remained faithful to his family's vision for him. 'My father always pushed me; he always wanted me to be a professional footballer. I didn't have too much choice.' It wasn't just athletics that Henry could have considered as he had the essential attributes required for a potential career in almost any sport: speed, strength, endurance and coordination. Toni Henry knew these skills could help him escape the mundane existence of many of his contemporaries and he was not going to let his son's talents go to waste.

'A lot of Titi's old pals are out of work and in odd bits of trouble with the law now,' Toni Henry said recently. 'There are some kids there who could have been top pros but they fell among the riff-raff because their parents did not care enough. I was determined that would not happen to Titi. I told him either school or sport were the only ways out. He was not too interested in school, so it had to be football. That is what we fell out about at times.'

Similar rows echo in countless households throughout the world – mothers and fathers who know best, children who refuse to listen. Despite his fabulous skills, Thierry Henry was just like any other boy; he wanted freedom to do what he wanted, to express himself and to make his own mistakes.

'I must admit we had some big shouting matches,' Toni continues. 'It is hard for kids to concentrate and Thierry was no different. Perhaps I was a bit suffocating, but I felt I had to keep on top of him. It was when Titi signed on for Monaco at 15 that he understood why I had kept on at him.'

Long before Monaco came knocking, young Henry could be found playing his first games with his friends after school and at the weekends, just like any other boy. The park pitches are still there with goal mouths which are bare of grass after lots of wear and tear from youngsters who, these days, run around pretending to be Thierry Henry. When Henry himself was playing there, it was always Marco Van Basten whom he would try to emulate. The Dutchman was graceful yet powerful, two-footed with tremendous close control, quick on the turn and supreme in the air. Most of these skills are evident in the Frenchman's game today, but it took a lot of hard work in the early days to get him where he is now.

'Henry is now a top player himself,' Van Basten has said in praise of his long-time fan. 'Everybody grows up with idols. For other people Henry will be an idol too. That's how it works; it goes from generation to generation. Henry is a very good player with special qualities; he scores a lot, he has unique acceleration and with his qualities he can be decisive in matches.'

'I would have enjoyed playing alongside him,' the new Holland coach added. 'It is easy to play with Henry, he anticipates very well. Together we would have been very "dangerous".'

As a kid, Thierry Henry was not always the team player he is at Arsenal. When he played park football, he admits he had a tendency to keep the ball all to himself. Some of his early coaches tried to explain the concept of collective play to him, to get him to pass the ball and to take on his share of defensive work. He listened to them and pretended to agree, but inside he was thinking, 'I am the one who scores the goals, let the others defend.' It was a far cry from the player who is often seen tracking back into his own penalty box for the sake of the team. But he had a lot to learn. The more Thierry played, the more he realised that football is a team game.

Henry started playing organised football with Les Ulis Under-10s for Claude Chezelles, his first real coach. He already had good ball control and pace in abundance. Chezelles remembers him well. 'He had all the attacking qualities. He just wanted to run at the goal with the ball. You couldn't get the ball off him. He was a small boy then, who already loved football. That's what stood out about him, though, those attacking qualities and his ability to race away with the ball.'

Chezelles had also played football with Henry's father Toni and, like all who have met him, he remembers him vividly. 'Thierry was all sweetness but his dad was very aggressive,' says Chezelles. 'Not in a bad way but it was clear what he wanted for Thierry.'

Indeed it was clear that Toni Henry wanted his son to play for the best team around and, when the opportunity arose, Thierry said goodbye to Les Ulis and joined Palaiseau, a small town ten miles up the road. The Palaiseau club president is Andre Decaux who vividly recalls a match that highlights the 'pushy parent' in Antoine Henry. 'Toni was very vocal,' Monsieur Decaux told the *People* newspaper. 'He felt that Thierry was not getting looked after by the ref.

It developed into a real scene. Toni and the coach got on to the pitch and the upshot was that we were disciplined and the coach was banned from the return game.'

Back then, according to Toni Henry, the junior leagues weren't too well regulated. 'Titi used to play against giants who would try to rough him up. There were a lot of young Africans in the junior leagues around Paris and, because many of them did not have birth certificates, some clubs used to claim they were a lot younger than their true age. Paris St Germain had a lad playing in the same age group as Thierry and he was found to be 23. It was pure mayhem.' It could get out of hand. 'Neither of us will ever forget a couple of games he played for Palaiseau against their closest championship rivals Villepinte. Titi was getting kicked to bits by a lad who looked at least five years older. It was sheer murder, but the ref would not give him any protection.'

As such a large influence in Thierry's life, Toni was not going to stand by and watch some brute of a defender attempt to end his son's career before it had started. In what must be considered an understatement, Toni says, 'I must admit I am more hot-headed than Thierry and, when he went down hurt from another bad foul, I could not take any more. I rushed on the pitch to sort things out and the coach came with me. It developed into a right punch-up. The upshot was the ref abandoned the game, the coach got suspended and we lost the points at a disciplinary hearing.'

Thierry's reaction showed the mental strength that has taken him to the pinnacle of the world game. Toni's eyes still light up when he talks about it. 'Titi decided the return match would be different. He told me he was going to destroy the opposition. The same huge lads were still there, but they could not get anywhere near him. He was brilliant. He ran the show on his own, scored both goals in a 2-1 win and told the coach the victory was for him. I had always known he had the talent. Now I knew he had the guts to go all the way.'

It is a testament to Thierry that he has never forgotten the people who helped him get where he is today, and he remains friends with his coach at Palaiseau, Jean-Marie Panza, whom he recently invited to Highbury for an emotional reunion. But Palaiseau were not the biggest of local clubs and Thierry eventually moved on to Viry Chatillon.

Viry Chatillon was a semi-professional club with a burgeoning reputation for improving aspiring young footballers. In the last decade, the club has provided 25 youngsters for the prestigious French football academy, 'L'Institut National de Football' in Clairefontaine, a treasure trove of world-class footballing talent. Thierry Pret, who now works as a scout for AS Cannes, was then the Under-15s coach at Viry Chatillon. Pret first saw Henry playing for Palaiseau, and approached his family about a move. Toni Henry was persuaded and Thierry soon became a member of the Under-15s squad.

Pret told the *Daily Telegraph*, 'His papa was a very present force in his footballing life, even though by then his father had divorced from his mother. Thierry was taller than boys his own age and was technically gifted. There were no signs then that he would be the hard player that he is today, chasing back to defend as he does at Arsenal and fighting for the ball. Back then he didn't work hard as a player, even though he had all the skills with his feet. What he didn't do very often was use his head, but he was an out-and-out goal-scorer.'

Pret's opinion is backed up by the statistics: in 26 matches for Viry-Chatillon, Thierry Henry scored 77 goals. 'He was a match-winner and he had a winner's attitude.' Speaking about Henry's retiring character – already he preferred to let his feet do the talking – Pret continues, 'Thierry was seen as shy by some people but I think he was just naturally reserved. He always came across as a likeable kid. I think even at that age he knew what he wanted and was intent on going out there and achieving it. The thing I will always remember about him is how much he wanted to play football. He was only 12 years old then, and the rest of the boys in the squad were 14 or 15. That didn't stop him wanting to play in every match.' Henry was already used to playing with older, bigger boys.

Pret also remembers Thierry's family. 'Maryse Sandia never came to matches. I spoke to her only on the phone. Toni was like two different people. He could be adorable. Then he would be pushing and pushing for Thierry, even when he didn't need to. He was always focused on what his son was doing, very focused on him, not the team. He was also very critical of the other players. It was evident that he had a deep love for his son. He pushed him and protected him.'

Another coach at Viry-Chatillon reckoned Toni Henry 'had more ambition for Thierry to be a professional player than the boy himself had at a young age'.

On top of the pressure Thierry felt from his father, he

found his mother was pushing him to improve his academic performance. Maryse was a popular member of the local neighbourhood and involved in the Antillean community. It was about this time that Henry's parents separated and Maryse left Les Ulis. She moved to Orsay, a pretty, quiet middle-class town, where she worked as a receptionist at one of the university halls of residence. She enrolled Thierry at Alexander Fleming College in Orsay. It was a good school and Maryse was determined that her son would have a good education. He was at the school for only two years, from the age of 11 to 13, before he was selected for the French football academy in Clairefontaine. His teachers at Alexander Fleming recall a quiet boy who mixed easily with the other children but did not stand out. It was a different matter, however, out on the football pitch.

'Titi lost count of the goals he scored,' Toni tells us. 'There were more than a hundred every season as a kid but he still remembers the ones he scored when the Monaco scout came to watch. I forget the score now but Thierry hit seven goals in that match. He was playing then for Viry Chatillon, a step up from Palaiseau, and his future with Monaco was sealed that day.'

It seems it was not just Thierry who lost count of the goals, as we hear from the Monaco scout Arnold Catalano who told *The People*, 'Word reached me about this skinny 13-year-old kid who could not stop scoring goals and I had to check him out for myself.

'I remember standing with his dad on the touchline waiting for the game to start. I was planning to get Thierry signed long before the game finished. Viry Chatillon won 6-

0 and he scored the lot. What struck me was how effortless he made it all look. He hardly appeared to strike the ball at all. He was so naturally gifted at placing it into the net. Just like he does so often now, he would pick up the ball on the left side of attack, move it inside at speed and score with his right foot. I see thousands of kids play football. But once in a while, you get a very special feeling.'

The exact details are lost to memory, but the fact remains he played a blinder and scored more goals than you could count on one hand. Having been scouted by Monaco, Thierry headed off for what is considered to be one of the toughest trials in world football. In March 1990, the young master Henry arrived at France's esteemed football academy, L'Institut National de Football (INF) in Clairefontaine. The successful French equivalent of the FA's now-defunct national football school at Lilleshall, the French Football Federation set up the INF in 1988 and it has since developed a reputation as one of the world's finest training centres. It has outstanding facilities, including grass, artificial and indoor pitches, saunas, a gymnasium, and tennis courts. But the children also continue their academic studies and, on the pitch, the coaches concentrate on technique above all else.

Henry was joined at Clairefontaine by 800 other 12- and 13-year-old boys, all hopeful of being selected as one of only 24 lucky recipients of a 3-year scholarship. After three months of intensive tests, Thierry Henry emerged as one of the chosen few, but his skills on the pitch were nearly undermined by poor results in the classroom. 'We really had to convince the college principal to take him because he was such a super player,' Claude Desseau, the former Director of INF, told the *Observer Sports Monthly* magazine. 'He finally agreed to make a rare exception for Thierry. And, happily, Thierry got more serious about that side of things and went on to do very well with his education.'

Despite his early academic troubles, Henry packed his bags to leave home at the tender age of 13 and board at the 'finisher's finishing school'. He joined a class full of now famous names: Nicolas Anelka, Louis Saha, David Trezeguet, William Gallas and Jerome Rothen were all contemporaries in his time at what Michel Platini calls 'the house of French football'. Each one has gone on to play for France.

Saha, now a striker with Manchester United, recalls their arrival. 'When we first got there, our only dream was to become professional. Then the coaches told us, "You don't know how to play football. We will teach you."'

Henry talks equally wistfully about those formative days. 'To be a footballer was just a dream and I don't believe in dreams. I only deal in what is real. To be honest, I've never thought about what I could get out of football or where it would take me. I just wanted to play.'

It was this devil-may-care attitude that initially got him in trouble with the coaches. Andre Merelle, one of Henry's three mentors at Clairefontaine, remembers the teenage striker very well as he told the *Daily Telegraph*. 'He was very intelligent, but at the start one of the few who didn't work well. That changed. He quickly became more diligent.

'I remember his parents were divorced when he came here and he was living with his mother, but there were no signs that he was homesick. His father was always close to him, visited quite often and came to matches. His father was a big influence, but sometimes too close.'

If there had been any worry about the young star getting homesick it was quickly dismissed, as he became good friends with Saha and Anelka, boys from similar backgrounds. All three were born in Paris, have Antillean ancestry, and are familiar with Creole, the bastardised French language of the Franco-Caribbean.

Saha explains, 'Our families are all from the Antilles in the West Indies, and we always used to hang out and speak Creole to each other. The three of us used to sit around and dream about playing in the World Cup.' They're still friends now as Saha confirms: 'My parents know Thierry's parents well and I sometimes go to stay at their place for my holidays.'

Having settled in at Clairefontaine, Henry had to knuckle down to some hard work, in the classroom, and more importantly on the pitch. One of his coaches, at 'L'Institut' was former Fulham and Liverpool trainer Christian Damiano, who says, 'Football is like school. For a young player, technique is more important than speed, strength or physique. Thierry already had great balance and coordination, but some bad footballing habits. So we worked on his technique for three years.'

By now, Thierry Henry was turning into the man we know today: with the virtue of respect instilled in him by his mother, he admits to getting angry when 'somebody doesn't hold a door open for someone else'. The mantra to 'never settle for what you have', drummed into him by his father, drove him on – 'Even if I scored four goals in a match he would say, "But you missed a cross in the 70th minute."'

After three years boarding at Clairefontaine, he had developed the mental strength required to live away from home or even in another country and, with three years of the best coaching France has to offer behind him, Thierry had now fine-tuned his football skills and was ready for the top flight in France.

After a brief stint at FC Versailles and having been scouted by Arnold Catalano years earlier, Henry joined AS Monaco. More significantly, he now began playing for a man he has since referred to as 'his spiritual father', a bespectacled man from Alsace by the name of Arsene Wenger.

Chapter two
Monte Carlo or Bust

'I was speechless. Just imagine, I was 16, I had grown up in a poor neighbourhood in Paris, I had never seen anything like it... we hardly ever saw bikes in my neighbourhood, never mind cars and boats. Here there were big boats everywhere, big cars, beautiful women, the sun, the sea, famous people everywhere – I thought I was in a movie.'

The kid from the backstreets of Paris had arrived in Monte Carlo and his head was spinning. The Principality, a millionaire's playground, tax haven and home to countless film and sports stars was now the stamping ground of a young man whose star was very much in the ascendant. And his footballing career would continue to progress with the help and advice of the AS Monaco coach.

'Arsene Wenger is a man I trusted and respected instantly,' Henry told GQ magazine. 'It's funny, but Arsene can make you do things without you noticing. When he spoke to me I

felt something for him and I think he felt something too.'
And so began the relationship many Arsenal fans would say
was made in heaven.

As a 16-year-old, Henry was playing as a striker in the
Monaco youth team and the French Under-17 team, which
was managed by the French FA's then director of coaching
Gerard Houllier, who was impressed from the start. 'I
knew Thierry could be special from the first time I played
him in the Under-17 national team,' Houllier admitted
recently. 'He had speed and technique, power and finesse.
Unusual combinations.'

It was two weeks after Thierry's 17th birthday when
Wenger gave the youngster a chance to shine. In the derby
match at home to Nice, Henry started at centre-forward, but
could not prevent *les Monegasques* going down 2–0. He was
also unable to stop Arsene from losing his job. Wenger was
sacked on 17 September 1994, just over two weeks after
giving Henry his debut. Monaco were in 17th place in 'Le
Championnat' and Wenger was in the final year of his
contract. Ironically, Wenger had turned down Bayern
Munich when the German giants tried to sign him during the
previous summer break.

Wenger's position as Monaco coach was initially taken
over by two of the club's former players, Jean Petit and Jean-
Luc Ettori. This double act did not last long and Ettori soon
took sole command but only until March 1995 when he was
ousted, and self-confessed 'old-school' coach Gerard Banide
took over for the rest of the campaign. Banide refused to
believe that results mattered above all else, a controversial
thought for someone taking control of a big name in the

wrong half of the division, and he went on to impose his brand of the beautiful game on Monaco. In a season of so much upheaval, it was difficult for Thierry to shine through and, when first-choice striker Sonny Anderson returned from injury, it was he, not Henry, who played up front with Mickael Madar, the French international striker who went on to play so unmemorably for Everton in the Premiership. Thierry was young and full of enthusiasm and he refused to be dismayed. 'I was just glad to be in the team. Someone said to me to "play on the left" and I did.'

It was this move to the left flank that helped Henry make a name for himself, as fourth-choice attacker behind Anderson, Madar and the Nigerian Victor Ikpeba; at first he was finding first-team appearances few and far between. But on the wing he started playing more regularly and on Saturday, 29 April 1995 he grabbed his first professional goals, scoring twice in the home game against RC Lens which Monaco won 6–0. Thierry finished his first senior season with three goals from eight games, having notched his first away goal in a 3–3 draw in Nantes. Not a bad statistic when you consider he only started in half of those games.

Monaco crashed out of the Coupe de France (French Cup) in the last 32 against Poitiers from National Ligue 1A, the French third division, and lost to Montpellier in the quarter-final of the Coupe de la Ligue (League Cup). In the league, they finished the season in sixth position, a massive 22 points behind champions FC Nantes Atlantique – a disappointing campaign for a club of Monaco's stature – and Gerard Banide was replaced as manager by French footballing legend Jean Tigana.

Tigana was an integral part of the French national side of the mid-1980s, winning the European Championship in 1984 and coming within a whisker of World Cup glory. He played in one of the greatest-ever French midfields alongside Michel Platini, Alain Giresse and Luis Fernandez, a perfect blend of individual talents. In the previous season in only his second year as a coach, Tigana had guided Olympique Lyonnais to second place in the league.

With the new manager in charge, the 1995–96 season began in hope and, keen to give youth a chance, Tigana started with Thierry Henry on the left wing in the first game. Henry repaid the faith of his manager by playing well and winning a penalty, which Anderson converted in a 3–1 win, at home against Stade Rennais. But this sound performance wasn't enough to keep Thierry in the starting line-up. He was in and out of the team after that, making a lot of appearances from the bench including his first taste of European competition.

On Tuesday, 12 September 1995, Henry came on with 20 minutes left to play in Monaco's UEFA Cup first-round match at home to Leeds United. *Les Monegasques* lost 3–0, and the game was overshadowed by a sickening clash of heads between two of the Monaco players. Centre-back Basile Boli crashed into substitute keeper Marc Delaroche as Leeds' Ghanaian striker, Tony Yeboah claimed the goal that completed his hat-trick. Both home players were stretchered off and rushed to hospital where they remained overnight. Having already made two substitutions, Monaco had to play the last ten minutes of the game with only ten men. Henry understandably failed to make an impression, but had his first experience of English football which he would grow to dominate within a decade. Henry didn't feature in the return leg, which Monaco won 1–0 at home, but it was not enough to progress.

The season continued with frequent substitute appearances, occasional goals and intermittent starts. Henry was even playing second fiddle to Christopher Wreh, a player who, despite scoring crucial goals in Arsenal's 1998 League and Cup double, is still best known for being the cousin of George Weah (World, European, and African player of the year in 1995).

At the end of the 1995–96 season, Monaco were third in the league, having failed to make much impression in any of their three cup campaigns. As well as their first-round exit from the UEFA Cup, Monaco lost to Lille in the last 16 of the French Cup, and to Lyon in the quarter-finals of the League Cup. On a personal note, Thierry had continued his development at a steady rate, scoring three goals in 18 league appearances and making his UEFA Cup debut. In June he was selected as captain of the France Under-18 squad, along with schoolmates Trezeguet and Anelka, for the 1996 UEFA European Under-18 Championship in France. Henry enjoyed his introduction to international tournaments as the French squad won the trophy, and he led by example, scoring the only goal in the final against Spain.

Henry returned to Monaco with his first medal round his neck, but the new season started much the same as the last – he came off the bench for most of his appearances. One new face in the Monaco squad was John Collins. The cultured Scotland midfielder had joined on one of the first Bosman free transfers from Glasgow Celtic, and he remembers the Frenchman as he was then, with room for improvement in his game. 'Henry wasn't a pure winger because he didn't have enough quality when he delivered with his left foot. He always wanted to come inside the full-back,' says Collins, before admitting his admiration for the Frenchman's current ability. 'Thierry wasn't complete then. It's a credit to him and to Arsene Wenger that he's reached such a standard. These days he can go both ways.'

He may have been one-dimensional according to his Scottish team-mate, but Henry still managed to weigh in with goals, becoming something of a 'super-sub' as Tigana liked to utilise the impetuosity of youth, allowing him to 'boil with impatience on the bench'. Despite a lack of playing time at Monaco, he still managed to force his way into the French Under-21 squad, *les Espoirs* or 'the hopes'. He made his Under-21 debut against Norway, two years to the day after Arsene Wenger had given him his league debut. It was about this time that the French press started to wax lyrical about the talents of their young winger. L'ATTAQUANT DE DEMAIN (the attacker of tomorrow) read the headline in *Le Monde*, and it wasn't just the journalists who were taking note.

Coaches and scouts from across Europe were keeping tabs on the talented youngster. Henry was often watched by Manchester United scout Les Kershaw. 'I saw him play for Monaco several times and, although he had phenomenal pace, he looked raw. But now I think he's a wonderful player.' Manchester United may have had their reservations, but former Chelsea manager Claudio Ranieri was far keener to sign him up. 'I watched him a long time ago when I was manager of Fiorentina and he was playing for the French Under-21 team. I said to my chairman, "He is the Muhammad Ali of the football pitch because he has such elegance, such speed. He does everything with such style." I said, "Please buy him because he is one of the best," but it did not happen for some reason.' With interested clubs from England and Italy in the offing, attention was sure to come from La Liga, and it was Real Madrid who came in with the sting.

Under French League policy, young players sign three contracts: one as an apprentice, another as a trainee and a third as a professional. A player is obliged to sign professional forms with the club at which he trained, but since the infamous Bosman ruling, it is seen as a restriction of trade not to allow that player to sign for another club overseas. It is because of this legal loophole that Henry signed a contract with Real Madrid, in the same way that Arsenal managed to sign Nicolas Anelka, as a 17-year-old from Paris St Germain for only a nominal fee. Unfortunately for Real Madrid, Henry would not be wearing the famous white shirt the following season.

After signing his agreement with Real Madrid, he then signed another contract, this time with Monaco. Reports suggest there may only have been a couple of hours between these two pieces of business, completed with two different agents. The problem for Real was that the contract he signed for them was negotiated by Jean-François Larios, despite the fact Thierry was already contracted to another agent, Alain Migliaccio. The football world's governing body, FIFA, stepped in to resolve the argument between the two clubs. FIFA fined Henry £40,000, also fined Real Madrid and finally cancelled the agreement because it had been fixed up by an agent not registered with FIFA. According to one friend, the proposed move was set up by the player's father, Toni Henry, and the fall-out from the failed transfer caused a temporary rift between father and son.

Having fought off the attentions of arguably the world's largest club, Monaco were determined to keep hold of their brightest young player. Thierry was regularly playing alongside Patrick Vieira for the French Under-21s and Monaco hoped the colossal midfielder would advise Thierry against moving abroad at too young an age.

After two impressive years at AS Cannes, Vieira moved to AC Milan, aged just 19. During his time in northern Italy he made only a handful of appearances for the *Rossoneri*. Vieira was hampered by the three-foreigner rule in place in the Italian League at the time, so as a foreign midfielder he had double the obstacles ahead of him to break into the first team, and he was not helped by the impressive form of his compatriot Marcel Desailly, Dejan Savicevic of Yugoslavia, and Croatia's Zvonimir Boban in midfield, and Liberian George Weah up front.

In Milan's squad of household names and global stars Vieira struggled to feature in his manager Fabio Capello's thoughts, and failed to make an impact on Serie A. At the end of the 1995–96 season, Arsene Wenger snapped him up and gave him a chance to shine at Arsenal. But the man who would one day captain Henry for club and country did not feel the need to advise his fellow countryman, and Henry said at the time, 'I do not speak to him [Vieira] about Milan.'

Despite any off-the-field disruptions, Henry and Monaco continued to grow together. At the end of 1996 Thierry was named France's Young Footballer of the Year, by *France Football* magazine, on the back of his fine performances for the French Under-18s and Monaco. The Principality side were going well in the UEFA Cup and jostling for top spot with Paris St Germain in Le Championnat. Henry had scored eight league goals by Christmas and made another five appearances in Europe, breaking his scoring duck against Borussia Monchengladbach in a game that Monaco won 4–2. Henry's performance was described as 'the difference between the two sides' by the French newspapers after he bagged the decisive third goal. With the scores level at 2–2, Henry came off the bench and within ten minutes had put Monaco ahead. It was a beautiful goal: he sprinted 50 metres, racing away from Stefan Effenberg, to finish with aplomb. Ikpeba added the fourth in injury-time and Monaco were in control of the tie and looking forward to an extended run in Europe.

As the New Year began, Monaco were hoping to continue their good pre-Christmas league form in the Cup, but in their second game back after the month-long winter break, they crashed out of the French Cup 1–0 away to lowly Laval. It was quite an upset, the Principality's big fish losing to minnows from the French second division. But Henry was in no doubt as to how it had come to pass. 'They wanted it more than us, and they won,' he said philosophically. The press had their own theory as to why *les Monegasques* had fallen at the first hurdle; the match against title rivals PSG was only a week away and looming large on the horizon: surely the Monaco players were getting ahead of themselves and ignoring the football cliché of taking it 'one game at a time'. Talking after the cup defeat, Monaco's Belgian midfielder Enzo Scifo was having none of it. 'In the two weeks we have been back in training, no one has mentioned the match against Paris St Germain. It's true that everyone thinks of it a little because there's so much at stake, but that has nothing to do with today's game. This week we will prepare for the match very seriously.'

Henry agreed with his team-mate: 'There's no more pressure on us [for next week] because we lost today. We will recover for the match against Paris, and try our hardest. The true preparation was done in the break. We won in Le Mans [in the League Cup] and lost in Laval, but we'll try and get back on track against Paris. As for knowing who is the better side, we'll see that on Sunday.' On the Sunday in question it was obvious to all present as Monaco triumphed 2–0 in le Stade Louis II. Henry was a lively presence on the left wing, repaying the manager's confidence for such an important match, and the win put Monaco seven points ahead of the Parisian giants. They now enjoyed a healthy lead with 14 league games left to play, which was testament to the development of Monaco's true title credentials, having overhauled the eight-point lead PSG held over their rivals the previous October. With their place at the top of the league cemented and the memory of the cup shock wiped out, the Monaco players' thoughts turned again to European competition.

In the UEFA Cup, they were drawn against Newcastle United, and had the unenviable task of attempting to become the first French team to beat an English team in 20 years of European competition. The Geordie 'Magpies' were flying high, having finished a close second behind Manchester United in the league the previous season, and they were hard on their heels once more heading into the quarter-finals of the UEFA Cup. Newcastle had already disposed of another French side in the previous round, having beaten Metz 3–1 on aggregate, and they went into the first match against Monaco full of confidence but short on strikers. Alan Shearer, Les Ferdinand, Peter Beardsley and Faustino Asprilla were all out injured, and this lack of firepower up front was to prove costly as Monaco won the first leg 1–0 in Newcastle.

Henry played the whole game, and created the solitary goal, running to the byline and cutting back a sumptuous ball for Sonny Anderson to slot home. But it was the Geordie faithful who left a lasting impression on the young winger. 'When they all shout the same thing at the same time, it is really incredible; the atmosphere was extraordinary,' he said in awe. The noise and colour of St James's Park's massive crowd was a culture shock to Thierry, who was used to playing a lot of home league games in front of Monaco's meagre hardcore of 2,500 fans.

In the return leg, it didn't get any better for the 'Toon Army' as their team were crushed 3–0 in Monaco. Henry started again, playing well and building on his reputation for being a big-game player. Newcastle suffered the ignominy of being the first English side to be knocked out of Europe by a French side in 20 years, ironically for the first time since Bastia defeated Newcastle in October 1977 when Thierry was just two months old.

In the league Monaco continued their march towards the title in first place and, in the semi-finals of the UEFA Cup, they were drawn against Internazionale of Milan. During the first leg in the San Siro, Henry was well shackled by the veteran Italian right-back Beppe Bergomi. Their duel was representative of the game as a whole as Monaco were well beaten by a 3–1 scoreline.

In the return leg, Henry started on the bench and Monaco defended more solidly than in the first game, under little pressure from an Italian side happy to keep nine or ten players behind the ball in typical *catenaccio* style (a system of playing football, with an emphasis on defence and tactical fouls – *Catenaccio*: from the Italian meaning 'door-bolt'). Henry finally entered the fray with half an hour to play as Tigana went for the 2–0 victory that would see Monaco into the final. With almost his first touch of the ball, Henry ran through and put the ball in the back of the net, only to see his effort ruled out for offside. When Victor Ikpeba scored ten minutes later, the whole stadium erupted in celebration and fans urged their side forward for the second goal that would see them progress to the final. Unfortunately for home supporters, Inter's keeper, the legendary Gianluca Pagliuca, was proving tough to beat and in the final minutes even Monaco's eccentric goalkeeper, Fabien Barthez, was going forward for corners. But the vital second goal proved elusive, even with six minutes of injury-time, and Monaco were out of the UEFA Cup.

Back in Le Championnat, Monaco refused to give up their lead, and on Saturday, 3 May 1997 they won the league without even playing. Paris St Germain were held to a 2–2 draw in their home game against Bordeaux. With only two games left to play, the eight-point gap between PSG and

Monaco was unassailable and the trophy was heading south. With the title secured, *les Monegasques* went out the next day to play Caen at home in a carnival atmosphere; their fans were still celebrating on the way to the stadium and looking forward to some champagne football worthy of the occasion.

After a goalless first half, the match sprang to life with four goals in 20 minutes. Monaco were twice ahead, first through Victor Ikpeba and later through Henry, scoring his first Monaco goal for five months, but Caen drew level each time as they continued their battle against relegation, and the game finished 2–2. The players would have preferred to celebrate with a win, but the fans did not care and hundreds of them poured on to the pitch at the final whistle.

It was Monaco's first league title for nine years, since Wenger's troops had triumphed in 1987–88, and their first trophy since winning the French Cup in 1991, again under Wenger. Monaco had the tightest defence in the league, and the most prolific attack; they finished the season 12 points ahead of PSG, and Henry was voted '*meilleur espoir*', or best young player, by his fellow professionals l'Union Nationale des Footballeurs Professionnels Francais (UNFP), the French equivalent of England's Professional Footballers' Association, the PFA. Henry had 9 league goals from 36 games, and 1 goal in the UEFA Cup from 9 performances.

After a long and tiring season the beaches of Guadeloupe must have seemed very inviting, but Thierry was called up for the annual Toulon international tournament, possibly the most prestigious of friendly tournaments for young footballers. Henry was captain of the French Under-21 squad which dominated the opposition, winning every game en route to the final, where they beat Portugal 2–1 after extra-time. Thierry was joint top scorer with three goals, and was named player of the tournament. But his season still was not finished.

After such a brilliant showing at 'le Tournoi de Toulon', the media were calling for Henry to abandon the French Under-20s, who were on their way to the World Youth Cup, and join the full French squad for 'le Tournoi de France', the dress rehearsal for the World Cup that was to be held the following year. The national coach, Aime Jacquet, was asked, 'Why haven't you called up Thierry Henry?'

'With regard to the attack, I'm keeping my options open. If a player is good enough, they can get in the French team. I made that clear to young Henry,' Jacquet said. 'You ask me why I've made this decision. You want me to take away from this kid the chance to win the World Youth Cup? Do you think that I would take him with me and leave him on the bench. That I'd make him play scraps of matches while his buddies become world champions, he'd never forgive me!'

So in early June, while France were playing hosts to Brazil, Italy and England, Henry, on the edge of the full squad and in the thoughts of Jacquet, headed off to the World Youth Cup in Malaysia, as captain of the French Under-20 team. The squad contained all the players from the Toulon tournament including his 'buddies' – Trezeguet, Anelka, and Gallas – but France could only finish second in their group, behind Brazil, and lost in the quarter-finals to Uruguay, 7–6 on penalties, after the match finished 1–1, with Trezeguet missing France's vital eighth spot-kick. His season finally over at the end of June, Henry could now take a holiday and bask in the glory of his successful season.

Chapter three
Top of the World

'I told everyone when Thierry was eight he would play one day for his country. They thought it was just another father talking at the time. But I was at Lens to watch him play his first international for France against South Africa at the age of 20. I cried like a kid, seeing him out there as they played the *Marseillaise*.' These were the tearful words of Toni Henry, who has since returned to his childhood home in the French Antilles, and who added, 'I get to watch Thierry on TV now. He is a living god here in Guadeloupe.'

Thierry Henry made his international debut on 11 October 1997 at le Stade Felix Bollaert, Lens. France beat South Africa 2–1 and Henry played the whole game on the left wing in Aime Jacquet's 4-2-3-1 formation. It was the first international of the season and the press had been clamouring for Henry's inclusion ever since the summer's *Le Tournoi de France*. The tournament had been a great success off the pitch with everything running smoothly: all the games were sold out; there were no problems with transport or fans. But on the pitch France had been far less impressive, losing to England and only managing draws against Italy and Brazil. With the home team finishing third out of four teams, the French press had been less than impressed, and as the new season began there was more and more talk about Henry as the 'great hope' of French football.

'Titi' had returned to Monaco to join a new-look squad for pre-season training. The title-winning team had broken up and a number of key players had moved on to pastures new: left-back Emmanuel Petit had gone to Arsenal, along with the versatile Gilles Grimandi; right-back Patrick Blondeau had also moved to England, where he spectacularly failed to impress with Sheffield Wednesday; and star striker Sonny Anderson had moved to Spanish giants Barcelona. A number of other squad players had also left, making space for new recruits such as midfielders Stephane Carnot from Guingamp, and Fabian Lefevre of Montpellier, bright young full-back Willy Sagnol from second division side Saint Etienne and Nantes' veteran striker Japhet N'Doram.

It was not just the new signings who were excited about the new season, as the exodus helped create space for Henry's schoolmate and France Under-21 buddy David Trezeguet, who had been limited to just a handful of first-team outings in the previous campaign. The 1997–98 season also heralded AS Monaco's first outing in the UEFA

Champions League as well as Thierry Henry's arrival as a football superstar.

Monaco got off to a bad start on the domestic front, only picking up four points from the opening five games. Tigana was only using Henry sparingly as the youngster recovered from his long and hectic previous season. That was why he did not feature in Monaco's first-ever Champions League match. In Group F with Sporting Lisbon, Bayer Leverkusen, and Lierse SK, Monaco went away to the Portuguese champions and lost 3–0.

A fortnight later it was a different story altogether. Monaco were at home to Bayer Leverkusen, Henry started and the German title-holders were beaten 4–0. Henry was a constant menace to the Leverkusen defence, opening the scoring after half an hour and running Robert Kovac ragged. The Croatian international defender, was sent off, by English referee David Elleray in the 70th minute after one foul too many on the magnificent French youngster. Playing the last twenty minutes against ten men, Henry exploited the extra space, using his pace and vision to devastating effect, creating two goals for Victor Ikpeba and claiming a second for himself. Tigana was understandably delighted with the performance of his starlet. 'Thierry Henry was very good,' the coach said. 'He found his legs, and now I'll be able to use him to the full.'

Henry's form was returning along with the pace, vision and passing that had set French football fans' tongues wagging the previous season. Again he was turning chances into goals and national coach Aime Jacquet was taking notice. Two weeks after Henry's first Champions League appearance came his international debut, and his father's tears. Back in the French League, Monaco's indifferent form continued, but in European competition *les Monegasques* continued their recovery with home and away victories over the Belgian champions Lierse. Henry played in both games and scored the opener at le Stade Louis II.

After the home game against Lierse, Henry joined up again with Patrick Vieira in the French Under-21 team for a European Championship qualifier against Norway. The match was not particularly impressive; France won 2–1 and Trezeguet scored both goals – Henry was booked ten minutes from time. But in the dressing room at the end of the match, a far more memorable meeting took place. 'One day, during a France v Norway Under-21 game, Arsene came to the changing rooms looking for Patrick Vieira and told me, "You're wasting your time on the wing, you should ask your coach to put you back up front, then you'd have a brand-new career,"' Thierry recalls. 'I found that pretty tough to imagine. I had won a championship with Monaco playing on the left.' Lacking the courage of Wenger's convictions, Henry returned to Monaco and didn't speak to Tigana about it, ensuring he was stuck playing out on the left wing.

When Sporting Lisbon came to Monaco in late November, it was a game the Portuguese had to win; they were third in the group, five points behind Monaco and Leverkusen, with only two games left to play. Monaco had put their patchy league form behind them and came into the game on the back of four straight wins. The hosts' confidence was understandably high at the start of the game, but by half-time they were reeling on the ropes. After 15 minutes, Monaco's defensive lynchpin, centre-back Martin Djetou, had gone off injured, and Sporting took advantage of the disorganisation that followed, scoring twice before the break through Luis Miguel and an Oceano penalty. At half-time, Tigana had what would be diplomatically called 'an honest and constructive discussion' with the players, admitting, 'I was not too hard, but I had to shake them a little.'

Whatever he said had the desired effect on his team as they came out for the second half with more purpose and desire. *Les Monegasques* were helped by the tentative approach of their opponents. Desperate for the three points and 2–0 up, the men from Lisbon sat back and defended their penalty area, but they were ruthlessly punished by Henry and his young accomplice Trezeguet. Midway through the second half, Trezeguet pulled Monaco back into the game and, ten minutes later, they were level as Henry struck. Monaco still weren't finished and the onslaught continued into injury-time, when Henry grabbed his second and Monaco's third to take the Principality club to the top of the group and send the fans home happy. The captain, goalkeeper Fabien Barthez, was elated. 'We proved this evening that Monaco is a large team, of European standard,' he eulogised.

Monaco's final game in Group F was away against Bayer Leverkusen and, with both sides on 12 points, it seemed a draw would guarantee the two clubs going through to the knock-out stages. In the 1997–98 season of the Champions League, there were six groups and the six group-winners went through to the quarter-finals, along with the two runners-up with most points. Bearing this in mind, it was hardly a surprise that the game petered out into a draw, with Henry grabbing one goal as the match finished 2–2.

Approaching Christmas, Monaco were top of the league again with a run of seven straight wins behind them, and they flew to Metz, also known as *les Messins*, full of confidence. Metz were also riding high, having gone eight games without defeat and, when Monaco's plane was diverted to Luxembourg due to a storm, *les Monegasques* had to finish their journey by coach. They could be forgiven for thinking it was not going to be their day.

The match started scrappily as might be expected in such adverse conditions. The home side were first to find their feet, with a young Robert Pires pulling the strings from midfield. Midway though the first half, *les Messins* took the lead through centre-back, Philippe Gaillot. In the second half, Monaco fell further behind against the run of play, when the referee awarded a highly dubious penalty against them, which was converted by Bruno Rodriguez. Monaco chased the game and it was no surprise when they conceded a third, a splendid lob by Belgian midfielder Danny Boffin.

The result meant that Metz overtook Monaco at the top of the League going into the winter break, and both sets of players were more than happy to leave the rain-swept pitch of le Stade Symphorien for sweeter climes. Henry had enjoyed a successful autumn, making his international debut and scoring four goals in 19 league games, but it was in the Champions League that he had really made a name for himself with six goals in five games. The whole of Europe, it seemed, was taking note.

But in the first games back after the holidays, *les*

Monegasques may have felt a bit more 'wish we weren't here...' as they first crashed out of the *Coupe de Ligue* at home against Niort, who were 12th in Division Two, and followed that up by losing in the league to AS Cannes, who were firmly rooted at the bottom of the top flight, again in le Stade Louis II. To add insult to injury, the Cannes goalscorer was the Swiss striker Marco Grassi, whom Monaco had released the previous summer after he failed to score in 12 league games in the Principality.

In the wake of these two defeats, Tigana took the opportunity to bolster the squad with the signing of the diminutive Ludovic Giuly from Olympique Lyonnais. The coach felt Giuly's pace and ability down the right would complement Henry's natural width on the left. Monaco's form did improve with eight points from the next four games, but only days before the first leg of the Champions League quarter-final, Monaco lost 1–0, away to Bastia.

In the draw for the last eight, in December, Monaco were paired with English champions Manchester United. The Red Devils had dominated Group B, winning their first five games to qualify before losing away to Juventus, and were at the top of the Premier League back in England. It was a daunting task for Monaco, playing against one of the world's largest clubs, and the defeat at the hands of lowly Bastia did not help their confidence as they headed into one of the biggest games in the club's history.

Manchester United travelled to Monaco with only Gary Pallister and Roy Keane missing. David Beckham played on the day of baby Brooklyn's birth. With just defensive absentees, it was a surprise that Manchester United did not play their normal game full of attacking menace, but manager Alex Ferguson was determined to take a clean sheet back to Old Trafford, and they were happy to absorb Monaco's attacking threat with a blanket of defensive resilience. With Monaco's defending equally resolute in the desire to prevent an away goal, it was not until the 25th minute that either goalkeeper had a shot to save, as Peter Schmeichel dived to his right to turn aside a long-range shot from Monaco's Belgian left-back Philippe Leonard. Since both sides were more concerned with defence than attack, 0–0 was always a likely score-line, and Henry could do little or nothing to change it.

The Champions League continued to affect Monaco's league form as they lost the next two games. The added concentration required at the top level of club football was clearly taking a toll as they were beaten at home by Lens and away by Auxerre. It was not just the French champions who were struggling to maintain good form domestically and abroad. Four days before the quarter-final second leg, Manchester United lost at home to Arsenal, with Henry's compatriots, Vieira, Anelka and Petit, all playing key roles in a 1–0 win for the Gunners.

With the Manchester United players low on confidence after conceding crucial ground in the title race at home to their closest rivals, and missing key players, Keane, Pallister, Giggs and Schmeichel (who injured himself going up for a last-minute corner against Arsenal), Monaco attacked from the outset and got their reward. After only five minutes Trezeguet rifled home an unstoppable shot from the edge of the area, and gave Monaco a vital away goal. Reeling from the early goal, the English side did well to compose themselves as they responded by putting pressure on the French defence. Monaco were delighted to go in one up at the break, but in the second half the attacks continued against them and eventually Ole-Gunnar Solskjaer found a way through Tigana's well-organised back line.

Less than ten minutes into the second half and the scores were level through the Norwegian striker, but fortunately for Monaco they still had the upper hand by virtue of their away goal. With Victor Ikpeba's legs tiring, Henry came on for the last 30 minutes, forcing the Manchester United defenders to drop deeper, wary of the damage his pace could inflict on their floundering cause. In defence, Monaco continued to frustrate the Reds and, with Ferguson's troops failing to add the necessary second goal, *les Monegasques* went through to the semi-finals of the Champions League for the first time in their history.

Monaco's midfielder John Collins didn't want it to stop there. 'We're in the last four, so it's possible that we could win and we'll give it our best shot,' the Scotsman said. He thought the opposition's injuries had helped lift Monaco. 'They put us under a bit of pressure,' he added, 'but we scored and it's important to get away goals in Europe. The fact that they were without Ryan Giggs, who has been in fine form this season, and Peter Schmeichel, who has a great influence on their back line, was a massive boost for us.'

Ferguson agreed, injuries had affected his side. 'It was a blow to us; there's no doubt about that. If we'd had some more regular, consistent team selections, I think we'd have beaten them.' The Reds boss went on, 'I don't think they were on top; they only had one shot on goal and that was the goal, but it was a good start for them and it meant they were quite comfortable on the ball. They got an away goal after five minutes and it was a killer.'

Manchester United's European campaign was indeed dead and buried, and Monaco were through to a semi-final clash with Juventus, the Old Lady of Turin.

Juventus had finished second in Group B behind Manchester United and had progressed further than the Reds after overcoming the Ukranian champions, Dynamo Kiev, 5–2 on aggregate. After a short flight from Monaco to northern Italy, the Principality club were on the wrong end of an Alessandro Del Piero masterclass. In the first leg in Turin, the Italian virtuoso, aged just 23, was at his dominant best, scoring a hat-trick in a 4–1 win for the Italian side.

With defenders Franck Dumas, and Philippe Leonard missing, Monaco were below strength at the back as Juve went on the attack from the start. The French side were also – mistakenly as it turned out – on the front foot, in the belief that attack is the best form of defence. It really was end-to-end stuff, as Del Piero and Zinedine Zidane probed at one end, and Italian keeper Angelo Peruzzi kept *les Monegasques* out at the other.

It was only a matter of time before one defence gave way and, in the 34th minute, Juventus made the breakthrough. Martin Djetou brought down Zidane, and up stepped Del Piero to drive a superb free-kick into the corner of the net from 20 yards, giving Barthez no chance. Monaco pressed forward in search of an equaliser, and got one just before half-time when Costinha rifled a low shot through a crowded area beyond Peruzzi's flailing left hand. Juventus refused to be shaken and hit back barely 60 seconds later, Del Piero converting a penalty after Barthez brought down Zidane.

Monaco came out fighting in the second half, but were two down after an hour when Del Piero brought up his hat-trick with a second spot-kick after Muhamed Konjic tripped Filippo Inzaghi. Looking for a footballing miracle, Tigana sent Henry on in a bid to get Monaco back in the game, but it was not to be for the mercurial Frenchman as fellow countryman Zidane completed the rout shortly before the final whistle with a superb strike from the edge of the area.

Tigana admitted Monaco were simply out of their depth. 'I think we played all right in the first half,' he said. 'But we cracked inevitably in the second. We didn't keep the ball moving forward and they ate us alive in midfield, where Deschamps and Davids were dominant.

'This is a very young team,' Tigana continued, 'and tonight they realised we've got a lot of hard work to do to try and reach the level of Juventus. Tonight they got an idea of what top-level football is all about. We weren't at that top level; we were always under pressure and were dominated in many departments. Now we have to try at least to go out with our heads high – put on a fighting performance and go out with a win.'

In the return leg, Monaco's young side did just that. With six first-team regulars missing through injury and with Giuly cup-tied, Tigana had little choice but to field six players aged 23 or under. But his attacking line-up really took the game to the Italians, with Henry the inspirational figure-head and an incessant menace on the left wing.

It was Juventus, though, who took the lead. After weathering Monaco's early storm, they extending their 4–1 advantage through Nicola Amoruso who stabbed home after good play by Del Piero and Zidane. Monaco refused to lie down, however, and they hit back in the 39th minute when Philippe Leonard smashed a free-kick through the defensive wall and past Peruzzi.

Things improved for Tigana's men five minutes into the second half, as Henry beat the Juventus offside trap and chipped the ball over the grounded keeper to give the French side the lead. With Ali Benarbia impressive in midfield, *les Monegasques* sensed their chance but Alessandro Del Piero had other ideas. Not content with a hat-trick in the first game and a hand in the opener, Del Piero extinguished Monaco's slim hopes with a thunderous right-foot volley that gave Barthez no chance after 74 minutes. Monaco's Croatian striker, Robert Spehar, headed a winner seven minutes from time to make it 3-2 and restore some pride and the sell-out crowd applauded their heroes off the park. But the damage had been done in Turin...

'You can't have any regrets losing to a great team like Juventus,' conceded Tigana afterwards, his youngsters having done him proud. 'That match will be my point of reference,' said a determined Henry, whose 51st-minute goal set a French scoring record for the European Cup. It was his seventh in Monaco's campaign, one more than the old mark held by the legendary Raymond Kopa.

Finally out of Europe, and following elimination from the *Coupe de France* three weeks earlier at the hands of eventual winners Paris St Germain, Monaco tried to keep their remote title hopes alive. At home against Toulouse, the possibility of a trophyless season became a grim reality as Henry and his team-mates lost 1–0, with the European Cup hangover in full effect.

With nothing left to play for at club level, Henry joined up with the French Under-21 side for a friendly in Sweden. Having failed to add to his solitary senior cap in October, he still harboured realistic hopes of making France's World Cup squad. 'It's every player's dream to play in the World Cup,' he said.

Henry failed to find the net against the Swedes, or in the final two league games of the domestic season, but his dream came true when on Saturday, 23 May, he was named in Aime Jacquet's 22-man squad for the 1998 World Cup Finals.

One of the unlucky men to miss out on the final cut was Henry's schoolmate Nicolas Anelka. It was somewhat ironic that Henry took the place of the man he would one day replace at Arsenal in the first-team squad at Highbury. At the end of a tough season, Henry had only scored once since Christmas, in the Champions League against Juventus, but it was his great form in Europe that had helped him into the squad, with a total of seven goals in nine games. After Jacquet's vote of confidence, Henry was looking forward to the World Cup. But he had little faith in his own chances for glory as he told the *Sunday Mirror*, 'Everyone says Brazil are favourites, but for me it's England.'

Henry had two major reasons for his faith in England: England boss Glenn Hoddle, along with his and Hoddle's shared mentor Arsene Wenger. Henry explained his thinking as follows: 'I remember seeing Hoddle play for Monaco on television when I was a young boy in Paris. But I have something in common with Hoddle; Arsene Wenger was still Monaco's coach when I joined the club. Wenger was a big influence on Hoddle and he was on my career, too. I have a lot to thank him for.

'He was a big influence on me before he left Monaco to go to Japan. And it's obvious that he's been a guide for Hoddle's coaching career. Since Hoddle became England's coach, they have changed their style of play. They are well organised and there's no kick and rush. It isn't all long balls. That's how people in Europe used to think of the English game. But England's style now is right to win the World Cup, even in France.'

Henry's choice as the key man in the England side was a surprise. He ignored the prolific Alan Shearer and instead went for his Newcastle team-mate David Batty. 'I played against Batty twice last season in the UEFA Cup and he left his mark on me. On one occasion, when I was lying on the ground, he stamped on my arm and walked all over me. He is the type of midfield player English teams like to have. He reminds me of Manchester United's Roy Keane. They are so aggressive I call them mad dogs. When we played United in this season's Champions League, I was glad Keane was injured and we didn't have to face him. I had already experienced Batty and I didn't really want to experience Keane, too.'

Fortunately for Henry and his shins, the Irish did not qualify for France 98 and he would have to wait to play against Keane another day. In the first of the French squad's three World Cup warm-up games, Henry played the last half-hour in a 1–0 win over Belgium. Two days later Thierry started the 2–2 draw with Morocco as Jacquet gave the whole of his squad a workout and experimented with his formation. Henry did not play in the final warm-up game against Finland, where his Monaco team-mate Trezeguet scored his first international goal.

Despite not playing against Finland, Henry had done enough to get himself into the starting line-up for France's opening game against World Cup first-timers South Africa in Marseille. Jacquet's selection was rewarded by Henry scoring a goal in the final minutes of a game the hosts dominated from start to finish. Roared on by vocal support from a partisan crowd, France took the lead when the much-maligned forward Christophe Dugarry headed home a Zidane corner after 34 minutes.

The score remained at 1–0 for most of the second half before South African centre-back Pierre Issa put through his own net, under pressure from Dugarry with 13 minutes left. Henry put the icing on the cake with the third goal in injury-time when he chipped keeper Hans Vonk. It was Henry's first goal for *les Bleus* in his fourth game and, allied with his goal-scoring form in the Champions League, showed the youngster's ability to deliver on the big stage.

It was a very satisfying start to the tournament by the hosts and, with Zidane imperious in midfield, the thousands of French football fans could start thinking for the first time about the possibility of the World Cup trophy staying in France beyond the final. It looked like they could win it.

In France's second game against Saudi Arabia the feeling of hope increased after a 4–0 win, but it came at a cost. After half an hour, Dugarry went off injured, and things got worse in the 70th minute with the sending-off of playmaker Zidane. The midfield maestro was shown the red card for stamping on Saudi captain Fuad Amin, but he protested his innocence. 'I didn't deserve this,' Zidane said. 'I did not mean to hurt the man. I just fell on him.'

On the playing side everything had gone swimmingly for the French. They were 1–0 up shortly after Dugarry's injury when Henry converted Bixente Lizarazu's pull-back with ease. Trezeguet got France's second before Zidane's aberration, and Henry scored the third shortly afterwards, before Lizarazu topped off another sparkling performance with number four. The 80,000 people in the Stade de France loved it and began an impromptu chorus of the *Marseillaise*.

Such nationalistic pride could not make up for Jacquet's loss of two key players. 'All would be great if not for Dugarry's injury. All would be great if not for Zidane's expulsion,' the French coach said. 'He will pay for it. His gesture had to be punished. We have been talking to our players about this for a long time. They must stay calm. They must show self-control.'

Zidane was handed a two-match ban by the FIFA officials, and France faced Denmark without him. With France on six points and assured of progression to the next round, Jacquet took the opportunity to rest some of his first-team players and give a much-needed run-out to some of the reserves. The second string acquitted themselves admirably against a strong Scandinavian side, in a 2–1 victory. Youri Djorkaeff put in a sterling performance as Zidane's replacement and scored the first goal, a penalty past Schmeichel. Emmanuel Petit got the second, shooting home through a forest of legs after Michael Laudrup had equalised from the spot. Henry played the final 20 minutes, coming on for Robert Pires and, as the final whistle blew, France topped Group C.

A rendition of the *Marseillaise* ensued, this time in front of the French president Jacques Chirac. 'I'll be there again [for France] at the final,' he said, caught up in the mood of national optimism. The coach was equally upbeat. 'We're doing well and we're going to get better,' Jacquet said. France met Paraguay in the last 16, the South Americans had came through Group D by beating a weakened Nigeria side 3–1, following goalless draws against Spain and Bulgaria. Having progressed largely through resolute defending, it was no surprise when the South Americans, from a country with less than 10 per cent of the population of France, offered little in attack.

Jose Luis Chilavert in the Paraguay goal was enjoying a good tournament and he had boasted that his was the 'best defence in the world'. For a long time, the imposing keeper seemed to have a point as the French attacks broke on the solid foundations of Celso Ayala and Carlos Gamarra. The best chance of normal time came in the 40th minute when Henry raced through and sweetly lifted the ball over the spread-eagled bulk of Chilavert, only to see his effort crash against a post.

As the second half wore on without a goal, it seemed Zidane's lack of self-control was going to cost the French. Jacquet took the drastic decision of removing Henry in the second half as he tried everything he could think of to get a goal, but after 90 minutes it still hadn't come and France 98 had its first taste of extra-time. This World Cup was the first high-profile tournament to feature the controversial golden-goal rule and, after 24 minutes of extra-time and 114 minutes of play in total, Paraguay were out of the World Cup as centre-back Laurent Blanc volleyed home venomously from Trezeguet's knock-down.

The Olympique Marseille defender was understandably overjoyed. 'It's the most incredible joy to score in this way,' Blanc said. 'We have criticised the golden goal in the past, yet here we profited from it. What went through me when I scored was just indescribable. We were fighting, fighting, fighting and we got our reward in the last few minutes. I promised myself that I would score in the World Cup and I did.'

After grinding out such a tough result, the French side were happy to welcome back creator-in-chief Zidane for their quarter-final clash with Italy. 'Zizou' and Christian Karembeu came in at the expense of Henry and Bernard Diomede. Henry's omission was largely due to a minor ankle sprain as Jacquet went for a more cautious team selection. The Italy side was typically defensive, with Zidane shadowed by Gianluca Pessotto throughout. It was a rough game, with fifty fouls and five yellow cards, and Italy did not manage a corner until the third minute of injury time at the end of the second half. Of the two sides the French had the better opportunities, but there were no clear-cut chances and penalties were on the cards long before the end of extra-time. When the spot-kick lottery came around, the Italian's 'curse' struck again.

Defeated on spot-kicks in the 1990 semi-final against Argentina and again in the World Cup final by Brazil in 1994, the *Azzurri* made it a hat-trick of penalty losses in France. Zidane and Italy's Roberto Baggio, the villain of the shoot-out in 1994, both scored before Lizarazu and Demetrio Albertini both had their shots saved, by Pagliuca and Barthez respectively. Trezeguet and Henry, both on in the 65th minute as substitutes, scored their kicks too, and Alessandro Costacurta and Christian Vieri were also successful, setting up the last two kicks perfectly. Blanc walked up and finished as coolly as you would expect from the man who had scored the golden goal only six days previously, and all the pressure was on Luigi Di Biagio. Unfortunately for Italy, it was all too much for the AS Roma midfielder and his shot crashed on to the bar.

Asked to take a penalty, Henry had not even hesitated, accepting the pressure of such a crucial shoot-out without a second thought; this was typical of the mental strength and self-confidence growing in this remarkable young man. 'When I was asked, I just said "yes" straight away,' Henry said. Thanks to his and his team-mates' spot-kick accuracy, France were through to the World Cup semi-finals for the first time in 12 years, where they would meet Croatia.

The Eastern Europeans were having an incredible World Cup journey: the country was only formed in 1991 when the Croats declared independence from Yugoslavia. At their first major football tournament, the European Championship of 1996, the Balkan team reached the quarter-finals and they had gone one better in the World Cup, reaching the last four by beating Germany 3–0 in their quarter-final. A strong sense of national pride and warrior spirit was combined with exceptional footballing ability in the feet of such players as Zvonimir Boban, the captain who liked to control the middle of the park, Davor Suker of Real Madrid who had scored four goals in six games before the semi and the remarkable Robert Jarni who made things happen down the left, both in attack and defence.

Ahead of the semi-final, public and media interest in Henry and France was growing incessantly. The French had never really regarded football as their number-one sport, but following a massive street party on the Champs Elysees after the quarter-final win, even Prime Minister Lionel Jospin followed the President's lead and came out in support of *les Bleus*. The public were now thinking ahead to the final and the possibility of winning the trophy, but Henry, his team-mates and the coach were taking it one game at a time. Speaking of their semi-final opponents Croatia, Jacquet said, 'I've been watching them with a very keen eye since Euro 96. Two years on, they are better performing, better balanced and more experienced.'

The French boss was right to be wary. After a goalless first half, the World Cup hosts found themselves a goal down straight after the break. There were only 26 seconds on the clock when Suker broke away and finished past Barthez, leaving the French fans with a horrible sense of déjà vu. Three times the French national side had reached the semi-finals of the World Cup – in 1958, 1982 and 1986 – and three times they had lost. On the back of two games that went to extra-time, *les Bleus* were struggling to break down a resilient Croatian defence. But luck was with the French that night, and their saviour came in an unlikely form. Right-back Lilian Thuram was winning his 38th cap against Croatia, and he had never looked like scoring in his previous 37 internationals. Choosing a spectacular way to break his duck, the uncompromising defender equalised Suker's goal within a minute, and then went on to score the winner 25 minutes later.

'This is fabulous. I don't even score during training,' Thuram said. 'It was 200 per cent luck. I am not a hero because I scored the goals. To be a hero – that's left for the final.' One man who would not be a hero, nor even play in the final, was Laurent Blanc. After his heroics against Paraguay and Italy, the defender guaranteed himself more headlines, as he was sent off 15 minutes from time for pushing an opponent in the face. Henry, meanwhile, continued his record of appearing in every game as he replaced Karembeu after half an hour, but it was a very tight game, as one would expect of a World Cup semi-final, and Henry failed to lift the lethargic French attack.

So it was that on 12 July, '*le jour de gloire est arrivé*' – 'the day of glory arrived' – to borrow a line from the *Marseillaise*. In the final, France met the favourites, Brazil. It was the final that World Cup organiser and French footballing hero Michel Platini could only have dreamed of when the bidding for the Finals had begun, and now it was here. The final started in bizarre circumstances as Brazil's star striker Ronaldo was dropped from the team and then reinstated after suffering from convulsions, which have never been fully explained to this day.

France, possibly buoyed by the news that the biggest

threat to their defence was not 100 per cent fit, started brightly and got their reward after 27 minutes when playmaker Zidane headed home Petit's corner. He repeated the feat in first-half injury-time by heading in Djorkaeff's corner from the other side. Going in at half-time two down, the Brazilians couldn't recover. Even when Marcel Desailly was sent off in the 68th minute, the kings of samba football failed to make the extra man count. And when the third goal came, it was France who got it as Petit ran on to Vieira's through ball in the last minute and slotted home.

The final whistle from Moroccan referee Said Belqola, the first African to officiate at a World Cup final, sent the majority of the crowd and most of France into raptures. The Champs Elysees was again flooded with an estimated million revellers. The partying went on for days and Henry remembers it well. 'The day after the World Cup final, I was watching TV and saw, on the Champs Elysees, guys in suits getting out of their Mercedes to party with total strangers dressed in their underwear, and letting them dance on their car bonnets. I said to myself that it is fabulous to see Paris and the whole of France come together.'

Henry was man enough to put his personal disappointment aside; he had been on the substitute's bench for the final and was all set to come on before Desailly was sent off. But after losing his first choice centre-back, Jacquet decided to send on Vieira, a more defensive player. Henry remembers it well today as he told GQ magazine, 'I was 20 years old and I had no fear. I had played in all the games and then in the final I was due to come on until Desailly got sent off, and that was my chance gone. But I only felt sorry for myself for about a minute, and then I forgot about it. Once you touch that cup, you forget everything!'

He may have forgotten everything, but his performances in the earlier games had left an indelible mark on the world of football and FIFA named him in their 22-man World Cup All-Star Squad. As a tribute to his achievements in the World Cup, Henry continues to wear the number 12 shirt for France to this day.

In the 12 short months of the 1997–98 season, Thierry Henry had gone from international hopeful to international superstar, winning the World Cup, scoring more goals than any of his team-mates, being selected for the All-Star Squad of the tournament and coming of age in the Champions League. All this and he was still just 20.

Chapter four
Turin Breaks his Heart

On 3 August 1999, Thierry Henry left Juventus after less than seven months in Turin. It was supposed to be a match made in heaven: Italy's biggest club and France's brightest star, the Italian Champions and the French World Cup winner. So where did it all go wrong?

After Henry's impressive displays at the World Cup, he was again being linked with a move away from the Principality. Barcelona, AS Roma and Arsenal were alleged to have been in negotiations with Monaco throughout the summer with a view to signing football's most exciting young winger, but Monaco were not keen to sell and the club President, Jean-Louis Campora, even went on record to declare his desire for Henry to remain in the Principality. 'Thierry made his name at Monaco. We're counting on him. He's staying, period.'

Campora met Arsenal Vice-Chairman David Dein in

London, where he told him Henry's transfer was out of the question. Speaking in *France Football* magazine, Campora was quoted as saying, 'Arsenal are and always have been interested. I met Dein in London and he asked me if Henry was for sale and I said, "No." That's that.'

Campora was sure Henry's agents were to blame and claimed they had even made contact with Arsenal without Monaco's permission. 'I'm convinced that this umpteenth attempt at intimidation is the work of the agents,' Monaco's President said. Henry, meanwhile, told *France Football* his representatives had done nothing wrong. 'I'm being depicted as a baby, as if I can't make a decision on my own at my age. I just want to leave, that's all.'

Reluctant to sell after Henry's World Cup exploits, the Monaco board felt fully vindicated in driving up the asking price and they succeeded in scaring off Arsenal and the other predators. So it was that, on 7 August 1998, Henry was still a Monaco player as he took to the field against Lorient.

It wasn't just Henry who was being pursued. Of the 22 Blues who lifted the World Cup in the summer, there were only 8 left playing their football in France. The strong state of French football meant that Gallic flair was making an impression all across Europe, with more than 80 Frenchmen playing professional football abroad.

With so many transfers going on throughout the summer, it was no surprise when Jean Tigana made changes at Monaco. Gone were John Collins to Everton, Ali Benarbia to Bordeaux and Stephane Carnot, after just one season, to Auxerre. Coming in to replace the midfield trio were Franck Gava from Paris Saint Germain and Sabri Lamouchi from Auxerre.

The changes affected the side, and Monaco got off to a slow start away to Lorient. Ali Bouafia put the newly promoted side ahead midway through the first half and, although Gava volleyed home an equaliser only minutes into the second half, it took an 89th-minute penalty for Monaco to secure the points, Ludovic Giuly scoring from the spot after Gava had been brought down. Henry had a poor game and further distanced himself from his fans and employers after the game. 'I want to play in England,' Henry told a gathering of TV and newspaper reporters, 'and, more specifically, I want to play for Arsenal.' Fortunately for Monaco, Henry let his feet do the talking in the following match, at home to Sochaux, scoring one and creating two more in a 4–1 win.

A week later, Henry was happy to get away from Monaco and join up with the French squad for a friendly in Vienna. It was new boss Roger Lemerre's first opportunity to work with the French team. Lemerre had taken over from Aime Jacquet after the World Cup and, with only two games of the new season played, there weren't too many changes to the squad. Tony Vairelles and Frederic Dehu of champions RC Lens won their first caps, and Henry continued on the left wing as the World Champions drew 2–2 with Austria. Still aware of their public's newfound love of football, the French broadcasters TF1 showed the game live, and retransmitted the match again in its entirety hours later. This was unheard-of behaviour in France before the World Cup and it was considered bizarre by many people even after the national team's triumph. It was only football, after all.

Back in Monaco, Henry kept on playing and Monaco continued unbeaten. After five league games of the new season, Monaco turned their attention to their first game back in the UEFA Cup. As semi-finalists in their last two European campaigns, *les Monegasques* were looking to continue their good European form away to LKS Lodz. Things didn't go exactly to plan as Lodz got off to a great start. Having been knocked out of the Champions League in the second qualifying round by Manchester United, the Polish title-holders opened the scoring after only nine minutes through striker Piotr Matys and Monaco were struggling to get into the game.

It wasn't until the 57th minute that the French side were back on level terms, and then it was a fortuitous own goal from central defender Witold Bendkowski who deflected a shot from Giuly into his own net. Monaco were buoyed by the goal and got a second ten minutes later, David Trezeguet scoring from the penalty spot after Bendkowski had brought down Willy Sagnol in the box. Monaco's Croatian striker, Robert Spehar, added a third, half-volleying home with five minutes to play.

With their UEFA Cup future looking secure, *les Monegasques* ventured to the capital for a league game against fallen giants Paris Saint Germain. PSG weren't enjoying the best of form, but they still managed to inflict a first defeat of the season on Henry and Monaco, with midfielder Yann Lachuer scoring the only goal of the game. This defeat signalled the start of a poor run of form for Tigana's men, as they picked up just six points in five league games and drew two UEFA Cup games, the home leg against

Lodz, 0–0, and the first leg of the next round 3–3 away to Graz AK of Austria.

In this series of disappointments, there was one bright spot for Henry as he managed to get himself on the score sheet against Rennes. But even that one, a late consolation strike in a 2–1 loss, was taken away from him as it was later declared an own goal. Then, to make matters worse, Henry was sensationally dropped by France.

Having played in both of Roger Lemerre's first two games, the second as a sub in the European Championship qualifier away to Iceland, Henry found himself back in *les Espoirs*. Away to Russia, not even the presence of a World Cup winner could stop the French Under-21 side losing 2–1. Henry was not playing his best football, and it is unclear whether it was a back injury that kept him out of the next three club games, or the fact that Tigana had simply dropped the want-away winger. Whatever the reason for his absence, in his first game back Henry helped Monaco up into third place in the league as they won 3–1 win against Nantes. Gava scored the first and had another disallowed for offside against Henry, who was lying on his back after trying unsuccessfully to bundle the ball over the line. Typical of his bad luck and poor form at the time, Henry managed to sidefoot the ball wide of goal even though he was unmarked from seven yards out. Fortunately for Monaco, neither of these missed opportunities came back to haunt them as they secured the points through Philippe Leonard and Victor Ikpeba – despite Nestor Fabbri's equaliser.

Lifted by the win, Monaco demolished Graz 4–0 in the second leg of their UEFA Cup tie back on home soil. But

Henry was again relegated to the bench, and only entered the fray after the scoring had been completed; Gava grabbed two, Spehar and Djibril Diawara got one each. Monaco's reward for defeating the Austrians was a quarter-final clash with Olympique Marseille, their very next opponents in *Le Championnat*. Marseille were unbeaten after 11 games, riding high in the league after overtaking Bordeaux at the top of the table the previous week with a 3–1 win in Lorient.

The league game between the two Mediterranean sides in Marseille, which Henry again missed, was a physical affair and both sides finished the match with ten men. French midfielder, Peter Luccin, was sent off for the home side after half an hour, and Spehar was shown a red card for Monaco five minutes from time. Florian Maurice grabbed the solitary goal for Marseille in the final minute to give them a boost ahead of the European meeting. But this was the first time two French teams had been drawn together in the history of European competition and, following their bruising encounter, Tigana was asked if he was worried about more incidents ahead of their next meeting. 'Definitely not,' he said. 'There is mutual respect between the two clubs and, even if our recent matches have been competitive, it has never got out of hand.

'Concerning our match in the UEFA Cup, the presence of a foreign referee is an excellent thing,' he continued, 'In European competition, the referees are more severe, and the players are less likely to make bad challenges.'

But speaking ahead of the big all-French UEFA Cup tie, Henry again spoke of his wish to move to England. 'The only time I have mentioned another club was in August when I said I wanted to join Arsenal, and that is still the case.' To the delight of Gunners fans worldwide, Henry went on, 'They are the club of my dreams and I want to play there for footballing reasons alone. If my name has been linked with any other clubs, other people have been speaking out of turn on my behalf.'

Explaining what attracted him to the north London club, he continued, 'Arsene Wenger is the coach who gave me my debut, and my mate Nicolas Anelka is over there, too. Everything about the club set-up at Arsenal makes my head spin and nobody will ever prevent me from thinking differently.' But Wenger, frightened off by Henry's hefty price tag, was busy signing the Nigerian conjurer Nwankwo Kanu from Inter Milan.

So despite all his wishing and pleading to move, Henry was still a Monaco player by the time Marseille came to town and, because of that wishing and pleading, he was again on the bench. It was another lively match. Marseille took the lead after nine minutes through Robert Pires, David Trezeguet equalised from the spot after eighteen and Titi Camara put the visitors back in front six minutes before the break.

After a frantic first half, there was hardly time to catch breath before Giuly got Monaco's second equaliser just ten minutes into the second half. Henry replaced Ikpeba shortly after the equaliser as Tigana pushed for a win. The Monaco cause was helped by Marseille's reduction to ten men, following Florian Maurice's two-footed lunge at Fabien Barthez. But Henry couldn't make much impact before Monaco's numerical advantage disappeared, when Franck

Dumas was shown the red card for pushing Camara after he had collided with Barthez. The dismissal of Dumas disrupted the rhythm of the home side just as they were starting to impose themselves, and the first leg finished 2–2.

Henry didn't even get off the bench in the next two games as Tigana showed him who was boss, and Monaco's indifferent league form continued. So it was that Henry found himself among the substitutes for the return leg in Marseille. The home side started brightly and, after Muhamed Konjic was sent off in the 37th minute, Monaco didn't really threaten. The Bosnian defender was shown the red card for a foul on Dugarry, when the striker was clean through on goal, and Marseille made the extra man count.

Camara scored the winner for Marseille after 71 minutes following good work by Jocelyn Gourvennec and, even with Henry's customary late appearance, Monaco couldn't get back in the game. Marseille continued their fine run in the UEFA Cup all the way to the final where they lost 3–0 to Parma, a fine statement of the health of French football. Driven by Fabrizio Ravanelli, Pires and Dugarry up front, and Laurent Blanc, Patrick Blondeau and William Gallas in defence, Marseille were also top of the League at Christmas. Monaco, however, were struggling way back in seventh place, with only five points from their last six games as they approached the winter break. The pressure was on.

Monaco's club president decided to put some of the pressure on his under-performing World Cup stars, Henry and Trezeguet. 'I am shocked by their performances. The aftermath of the World Cup has had a very negative psychological effect on their spirit and our young internationals have experienced a slump in their form after their success,' Campora said.

'I am convinced they have been influenced by their entourage, who obviously want to profit from their glory but who are acting as parasites on them,' Campora continued, insisting neither player was up for sale. 'They can either get their act together or go and play in the reserves. Monaco are a solid club which can survive coming tenth; they can't if they want to put themselves in the shop window for the big clubs.'

The president may have had no qualms about finishing tenth, but seventh was not good enough for Tigana and, on 14 January 1999, he resigned as head coach of Monaco. The club president was 'surprised' but accepted the resignation from a man he described with admiration. 'Jean Tigana acted like a gentleman, in all dignity. He asked to leave without asking for any compensation, which is extremely rare and deserves respect.' Tigana was replaced by Claude Puel, a move that would have been well received by Henry.

Speaking during the World Cup, Henry had let slip that maybe he wasn't as happy with Tigana as might have been thought – after all, Tigana had brought him along as a player and had been his coach for all but two weeks of his professional career. 'To say that I owe a lot to Jean Tigana, as Aime Jacquet would have it, doesn't seem quite right. I'm grateful, but if I had to pick one person outside my family, it would be Claude Puel, the physical trainer at Monaco. He was the one who put me back on track.'

Henry had needed putting back on track after the proposed transfer to Real Madrid fell through and excessive press attention had left Henry feeling more isolated than ever. 'I was feeling alone on the pitch. It's a strange feeling; you get the impression that you have lost all that is important in this job. When you are adored, idolised, you run the risk of losing your head and, when you're down, everything conspires to make it worse.'

So having fallen out with Tigana to such an extent that the old pro felt he could no longer work with the man he had treated like a son, Henry had a chance to work with the man he credited with saving his career. In the first game under the new coach, nothing much had changed and Henry was again on the bench. When he came on for the final 20 minutes away to RC Lens, Henry didn't really look interested and, when the final whistle went with the score at 1–1, it signalled the end of Henry's career at the club.

In the 1998–99 season Henry had played thirteen league games, starting in eight of them but scoring only one goal. In Europe he had played five games, starting just two. It had been a tough start to the season, and with no signs of improvement Monaco decided to take the money while it was still on offer. Henry was on his way to Turin.

On 18 January 1999, only four days after Tigana quit, Henry signed for Juventus for a fee believed to be £12 million. 'He is a brilliant player but that's an amazing amount of money,' Wenger commented from Highbury, before adding that he was still an admirer, even offering Henry a safety net if all went wrong. 'Don't worry. If it doesn't work out, we'll sign you,' Wenger promised.

Juventus signed Henry, along with Espanyol's Argentine striker Juan Esnaider, to help make up for the knee injury that had cut short the season for Alessandro Del Piero. With a strong French contingent in Turin, Henry was made welcome by compatriots Zinedine Zidane, Didier Deschamps and Jocelyn Blanchard, all playing at his new club. But he would have to make an impression quickly on the pitch as the Italian giants weren't enjoying the best of seasons themselves – they were seventh in Serie A.

Ever since coach Marcello Lippi joined Juventus in the summer of 1994, the 'Old Lady of Turin' had enjoyed great success. The 1994–95 season ended with a domestic double and the following season saw Juve win the Champions League. In the 1996–97 season, they followed up their Champions League success with the European Super Cup and the World Club Cup, while securing another Serie A title and reaching the Champions League final. The 1997–98 season brought the *Bianconeri* another Serie A title, and an appearance in a third consecutive Champions League final, which they lost 1–0 to Real Madrid. After all his requests to move had been answered, Henry was joining one of Europe's biggest and most successful sides, but when he signed midway through the 1998–99 season, everything was going wrong.

It was well known in football circles that Lippi was going to leave Juventus at the end of the season to be replaced by Carlo Ancelotti, and in December Lippi himself made this public. Maybe this declaration had undermined his authority with the players. Perhaps, after four highly successful seasons, the players had lost their hunger for success. Possibly winning the World Cup had taken too much out of two key players, Zidane and Deschamps.

Lippi certainly wasn't helped by the knee-ligament injury

suffered by Del Piero, a player that any club would be hard-pushed to replace – he had been the catalyst to Juve's recent success. Whatever the reasons, Juventus were seventh in Serie A and in desperate need of a lift and, more importantly, goals, which Lippi hoped would come from Henry and fellow newcomer Esnaider.

The pressure was on. In Henry's first game, Juventus managed to score two for only the second time in ten games, and got all three points for a second win in eleven matches. Henry came off the bench for the final 22 minutes, as Juventus beat Perugia 2–1 in the Stadio Delle Alpi. The *Bianconeri* came from behind with a goal apiece for Zidane and Uruguayan striker Daniel Fonseca.

Henry got his first start three days later in the second leg of the Italian cup quarter-final away to Bologna. A 1–0 victory wasn't enough for Juventus to progress, however, as Bologna went through on the away-goals rule, having won the first leg 2–1. After this brief boost to their form, it was business as usual for Lippi's side as they lost the next two games with another pair of substitute appearances for Henry. The 4–2 defeat at the hands of Parma was too much for Lippi to bear in front of his own fans, and he quit.

'I have decided to resign,' Lippi said, after storming into the press room. 'If I am the problem, if the problem is linked to my December announcement about my future, then I'll say good day to you and leave.'

The defeat to Parma was Juventus' sixth league loss of the season, and left them in ninth place in Serie A, fifteen points behind leaders Fiorentina and ten points away from qualifying for the Champions League. Fortunately for

Juventus, Lippi's replacement was available and Ancelotti decided to start work immediately.

With all the chaos in Turin, Henry would have been happy to join up with the French squad for a friendly in England. But he was still in international exile and joined the Under-21s for a game in Derby. On the pitch, things were as bleak as ever as the young Lions beat *les Espoirs* 2–1, with goals from Lee Bowyer and Arsenal's Matthew Upson cancelling out Philippe Christanval's opener.

Back in Turin, Henry got off to a good start with the new coach as he made the starting XI for Ancelotti's first game away to Piacenza. It was Henry's first league start for three and a half months, and Juve got the three points they deserved for their efforts in a 2–0 win. Henry started the next two games as Juventus' Ancelotti-led revival continued, but at home against Olympiakos in the Champions League quarter-final Henry was ineligible as he had played in the UEFA Cup for Monaco.

Juventus made light of his absence as they beat the Greek champions 2–1. The Italian goals came from Filippo Inzaghi and Antonio Conte as Juve took control of the game. Olympiakos refused to lie down though and pulled a goal back in the third minute of injury-time to keep the tie alive. It was a goal that could have hurt Juventus, as in the return leg the Greeks were leading 1–0 until the 85th minute, and would have gone through on the away goal until Conte, continuing his run of good form, scored the equaliser.

Since Ancelotti had taken over the *Bianconeri*, they had had played six league games, winning four and drawing two, and had got through to the semi-finals of the Champions

League. Henry had started five of the League games, and come on as a substitute for the last half hour in the other – but he was still to find the net for his new employers and the fans were getting restless. So it was that he welcomed the chance to play again for the French Under-21 side and join up with his childhood friend and former team-mate Trezeguet.

The reunion was great news for the French youngsters as the two World Cup winners obliterated the Ukrainian defence; Trezeguet grabbed four goals, with two assists from Henry, in a 4–0 win. Five days later, Henry even managed to get on the score-sheet himself as Armenia were put to the sword in a game that finished 3–1 and he returned to Turin in high spirits. After his exertions for *les Espoirs*, Henry was rested for the next game away to Empoli. Stefano Bianconi scored in a 1–0 win for Empoli that was marred by the two red cards shown to Stefano Morrone of Empoli and Juventus midfielder Alessio Tacchinardi.

After suffering their first loss under the new coach, the Juventus players had to pull together for their biggest game of the season, the Champions League semi-final away to Manchester United. Henry watched on television as his team-mates played the Reds off the park and led deep into injury-time at the end of 90 minutes through Conte's well-struck goal. But the football gods were smiling on Manchester United that season, and Giggs equalised very late in the game to send the Old Trafford fans back home happy with an undeserved draw.

Henry was back in the starting line-up for the league games that followed and, on 17 April 1999, he grabbed his first goals for Juventus in a 3–1 win over Lazio. His first goal after 34 minutes was a pretty lucky effort as Luca Marchegiani, Lazio's veteran keeper, left the shot, believing it was going wide, only to see it roll slowly into the corner of the net. Having finally broken the drought, Henry managed to double his tally in the second half after Nicola Amoruso extended, and Roberto Mancini later halved, Juventus' lead.

Henry was happy to have scored, and it would have helped to get the fickle Italian fans off his back. But Henry was no longer playing as an out-and-out winger – he was in more of a wide-midfielder role – and he was expected to help out his full-back. It was a role he probably didn't gain pleasure from, thinks former France boss Jacques Santini, who said, 'With Juventus, they told him to play on the left. It was part of a game scheme; it was all very tactical and he probably didn't like being told to play there. But when you watch him now, he'll often go on the left because he has the freedom to do so. He's not being shut into a strict plan.'

It wasn't the lack of independence, but more the added responsibility that meant Henry couldn't enjoy his football in Serie A. 'In Italy, I didn't get any pleasure from playing,' he recalls. 'I had to do a lot of defensive work during matches and there were some really dull games, games with no action, no attacking play.'

The second leg against Manchester United in Turin goes down in history as one of the most dramatic nights in European football as the Reds overcame a 2–0 deficit on the night, following Filippo Inzaghi's two early strikes, to win 3–2. Henry was still cup-tied and therefore not involved in the game, but a defeat like that must have affected all the players at the club and it effectively ended the season for the

Bianconeri. Sixth in the league and out of all the cups, the only thing left for Juventus to play for was qualification into the UEFA Cup, an almighty fall from grace for the side that had appeared in the last three Champions League finals.

Henry started the remaining five league games of the season, including a 2–0 home defeat at the hands of AC Milan. 'I must still improve my striking, even if I'll never reach the calibre of (Filippo) Inzaghi,' Henry said at the time. 'I fill a different role and I've started to get used to playing on the left side and to liaise better between defence and attack. That takes up a lot of my energy and, by the time I'm in a position to shoot, I'm running out of steam; that's what happened to me last Sunday against AC Milan.' Being all over the pitch may have been running the fleet-footed winger down, but he still managed to grab one more goal for Juventus in the final game of the season at home to Venezia.

At the end of the season, Juventus were sixth in Serie A, sixteen points behind champions AC Milan. After a tough season, much of the first half of which was spent on the bench at Monaco, Henry joined an under-performing team in a new country on the back of winning the World Cup the previous season. It had been very difficult for Henry to impress in Italy. He summed up the time well in an interview with *GQ* magazine. 'When I arrived, Juventus were sixth or seventh in Serie A and they thought I would be the saviour. But everyone was having a bad time, even Zinedine Zidane. I played in 13 games out of 16, and I only played well in 3 of them!' he laughed.

Henry joined up with the French Under-21 team again at the end of the season and, possibly frustrated at the tough year he had endured since the World Cup, he received his first professional red card in a 2–0 win over Russia. In the close season, Juventus were busy in the transfer market in a bid to return to their previous glories, and one player they went after was Henry's old schoolfriend, Nicolas Anelka.

Anelka had enjoyed a successful time at Arsenal since his controversial move from Clairefontaine in 1997, winning a Premier League and FA Cup Double in 1997–98, and top-scoring for the Gunners in 1998–99. But, along with his advisers, he had decided it was time to move on from Highbury, with Real Madrid his intended destination.

Arsenal, however were refusing to deal with the Spanish giants, claming they had made an illegal approach for the player. So the epic turned to Italy where Lazio and Juventus were alleged also to be interested. Juventus were keen to use Henry as bait to sign the other Frenchman, but Henry advised his young friend against a move to Turin, and Lazio pulled out of the running saying Arsenal's quote was too high. The 'Anelka Saga' finally ended in August when Arsenal went back to Real Madrid, content with their explanation of what had happened, and sold him for approximately £23 million.

In need of a replacement up front and with the money clearly burning a hole in his pocket, Wenger signed Henry from Juventus on 3 August 1999 on 'a long-term contract for an undisclosed fee'. Arsenal may have been reluctant to reveal the details of the transfer fee, but it is widely believed to have been £10.5 million.

Henry was very happy to have got his wish at last almost a year after first talking about moving to Highbury, but what was wrong with life in Turin? 'Italy was very different and things behind the scenes were not right... things that have nothing to do with football. Maybe if I had had more time there, things might have been different, but I had to go [to Juventus] and I don't regret that. In the long term it made me stronger.' After another chance meeting with Wenger, Henry was adamant Arsenal were the club for him. 'Straight away after what happened at Juve, I told the board, "Don't even try to set me up with another team. I want to go to Arsenal."'

Henry was involved in pre-season training with Juventus who wanted to get rid of him, when his transfer was completed. In a recent interview with *TheFA.com*, Arsenal Chief Executive and Vice-Chairman David Dein revealed, 'Thierry Henry was going to go out on loan from Juventus to Udinese, and Arsene sort of plucked him from obscurity.'

Many times since he joined Arsenal, Henry has been asked what is so special about the north London club. As he told *GQ* magazine, 'It's just a feeling. Sometimes you can't describe why you feel a certain way. I saw them play a couple of games against French teams years ago, I like the shirts, Highbury... and Arsene helped of course.'

Despite only playing one league game under Wenger at Monaco, Henry often spoke to his mentor and was always told the same thing. 'You are a number nine, you are wasting your time on the wing.' Henry is very grateful for the faith placed in him by Wenger. As he tells us, 'Arsene believed in me, I cannot forget that. When I was down, when things went wrong at Juve, when I was back in the French Under-21 team, he held out a hand to me.'

Henry had not enjoyed his time in Italy and took that

hand very quickly, happy to be moving on. 'Had Arsene not signed me, I don't know what would have happened. It's very difficult for me to say. I like to go forward and not look too much into the past or at the bad moments I have had. When things were not working out for me at Juventus, I met Arsene on a plane and told him I wanted to play for him. I then phoned him. I just wanted to go with him again. It was special to work with him at Monaco – that left a good taste in my mouth. Arsene laughed and said he was more than pleased if it happened. Now here we are. It's the beginning of a long story – but I hope there will be more pages to add to the book.'

Chapter five
Hello Highbury

'I owe absolutely loads to Arsene Wenger. If he hadn't suggested that I play through the middle, I would never have thought of it. At the beginning, it wasn't easy for me because I could have chosen a club that wanted me to play on the wing. That would have been the easier option. I didn't doubt my ability to play in that position otherwise I would have rejected Arsene's idea. I had total confidence in him; it was that which tipped the balance in his favour. He has managed some great attackers in the past and he knows so much about football. However, I hadn't played through the middle since I was a kid. On the professional level, it was a new position for me.' Henry was in a new country and now he had a new position to get used to as well.

When Arsene Wenger signed Thierry Henry from Juventus, the world thought Highbury's professor of football had paid over the odds for a winger who had had a good

World Cup, but had done little since then. The Arsenal coach saw things differently and considered the young Frenchman a model of the perfect striker. The 1999–2000 season would prove once again that Wenger can see things in a player, even if the player can't see it in himself.

Fortunately for Henry, he was immediately made welcome at Arsenal by the north London club's strong French contingent. He had played at Monaco with Emmanuel Petit and Gilles Grimandi, and with Patrick Vieira for France and *les Espoirs*. 'Thierry had come from Juventus and had had a really hard pre-season,' says Vieira. 'We shared a room [on away trips] because we used to play together in the French Under-21s. I knew him well and tried to help him like other players helped me when I joined.'

Henry was not Arsenal's only new signing. Wenger had been busy over the summer securing the signatures of a host of fresh players. The pick of the new boys was Brazilian full-back Silvinho signed from Corinthians, but Wenger also picked up Ukrainian captain Oleg Luzhny from Dynamo Kiev to replace Sunderland-bound Steve Bould and German midfielder Stefan Malz from TSV 1860 Munich. To help share the goal-scoring burden following Anelka's departure, the Arsenal manager also signed the prolific Croatian striker Davor Suker.

Suker had missed pre-season training and was short on fitness, which meant Wenger decided to ease his expensive new signing into English football. Along with Marc Overmars, Henry was one of two attacking substitutes for the game at home to Leicester City, and the Frenchman took his place on the bench. Wenger started the game with Dennis

Bergkamp and Nwankwo Kanu up front, so that Henry could see what he was letting himself in for.

The hustle and bustle of the English Premier League is a far cry from Italy's slower-paced Serie A or even *Le Championnat* in France, and Wenger felt it would help Henry if he saw close up just how frenetic it was.

At half-time, Henry came on for the injured Fredrik Ljungberg on the wing and his electrifying pace made an instant impression on all present. But it was the away side who made the first breakthrough as Tony Cottee knocked in Steve Guppy's cross from six yards out. It was Leicester's only meaningful chance of the game and Wenger was forced into making another change. Marc Overmars came on for Ray Parlour and, with two quick wingers pinning the Leicester defenders back, Arsenal were soon back on level terms as Bergkamp collected a poor defensive header and dispatched it past Tim Flowers in the Leicester goal.

Henry's pace continued to trouble the visitors' defence and he got into many good shooting positions on his debut, but a lack of composure in front of goal meant he missed a hat-trick of chances. He refused to give up, however, and in the final minute it was his header from Manu Petit's corner that Leicester's Frank Sinclair put past his own keeper to give Arsenal all three points.

Having started his Highbury career with a win, Henry admits that the physical side of the game in England took some getting used to. 'In my first match here, I received blows from everywhere,' he remembers. 'I was flying about. I was wondering where I had landed. Players were falling all over the place. It was a real battleground.'

As well as a slightly rougher game than he was used to, Henry also had to come to terms with the attitude of referees in England. 'I had a reputation for losing my temper every time I was checked too closely,' he admits. 'I learned to behave myself and, above all, to stop complaining. There is no other way here. If you do not accept tackling, you spend your time crying at the referee. Here, you are judged above all on your commitment.'

One player who epitomises that commitment was his Arsenal team-mate Martin Keown. 'Here you play in training the same as in a match,' says Henry, especially if your name is Keown. 'He was always after me; to the point that I thought he had something against me. But gradually I realised that every ball was worth a fight.'

With Arsenal spirit slowly working its way into Henry's system, often via Keown's boot, the Frenchman started the next four games flying up and down the Arsenal wing. But if anything his shooting was getting worse.

'I was more likely to hit the top of the stand than the corner of the net,' Henry says with a smile. It's something he can laugh about now but at the time it was a real concern for Arsenal fans. Author and celebrity Gooner Nick Hornby remembers it well. 'He was so hopeless... my brother said we'd spent our record fee on the French Perry Groves.'

Henry may not have been as bad as the ginger winger whose greatest contribution to a game – apart from setting up Charlie Nicholas to win the 1987 League Cup – was more often than not a very, very long throw-in, but his shooting was a worry for all. Hornby continues, 'His speed actually made things worse for him, because it constantly got him into positions where his ineptitude was revealed for all to see.'

Wenger was not concerned though and, in a bold move typical of his management, he selected Henry up front with Bergkamp for the away game against Liverpool. Henry was struggling to come to terms with his new role, when Robbie Fowler showed him just how it should be done. Fowler, the perennial scourge of Arsenal, grabbed a sumptuous first and was a constant threat in a 2–0 win for the home side. Suker even had a last-minute penalty saved for the Gunners after Ljungberg was brought down.

Henry was honest in assessing that Anfield performance, saying, 'Before I came to Arsenal I had not played as a striker for ten years. It was strange and it didn't work at first. I played there at Liverpool and the manager switched me back at half-time. He said I had been rubbish, and he was right.' After his poor display as front man, Henry found himself in the background as he took up a place on the bench for the next three games.

He made a late appearance at home to Aston Villa after the points were in the bag; Arsenal won 3–1 with goals from Kanu and Suker twice. Henry then made his first European appearance for the Gunners away to Fiorentina in the Champions League, coming on for the last ten minutes in a game remembered for another last-minute penalty miss. Unlike Suker's attempt against Liverpool, Kanu's saved spot-kick in Florence cost Arsenal valuable points as they drew their first game in Group B 0–0.

Away to Southampton in the next league game, another goalless draw was on the cards when Henry came on with

20 minutes to go. Following their midweek exertions in Italy, Arsenal looked lethargic and it took Henry's fresh legs to lift the Gunners. He quickly made his presence felt as his pace got him on to a long clearance from goalkeeper Alex Manninger and his shot produced a good save from Paul Jones. The Saints keeper could do little to stop Henry's next effort though, as he took a pass from Tony Adams 20 yards out with his back to goal. Using his strength to hold off the defender, Henry turned and shot in one movement, and the ball flew past Jones to give Thierry Henry his first Arsenal goal. Henry remembers it as if it was yesterday. 'It was a ball from Tony Adams,' he says. 'I controlled it and hit it in the corner of the net. It was a big relief because I was waiting for it. The most difficult thing is to start; after that you get confidence and then you can carry on. It is always tough to get the first one.'

Wenger was delighted for his young pupil. 'It will be a big boost for Thierry's confidence,' the manager said. 'He needed that goal because when he came on the first time against Leicester, he had three chances in 20 minutes and missed them all, and every time he missed one it looked a terrible blow to him.' The game finished 1–0 and, by breaking his Arsenal duck against the Saints, Henry had joined a prominent pair of Arsenal legends.

Ian Wright joined Arsenal in September 1991 and, although he scored in his first game away to Leicester in the Rumbelows Cup, it was in his very first league game for the Gunners that he really impressed. Wright grabbed a hat-trick in a 4–0 win away against Southampton and staked a claim for a place in Arsenal folklore. It was a place 'Wright,

Wright, Wright' later secured with a steady stream of goals as he became Arsenal's all-time top scorer with 185 goals in all competitions.

Dennis Bergkamp is another player who got himself on the Arsenal score-sheet for the first time against the South Coast side. But it took the Dutchman a little longer than Wrighty to find the net; it was his seventh Arsenal game when the Saints came to Highbury. But Bergkamp also found the Southampton defending to his taste as he broke his duck with two beautiful goals, the first of many brilliant strikes for him in the Arsenal shirt. Having joined such illustrious company of Saints-slayers, the omens were certainly good for Henry's Arsenal future.

Henry's next game for the Gunners was against AIK Solna at the FA's Wembley Stadium. Arsenal were playing their Champions League home games in front of the Twin Towers because Arsenal's relatively small capacity had been further diminished by UEFA advertising regulations. The Highbury hierarchy decided that, by playing the games at Wembley, more supporters would be able to get to see games, but the move was not popular with fans. In the previous season, Wembley had seemed to curse the Gunners as they effectively conceded home advantage – plus the fact that extra motivation was handed to opposing teams who tended to play out of their skin at such a world-famous venue. In their first season at Wembley, Arsenal had failed to qualify from a fairly easy group due to their poor 'home' form, and the fans were worried it was going to happen again.

Group B of the Champions League was made up of Arsenal, Fiorentina, AIK Solna and Barcelona and, after dropping two points in Florence, it was imperative that Arsenal picked up all three points against the Swedish title-holders. Arsenal started brightly and got some reward for their dominance when Bergkamp played in Ljungberg for the opener against his compatriots in the 27th minute. After Freddie's goal, Arsenal's composure left them and a number of chances went begging before the break.

In the second half, it seemed the Gunners' profligacy was going to cost them as Solna captain Krister Nordin beat the fabled Arsenal offside trap and equalised with a cool finish past Manninger. Desperate for the win, Wenger urged his men forward for the goal that would take the points back to Highbury, but it would not come and, with 20 minutes remaining, the Arsenal manager sent on reinforcements.

Henry and Kanu came off the bench to replace Ljungberg and Overmars and Arsenal adopted a 4-2-4 formation as Bergkamp and Suker completed the front line. Fortune favours the brave and, with everything but the kitchen sink being hurled forward, Arsenal finally got the breakthrough in the first minute of injury-time. Bergkamp passed to Kanu and, falling under a strong challenge, the Nigerian forward managed to roll the ball to an unmarked Henry who sidefooted home. Thinking the Wembley hoodoo had been broken, the crowd went wild but Solna weren't giving up. From the kick-off, they went straight back down the Arsenal end and won a corner.

When the corner broke to Bergkamp the relief in the stadium was palpable, but the game was still not finished and, in a move that would become very familiar to Arsenal-watchers, they grabbed a third, breaking from deep.

Bergkamp passed the ball into space for Henry, who had sprinted forward from the Arsenal box. Collecting the ball on halfway, Henry blazed his way through the Swedish half, leaving a trail of defenders in his wake. Approaching the Solna penalty area, the keeper rushed out at the Frenchman's feet and, ever-aware of a better-placed team-mate, Henry rolled the ball across to Suker for a simple tap-in. After such an exhilarating end to the game, the Arsenal fans headed home happy with the three points – they were also starting to think that Thierry Henry might be able to replace the talented, departed Nicolas Anelka after all.

With Henry's confidence boosted by two goals in two games, Wenger decided it was time to start him again, up front. At home to Watford, Henry's performance was an improvement on his Liverpool showing but he still couldn't find a way through, as the Hornets came to Highbury desperate for points and defended in numbers. By the time Kanu's late goal decided the result, Wenger had replaced Henry with Bergkamp and, following another failure up front, Henry found himself back on the bench for the trip to the Nou Camp.

In Barcelona, Arsenal dropped two more valuable points, drawing 1–1 in a game which they possibly deserved to win, even though they had to work hard following Gilles Grimandi's red card. But Wenger was determined to transform Henry into a striker and gave him a starting berth up front in the League Cup.

Since Wenger's arrival at Highbury, the League Cup – in its previous guise as the Coca-Cola Cup and again in its then incarnation as the Worthington – had been treated with increasing disdain. By the time Henry joined Arsenal, League Cup outings were seen as valuable match practice for squad players and a chance for Wenger to blood some of the more promising youth-team players.

This time against Preston North End Henry lined up alongside the likes of Paolo Vernazza and Stefan Malz as the Gunners triumphed 2–1. Henry didn't do enough to get himself back into the first XI and was on the bench for the next two league games against Everton and Chelsea. At Stamford Bridge, Arsenal were 2–0 down when Henry entered the fray, but Arsenal managed to get all 3 points through an incredible Kanu hat-trick in the final 15 minutes which will live long in the memory of all those who saw it.

By the time Henry next started a game, Arsenal were out of the Champions League. The Wembley 'curse' had struck again, causing them to lose at 'home' to Barcelona and Fiorentina. This interpretation possibly does a disservice to the excellence of Barca and the *Viola*, but after two consecutive seasons of crashing out at the first group stage, the Wembley experiment was over and Arsenal would return to Highbury for any future campaigns in Europe.

After the disappointment of their Champions League exit, the Arsenal players had to try and pick themselves up for the visit of Newcastle United to north London. In a bid to freshen things up against the Magpies, Wenger made six changes to the side that lost to Fiorentina and brought in Henry for another chance through the middle. Unfortunately for Henry and Arsenal, Newcastle had just changed managers – Bobby Robson had been installed to replace

Ruud Gullit – and the new boss was determined to get some points from his first game in charge.

In a game where Arsenal looked a little disjointed after making so many changes and with Newcastle happy to keep nine men behind the ball, it was always going to be difficult to break the deadlock. Henry's continuing reinvention as a striker lasted for only 45 minutes as he picked up a knock and didn't emerge for the second half. The game finished 0–0.

The injury kept him out of a couple of games and he missed the away trip to Solna, where Arsenal won to claim a place in the UEFA Cup, as well as what would have been his first north London derby. Henry was still out injured on 8 November as Real Madrid came to town for Lee Dixon's Testimonial match at Highbury. Many Arsenal fans were disappointed that Henry's schoolfriend, Anelka, was injured and unable to make a Highbury return, but another former Arsenal striker did make an appearance which would help in Henry's conversion from pacy front man to clinical finisher.

Ian Wright had left Arsenal in the summer of 1998 without a real send-off and he relished the opportunity to appear again at Highbury in an Arsenal shirt for his former team-mate's testimonial. 'At Lee Dixon's Testimonial, I was sitting next to Martin Keown and he asked me to watch Ian Wright. And I did,' Henry recalls. 'I have the tape of his goals with Arsenal at home and I sometimes watch it for fun: 185 goals in 288 matches. Solid, very solid.'

Having seen Arsenal's greatest-ever goal-scorer in action, Henry was again on duty for *les Espoirs* as his international exile for the senior side continued. Henry got his country's only goal as the French Under-21s lost 2–1 to their Italian equivalents in Tarente. Struggling to come to terms with a central role for Arsenal, and still playing with the youngsters for France when the European Championship was just six months away, Henry, the World Cup-winning winger, could be forgiven for thinking a move back to the flank would be the best thing for his career. 'One day I wanted to do it,' Henry says. 'I didn't do it because I had, and I have, a lot of confidence in Arsene. But it was so hard. In my mind it was so hard because I had always been in the French squad as a winger. And everybody in Europe knew me as a winger.

'So one day I thought I have to speak with the boss. Then when I arrived at the training ground I said, "No, it's all right." You know sometimes you have players who will stop when they have a little problem, but I thought, I have to keep going, and maybe we'll see at the end of the season.' In Henry's next game in the red-and-white shirt everything became clear.

'The day it clicked was against Derby at home. We were losing 1–0 and I scored twice and they were goals like a proper striker,' Henry says. 'I made a run, I can remember it was Marc Overmars who set me up twice. He gave me the first ball and I scored with my left foot. It was an easy goal, and I made a good run with Marc again [for the second]. I started to have more confidence and felt like a striker again.' Everything was falling into place.

The Gunners were buoyant after a 3–0 UEFA Cup win against Nantes Atlantique and finding European matches much more to their liking back at Highbury. Indeed they were unlucky to find themselves behind at home to Derby County, but Henry quickly cancelled out Dean Sturridge's early goal, taking Overmars's pass, racing past the defender and finishing coolly past keeper Mart Poom. after 51 minutes, was much like the first as with the equally rapid Overmars.

With his confidence lifted by his well-take started another game up front, this time away to Middlesbrough in the League Cup. Looking more and more like a striker, Henry equalised Hamilton Ricard's early goal with a 20-yard rocket after catching Paul Ince in possession, and he also had a hand in the second as Mark Schwarzer failed to hold Henry's free-kick and Suker followed up with a tidy finish. So Arsenal were 2–1 up with just over five minutes left to play, when Henry, with three goals in three days, inexplicably handled a ball close to the Arsenal goal-line, conceding a penalty. Ricard converted the spot-kick and the game stayed at 2–2 throughout extra-time and went to penalties. Henry didn't take any of Arsenal's four kicks as the Gunners continued their poor form from the spot, losing 3–1 with only Suker successful for the visitors.

In the UEFA Cup second leg in Nantes, Arsenal started slowly, possibly resting on their three-goal cushion from the first leg, and the carpet was pulled from under them somewhat with Antoine Sibierski's goal after 12 minutes. Happily for Arsenal's travelling supporters, it only served as a wake-up call, and the north Londoners soon stamped their authority on the match. Grimandi got the equalizer from a Petit corner, before Henry, playing his first game back in France since he left Monaco, put the tie out of reach for his compatriots.

Kanu watched Henry's run into *les Canaries* area, flicked a perfect pass over the defenders and into his path, and

Henry gave the ball the finish it deserved, hammering home from 12 yards out. With Overmars grabbing another goal for the English side just before half-time, it came as little surprise that Arsenal's second-half performance failed to live up to the first. Knowing that Nantes needed 6 goals in 45 minutes to knock the Gunners out, Arsenal relaxed, conceded 2 more goals and finished the game 3–3, taking the tie 6–3 on aggregate.

In goal-scoring form and starting to enjoy his striking role, Henry even attempted a bicycle-kick in his next game, his FA Cup debut at home to Blackpool – although he didn't connect with the ball, it resulted in a goal anyway as the loose ball fell to Overmars whose shot across goal was knocked in by Arsenal skipper Tony Adams. The game finished 3–1 as Grimandi scored his third in three games, and Henry set up Overmars for the third. Phil Clarkson had equalised Grimandi's opener to keep the FA Cup dream alive for the Tangerines but Arsenal were just too good.

Henry was getting better with each game, and scored in his last game before Christmas, slotting home Silvinho's pull-back to get a point in a 1–1 home draw against Wimbledon. Henry's goals were becoming a source of delight to the fans and he was enjoying playing in front of the Highbury faithful. 'When you play for a few seasons in front of empty stands in Monaco and you end up in Arsenal in front of these extraordinary fans, it's a radical transition,' Henry said. 'I'm still impressed when the stadium starts to vibrate. Only in England can you feel a thing like that. In these moments, on the pitch, you have the impression you're about to take off.'

Henry was certainly taking off with the fans and he even had his own chant. To the tune of a 1980s song, 'Tom Hark' by the Piranhas, like many football chants it started as a melodic repetition of the player's name before various made-up verses were added. The most popular runs along the lines of:

I met a bloke down the pub last night,
He said to me there's a new Ian Wright,
I said to him how can this be,
He told me a name. He said, 'Thierry Henry'
Thierry Henry, Thierry Henry,
Thierry Henry, Thierry Henry,
Thierry Henry, Thierry Henry.

After only a couple of months, Henry regularly had 35,000 people shouting his name in unison, a far cry from when he arrived at Highbury. 'I was lonely at first,' he says. Initially he was staying at the Sopwell House Hotel in St Albans and could even get the train home in full Arsenal kit without getting mobbed by fans. 'At the beginning, it's always difficult because you miss your friends, your family, all the things you used to do at home. Now I enjoy the life. I have a house and all my friends can now come over and see me so it's much better.'

Events off the pitch mirrored those on it, as Henry was mocked by his team-mates for missing the odd sitter. 'I had problems settling in England to begin with and I think I missed more chances than I scored at the beginning,' Henry told *Match* magazine. 'All the time, Patrick Vieira used to tease me about missing and at the beginning it was funny, but at the end it was true as well. And they weren't difficult chances, just a good shot for a normal striker and sometimes I would shoot and it would end up by the clock at Highbury.' The Clock End faithful are a loyal bunch and didn't object too much to the barrage.

'When I had to come on the pitch the fans were always clapping me and when I used to miss the goal they were still singing. That's why I was still happy even when I was not scoring.' Henry was finding England a more enjoyable alternative to his time in Serie A. 'In Italy, if you miss a goal, even if you are Batistuta or Bierhoff, they want to kill you. Here, they sing my name and I hope they'll do it next season and then the season after that as well.'

In their last game of 1999, Arsenal were at home to league leaders Leeds United and Henry worked his way further into most Gooners' hearts as he demonstrated exactly how lethal his famous turn of speed could be. Henry gathered a Kanu pass and headed for goal with Leeds captain, Lucas Radebe, in close pursuit. As Radebe stretched to make a challenge, Henry cut inside the defender and gave Nigel Martyn no chance with a crisp finish. After Ljungberg's opener, Henry's strike made it 2–0 and the game was safe as Arsenal closed the gap on Leeds to five points.

Arsenal were only in third place in the league, their title challenge having been let down by poor away form, but their home form was strong and Henry was enjoying himself at Highbury. He had scored in his last three home league games. Henry made it four in a row when Sunderland came to visit. Having terrorised Radebe against Leeds, his next victim was Steve Bould. The former Highbury hero found himself unable to deal with the young Gunner's pace and power as Sunderland found themselves one-down after only three minutes.

Henry gathered a pass from Overmars, raced into the Sunderland area, held off Bould and put Arsenal ahead. Henry went on to make the second for Suker and passed to the Croatian for the third, although he could claim little credit for the goal as Suker hit a fabulous looping half-volley from the corner of the 18-yard box into the top corner of the goal. After Niall Quinn had given the away fans something to cheer about, Henry found time to add a fourth for Arsenal as he turned Bould inside out before beating Thomas Sorensen in the Sunderland goal.

In the Fourth Round of the FA Cup, Arsenal struggled to break down a well-organised Leicester defence over 90 minutes at Highbury, and in the replay at Filbert Street Tim Flowers was in inspired form in the Leicester goal. Arsenal managed to create some chances but that, too, finished goalless. After 30 minutes of extra-time and a Leicester goalkeeping substitution, the tie went to penalties with neither side able to manage a goal in 210 minutes of football.

Leicester won the shoot-out 6–5, with keeper Pegguy Arphexad saving the second kick from Dixon and the vital seventh taken by Grimandi. Henry took the fifth penalty successfully to take it to sudden death, but it still wasn't enough to go through. With only two competitions left to concentrate on, Arsenal travelled to Old Trafford to play the new league leaders, Manchester United. Henry started up front with an unlikely partner in Freddie Ljungberg, as Bergkamp, Kanu and Suker were all out injured.

The partnership proved an instant success as Ljungberg opened the scoring after 11 minutes. The Swede had a history of scoring against Manchester United – he had put one past Peter Schmeichel on his Arsenal debut – but Freddie's goal wasn't enough to win the game and the Reds equalised with 17 minutes remaining. After dropping two points in Manchester, Arsenal were three points off top spot going into February.

Arsenal's dismal away form seemed to be continuing into the New Year, and Arsenal followed draws in Sheffield – against Wednesday – and Manchester with a defeat at Valley Parade against Bradford City. Henry managed to equalise with a half-volley from 30 yards, but Arsenal went down 2–1. Things got even worse for Arsenal as they suffered a rare home defeat when Liverpool came to north London, Titi Camara grabbing the only goal of the game in a 1–0 away win.

When the UEFA Cup resumed in March, Arsenal had to play the Spanish league leaders Deportivo La Coruna. It seemed an ominous task for a faltering Arsenal side, but if the team's confidence had been knocked after two straight defeats, it didn't show as the game started and Arsenal took the lead after only five minutes. Henry's left-wing cross was well met by Dixon. Henry himself doubled the lead after half an hour as he tucked away Overmars's pull-back from the byline. Djalminha scored from the spot to keep the game alive, but his dismissal after an hour's play gave Arsenal a one-man advantage which they used to devastating effect in the final 30 minutes.

The Gunners grabbed 3 goals in a pulsating 15-minute spell in the second half which effectively ended the tie and Henry even scored a rare header. After 67 minutes, he grabbed Arsenal's third, meeting Petit's right-wing free-kick at the far post with his loaf. Ten minutes later, Kanu scored one of the most memorable Arsenal goals of recent years: one-on-one with the Depor goalkeeper, he feigned to go one way with a drop of his shoulder and then went the other, leaving Jacques Songo'o in the visitors' goal on his backside as he rolled the ball into the unguarded net. Bergkamp got another for Arsenal with a deflected free-kick, and the Gunners travelled to Spain with a 5–1 lead.

With the tie dead in the water, the second leg was a bit of a non-event, and when Henry scored with less than half an hour to play, racing on to a Kanu through ball and rolling it past the keeper's outstretched arm into the bottom corner of the net, Depor needed six goals to go through. The Arsenal defence again got understandably complacent and they conceded two late goals to give the home fans in the Riazor something to celebrate. Following the 2–1 defeat, Arsenal had won a second UEFA Cup tie 6–3 on aggregate.

Arsenal had made easy work of qualifying for the UEFA Cup quarter-finals, but back in the Premier League things were proving a little trickier. Arsenal's poor form on their travels was undermining their whole campaign and two more points were dropped away to Aston Villa. Then Arsenal lost 2–1 in Middlesbrough, conceding further vital ground in the title race to Manchester United. Arsenal were 13 points behind their rivals with 10 games remaining, and they were relieved to turn their attentions back to the UEFA Cup.

Arsenal took control of the quarter-final first leg at home to Werder Bremen with another cool finish from our man Henry, this time from a Vieira pass, and Ljungberg got a fortunate second after Kanu miskicked the ball straight into his path as he ran into the area. After a comfortable 2–0 win against German opposition, Arsenal turned to the big confrontation against the team from the wrong end of the Seven Sisters Road, Tottenham Hotspur.

Having missed the journey to White Hart Lane, Henry was to enjoy his first north London clash on 19 March 2000. The derby debutant played a part in both Arsenal goals as they secured local bragging rights for another season. The opening goal arrived when Chris Armstrong put Silvinho's corner into his own net under pressure from Henry. Armstrong managed to make amends for his blunder with a goal at the other end when he equalised for the Lilywhites, but on the stroke of half-time Arsenal got a penalty. Henry showed no sign of nerves as he stepped up to take his first, non-shoot-out penalty for Arsenal. The fiery atmosphere of a north London derby failed to affect the Frenchman as he blasted the penalty low and hard past Ian Walker in the Tottenham goal.

The second half was goalless despite Grimandi's late sending-off and the Gunners won 2–1. The way the penalty-kick was dispatched typified the resilience Henry had developed since he first broke into the first team at Monaco. 'Before and during the World Cup there was a lot of pressure on me and I found it very hard to handle. I was only 19 and I felt my career was going to be over before it had even started,' Henry says. 'But I came through it and it made me a lot stronger in my mind.'

During the World Cup-winning season of 1997–98. Henry had scored 14 goals for Monaco and France in all competitions, his highest total as a professional until now. 'I have 16 goals and we are only in March. That is more than I have ever scored in a complete season,' he said with a smile. He was certainly enjoying himself up front now, positively benefiting from the added responsibility. 'I certainly think striker is the most difficult position to play in, with the goalkeeper as well, because when they make an error it is usually a goal,' Henry says. 'As a striker, when you do not score for one game or maybe two, three, any more than four, you lose confidence and people start talking about you. You must make sure you score all the time.' And he was doing his utmost to ensure he did just that.

So good was his club form, that he received a call up to the France squad – for the first time in over a year and a half – for the game against Scotland the following week. But Henry first had to play a second leg against Werder in Bremen. The game got off to a great start for the Gunners as Ray Parlour grabbed his first European goal for Arsenal with a fantastic shot from the corner of the German box after just eight minutes. Leading 3–0 on aggregate and with a vital away goal, things got even better for the Gunners when Parlour scored a second midway through the first half. Marco Bode gave his countrymen a glimmer of hope when he pulled one back for Bremen before the break, but Arsenal were too strong for them and the second half turned out to be more of the same.

On for a hat-trick, Romford Ray showed his generosity as he set up Henry for an open goal when he could have had a shot himself. Henry received his marching orders shortly after scoring for what the Danish referee Kim-Milton Nielsen controversially perceived to be serious foul play, although it seemed more of a yellow-card offence for a slightly clumsy challenge. The dismissal didn't affect the outcome of the game though and, after Rade Bogdanovic had scored another goal for the home side, Parlour completed a deserved treble as he broke on to Kanu's pass from deep.

Having notched up an aggregate of six goals for the third successive round, Arsenal found themselves in the UEFA Cup semi-finals where they were drawn against Lens, but first they had the chance to avenge a 3–2 away defeat inflicted by Coventry. The Sky Blues' visit to Highbury had an entirely different complexion; despite keeping it to 0–0 for the first 45 minutes, Gordon Strachan's men were overrun in the second half. Henry converted a Vieira through ball after 50 minutes and Grimandi and Kanu finished the rout. Arsenal ran out 3–0 winners.

When Henry travelled to Scotland with the French national side, he even managed to score the second goal as *les Bleus* beat the home side 2–0. It was a successful return to the international arena for Thierry and put him firmly back into Roger Lemerre's plans. Henry had always had a place in the French manager's thoughts, as Lemerre was well aware of how dangerous the newly prolific striker could be when on top of his game. 'I know Thierry very well and I have never been worried,' said the French boss. 'I was assistant to Jacquet during the World Cup and I saw then what Henry can do. For me, it's not a problem that he hadn't enjoyed his best form. I know his capabilities and his gifts.'

Henry's talents were again on display in a red-and-white shirt the following Saturday as Arsenal came from behind to beat Wimbledon 3–1, with Henry grabbing the third from the penalty-spot after Kanu had turned the game around with his two strikes. In the next Arsenal game Henry was conspicuous by his absence as Arsenal laboured to a 1–0 win against Lens at Highbury. Bergkamp got the Gunners off to a flyer as he rounded the keeper in the opening minutes, but no more goals were forthcoming and the game finished with just a solitary one-goal lead to take to France. Fortunately for Arsenal, Henry was suspended for only one game and would be available for the return leg.

Henry showed how important he was to the Arsenal cause when he scored in his sixth consecutive start for the Gunners in the next game away to Leeds United. The game was played on a Sunday following the midweek UEFA Cup action and the day after Manchester United had finally confirmed their retention of the Premier League trophy for another season with a 4–0 win over Sunderland at Old Trafford. Despite the disappearance of their title hopes, Arsenal produced one of their finest displays of the season as they beat Leeds 4–0. Henry got the opening goal when he completed a slick passing move with a crisp finish; he also played a part in the second goal somewhat unwittingly as Keown headed Silvinho's corner against him. The ball bounced off Henry and straight back to Keown who volleyed home the rebound. Kanu finished off some great work by Silvinho and Overmars completed the scoring late on.

Aside from the disappointment of Fergie's men confirming top spot, Henry was maintaining a fine end to the season.

When Arsenal travelled to northern France, Henry made it two goals from two return trips to his homeland, following up his goal in Nantes with the opener in the UEFA Cup semi-final second leg against Lens. With a strike reminiscent of his first-ever Arsenal goal, Henry received the ball outside the box with his back to goal, turned and hammered the ball home. Henry's team-mate, right-back Lee Dixon, was full of praise describing the goal as 'a great finish, unbelievable'. With only minutes to go before half-time and a slender lead from the first leg, it was a crucial away goal at an ideal time. Although Lens struck back in the second half through Pascal Nouma, Kanu added a second for Arsenal in the final minutes and north London's finest were through to the UEFA Cup final.

Having been knocked out in the semi-finals of the Champions League twice while at Monaco, Henry was delighted to have made a European final at last and he was determined to get his hands on the silverware. 'When I first came on the pitch I was worried,' Henry said. 'But I knew I would have some good opportunities so I just had to concentrate my mind on that and I did it. I have missed out on winning in Europe twice so I just hope I can bring the Cup back to London this time.'

Back in the capital, Henry scored for an eighth consecutive game, with a well-taken brace against Watford at Vicarage Road. The first was typical of many of the goals he scored that season, as he sped on to Petit's long pass and slotted home past the advancing keeper. But the second really was something special. With the game seemingly secure following Parlour's goal from Henry's through ball, Henry himself received the ball 40 yards from goal and waltzed past two Hornets defenders before curling home a sumptuous finish from just inside the area. That goal showed just how far he had come since the start of the 1999–2000 season and the beginning of his Arsenal career. He was now combining the cool finishing developed at Highbury with the dribbling perfected at Clairefontaine and his natural pace – and he was rapidly becoming a striker to fear and admire.

Henry's team-mate and compatriot, Patrick Vieira, was full of praise. 'He was a bit down at the start but scoring made him feel good,' Vieira said. 'When he got some responsibility it made him feel more important. He needed two or three games under his belt. But when he got a few goals, he got some confidence from the boss, the team and the fans. Now he scores goals for fun.'

Henry didn't manage to score in his next game for France against Slovenia. But he was continuing his international comeback, which made him happy with little more than two months until the European Championship. Wenger was less enthusiastic about the injury he picked up which kept him out of the next two league games. But Arsenal continued their good form without the Frenchman, and they overcame Everton and West Ham with Overmars scoring very Henryesque goals in both games.

In Henry's first game back after injury, it was as if he had never been away as he scored both Arsenal goals in a 2–1 win. Chelsea were the visitors to Highbury as he displayed opportunism and skill for the first goal, pouncing on Frank Leboeuf's error, then rounding Ed De Goey. Pace and power were the key ingredients for the second as he sprinted round Marcel Desailly before shrugging off his muscular international team-mate and shooting through De Goey's legs for 2–0.

It was Arsenal's eighth straight league win, a run that had coincided with Henry's fantastic form and, although Arsenal drew their next game at home to Sheffield Wednesday, Henry set a new Premiership record for Arsenal by scoring in his seventh consecutive league game. In an incredible match at Highbury, Dixon opened the scoring, stretching to convert Henry's cross from an unlikely angle. Unfortunately for Arsenal, this seemed to fire up the Owls, who came out for the second half determined not to be relegated at Highbury. With three quick goals from Gerald Sibon, Gilles De Bilde and Alan Quinn, Wednesday put themselves 3–1 up and left Arsenal wondering what had hit them.

With the Gunners looking to maintain their good form heading into the UEFA Cup final, Silvinho chose a good time to score his first Arsenal goal, returning a clearance with interest from the corner of the box. Henry completed Arsenal's comeback within a minute, sidefooting home an Overmars cutback, and the game finished 3–3. Wednesday were relegated.

In the last league game of the season away to Newcastle United with nothing but pride to play for, Wenger took the opportunity to rest some players ahead of the UEFA Cup final. Henry was one of nine first-teamers to miss the game at St James's Park as Arsenal crashed 4–2 to finish the season in second place, 18 points behind Manchester United. But Arsenal still had one chance of silverware left and, on Wednesday, 17 May 2000, all eyes were on the Parken Stadium, Copenhagen.

Arsenal were able to field the first XI with only Freddie Ljungberg missing through injury, and they went into the final full of confidence against the Turkish champions, Galatasaray, who had beaten Leeds United in their semi-final. Like Arsenal, they had also crashed out of the Champions League after the first group stage. Central to the confidence of Arsenal was the incredible form of Thierry Henry. Including scoring in seven consecutive Premiership games, the talented striker had scored at least one in each of his last ten games for the Gunners, notching up twelve goals.

Such prolific form surprised even the man responsible for putting the Frenchman up front. 'I did not expect such a success. I thought it would take much longer,' Wenger admitted. 'I tried it, and that's the credit I might have, but I'd be lying if I said I could have predicted this. In the first few games I was disappointed with him. I played him and Dennis Bergkamp up front at Liverpool and it didn't work at all,' he said acknowledging the early troubles. 'I thought it was too early to put him back on the wing but I was concerned as he didn't show any signs in that game of being a success in the centre. But he is intelligent and has learned quickly.'

Indeed the pacy young Henry did everything pretty quickly, much to the chagrin of defenders at home and abroad. And the Arsenal players and fans alike were hoping Galatasaray would soon be added to the list of teams to suffer at the hands, and feet, of Henry. The Turks had other ideas, however, and defended deep and in numbers, leaving only Hakan Sukur up front on his own, as the mercurial Gheorghe Hagi tried to create something in the middle of the park. It was Arsenal creating all the chances, though, and

Henry even had a header saved by the Brazilian Claudio Taffarel in the Galatasaray goal.

With chances few and far between, many Arsenal supporters would have been less than happy to see the best opportunity of the night falling to the less than prolific Keown with only a handful of goals in his hundreds of games for Arsenal. As Henry fired in a low cross from the left-hand side the Gunners' centre-back stretched for the ball as it flew across the six-yard box, but could only manage to put it over the bar from five yards out with the keeper beaten. Neither side could conjure up anything in the 90 minutes and, even when the Turkish side were reduced to 10 men following Hagi's dismissal, Arsenal failed to beat Taffarel. The destination of the trophy was to be decided by a penalty shoot-out.

With penalties the downfall of Arsenal in both of the domestic cup competitions and playing a major part in their Champions League dismissal, fate didn't look to be on the side of the Gunners. And in the stadium in which they had won the Cup Winners' Cup six years previously, Arsenal lost 4–1 on penalties. To make matters worse for Arsenal, Gica Popescu, formerly of Tottenham, scored the winning penalty.

Henry had gone off with a slight hamstring injury shortly after creating the chance for Keown, and he could only watch from the sidelines as Suker and Vieira both failed to beat Taffarel from 12 yards. So it was that Henry finished the club season without a trophy to crown his very successful conversion from winger to striker. But he did finish the season as Arsenal's top scorer with 17 league goals, 8 European goals and 26 in all competitions. He had made the transformation that only Arsene Wenger had thought possible at the start of the season and he could look forward to the rest of his career as a front man thanks to his mentor.

On the subject of the debt he owes to Wenger, Henry says, 'I have always given him credit for launching me, for relaunching my career; he's someone who believes in me, who believed in me at the time; he's a gentlemen, a really great man, and he's been a very significant person in my career. What he does is fantastic, and not just with me, but with all his players. He is a very honest, very loyal person and I don't think any player of his could ever say anything bad about him. Everything that I've got now is partly thanks to him. Yes, of course, I have to be out there, getting results, but he believed in me when no one else saw what I could do.'

And for that Henry is not alone in being very grateful.

Chapter six
Euro Hero

'It's a great feeling, a great achievement,' Henry said, understandably delighted with France winning Euro 2000. 'We had a very difficult group and we had very difficult matches against Portugal and Spain just to reach the final. Then we were losing until the very end, but we came back. We proved we can go behind and still win. Everyone was expecting us to fail because none of the European teams have ever done it before us: to win the World Cup and then to win the European Championship, and now we have done it.'

Having completed the metamorphosis from winger to striker at club level, Henry still had to convince the football world that he could perform his new role on the international stage. At the European Championship in Belgium and the Netherlands, Henry had the chance to show what he could do. Coach Roger Lemerre called up Henry for the French squad, and he went into the tournament as one of the most in-form players after his fine goal-scoring end to the League season.

Lemerre, however, did not always play Henry as a striker. The French manager instead favoured Anelka or Trezeguet up front alone in a 4-5-1 cum 4-3-3 formation, with Henry adding his pace and power to the attacks from the left flank. The relocation didn't affect Henry too much, though, as a player full of confidence; he still had licence to attack when in possession. He played well in the warm-up game that he started against Croatia, a 2–0 victory. In the friendly Hassan II tournament in Morocco, Henry took a successful penalty in the shoot-out after coming on as a substitute against Japan, and he scored the opening goal in a 5–1 mauling of Morocco, as Lemerre tried out different formations and selections, even playing Henry through the middle of a 4-4-2 on occasion.

In the European Championship, France were in Group D with Denmark, the Czech Republic and Holland. France, as World Champions, were among the favourites for the tournament along with all the usual suspects as far as European football is concerned: Italy, England, Portugal and Group D rivals Holland. The French group was quite tough with the exciting Dutch and the ever-improving Czechs, and it was imperative that Henry and his team-mates got off to a good start in their first game, against Denmark.

The Danes had the better of the opening exchanges in Bruges as Jon-Dahl Tomasson forced a good save from Barthez after only three minutes. Anelka wasted a good chance for France before he helped to create the first goal. Peter Schmeichel saved at the former Arsenal striker's feet after he had linked well with Henry, but the ball broke only as far as Laurent Blanc who calmly stroked the ball into the net to give *les Bleus* the lead after only 16 minutes. The goal helped to settle the World Champions; they remained composed throughout the first 45 minutes and took their 1–0 lead into half-time.

Denmark came out firing on all cylinders in the second half and managed to maintain the pressure for 20 minutes until France got the breakaway goal which had always been a possibility with the fleet-footed Henry on the park. The mercurial Frenchman was put in on goal by a pass from Zidane and had time to pick his spot before slotting the ball past Danish captain Schmeichel. Wiltord added a third in injury-time to put the gloss on the win for France.

After what became a comfortable French victory, Henry followed up his goal against the Danes with a man-of-the-match performance in his next game against the Czech Republic, which was also played in Bruges. There were only seven minutes on the clock when Petr Gabriel's weak back pass fell to Henry forty yards out. The Arsenal forward advanced on goal unchallenged and beat Pavel Srnicek to open the scoring. With his sky-high confidence lifted further by his goal, Henry was a constant menace to the Czech defence and managed to create a second French goal after Karel Poborsky had equalised from the penalty-spot. With half an hour left to play, Henry broke down the left and lobbed a ball into the Czech area which eluded everyone but Youri Djorkaeff. The Kaiserslautern playmaker hammered the ball home from ten yards and the Czechs were beaten.

Rather than celebrate his goal, assist and UEFA man-of-the-match award, Henry chose to dwell on the chances that got away from him, especially the one that was swiftly followed by the Czech equaliser. 'For the first goal, I went one-on-one, but I missed my control and I was very lucky to score,' Henry said. 'I should have scored another, but I didn't and that put my team in trouble. I have to keep working in training to make sure that when I have the opportunity I score.'

Having lost narrowly to both Holland and France, the Czech Republic were now out of the tournament but Henry was full of praise for the Eastern European side. 'The Czech team didn't deserve to go out. They are one of the best teams in Europe, but had to play against strong sides. They can't go through now, but they are a good side.' The French side were through and, faced with a hectic schedule, Lemerre took the opportunity to rest eight players from the side which beat the Czechs, including Henry, for the game against the Dutch.

The tournament co-hosts were too good for the French reserves in the Amsterdam Arena and their 3–2 victory left them at the top of Group D, leading to a quarter-final showdown with Yugoslavia in Amsterdam, while the French returned to their adopted home in Bruges for a game against their trans-Pyrenean neighbours Spain. It was the first time the two sides had met in the competition since the 1984 final and the match started at a frenetic pace. In keeping with the rest of the tournament, both sides were committed to attack and good chances went begging at either end before Zidane opened the scoring.

Djorkaeff was fouled five yards outside the Spanish

penalty area and Zidane struck the ensuing free-kick with pace and swerve into the top right corner to give Santiago Canizares in the Spanish goal no chance of a save. The French lead lasted for only five minutes, however, as the Spaniards produced a rapid response. Racing Santander's lively winger Pedro Munitis, who had been giving Lilian Thuram a torrid time down France's right-hand side, won a penalty after the then Parma defender's debatable challenge was deemed illegal by Italian referee Pierluigi Collina.

Gaizka Mendieta made no mistake from the spot, sending Barthez the wrong way in the 38th minute. But the French side made an equally swift riposte to their setback when Djorkaeff restored *les Bleus*' lead just before half-time after good work by Vieira. As is often the way after a pulsating first half, the second half descended into a much scrappier affair, with Collina brandishing the yellow card on five occasions. Playing for once in the centre-forward position, Henry was having a quiet game. He was receiving little support from Djorkaeff and Christophe Dugarry on the flanks, but one of the many second-half bookings went to Spanish defender Paco who had committed one of the most cynical fouls of recent years on Henry.

Following a Spanish corner, Henry broke from deep in his own half and was forced wide as he approached the centre-circle. Galloping down the touchline into the Spanish half, Henry went past Paco and was hauled to the ground in a manner more suited to the rugby pitch. With nobody between himself and the goalkeeper, the only reason the full-back escaped the red card, much to the disgust of the French fans, was the sheer distance between Henry and the goal – but considering the form the young striker was in, it could be argued that he was denied a clear goal-scoring opportunity.

In the final minute it seemed that the decision could cost *les Bleus* as Barthez conceded a last-minute penalty for bringing down Fernandez Abelardo. The goalkeeper had failed to hold Vieira's header back and tangled with Abelardo as he tried to recover the ball. With nominated taker Mendieta off the pitch, responsibility for the penalty fell to Real Madrid striker Raul. Fortunately for Barthez and France, the pressure was too much for the young Spaniard and he sent his penalty high and wide of the French goal.

Having progressed to the semi-finals where they would play against Portugal, Henry and his team-mates were determined to show the doubters that their World Cup success wasn't a fluke. 'Some people said at France 98 that we only won the World Cup because of an easy group, because we were at home, we only beat Italy on penalties and because there was the golden goal,' Henry said. 'But we proved ourselves by beating Brazil 3–0 in the final. People were not happy because they said the World Cup happened in France; we were told this was an advantage.'

Henry and his team-mates took to the field against Portugal in Brussels with something of a point to prove as well as a new formation. After his subdued performance as a lone striker, Lemerre paired Henry with Anelka as he switched to 4-4-2 and the striking duo's pace caused the Portuguese defenders all sorts of troubles early on, but it was Portugal who opened the scoring completely against the run of play. French captain Didier Deschamps was making his hundredth international appearance but this achievement counted for nothing as he was muscled off the ball by Sergio Conceicao, who then teed up Nuno Gomes, whose fabulous strike made it 1–0 to Portugal after 19 minutes.

The score didn't change until six minutes after the break when a move built in north London brought reward for the French team. Arsenal's Vieira found former Gunner Anelka in space on the edge of the area, who in turn fed his Highbury replacement Henry. Henry swivelled and shot low past Vitor Baia with the help of a deflection off Fernando Couto.

There was little to separate the two sides after that, although Henry twice broke on to through balls from Zidane but was blocked as he unleashed his shots – first by Couto, then by Jorge Costa. With the teams so equally matched, the game inevitably headed for extra-time, where chances continued to be scarce and it took until the 117th minute for the Golden Goal to arrive. Trezeguet, on as a substitute for Henry, had a shot saved by Baia, but he couldn't hold the ball and it fell to Wiltord whose shot was stopped on the line by Abel Xavier's arm. The referee Guenter Benko at first appeared to have awarded a corner but, after consultation with his assistant, awarded a penalty to France, much to the disgust of the Portuguese players and fans.

When the Portuguese protestations had finally died down, Zidane stepped up to put the penalty confidently into the top-left corner and give Vitor Baia no chance. The Portuguese complained long into the night but to no avail and *les Bleus* were into the final of the European Championship where they would face Italy. The *Azzurri* had reached the final by decisively breaking their penalty jinx in their semi-final at the expense of the equally woeful spot-kick-taking Dutch to prevent a repeat of the Group D decider in the final.

The World Champions had continued their strong tournament form from two years previously in France, where they won despite a lack of proven goal-scorers. Michel Platini was very impressed by the new attacking options at Lemerre's disposal. 'We have some prodigious talents in Anelka, Henry and Wiltord, but we must remain realistic. There are a lot of other great forwards in the world such as Nuno Gomes, Francesco Totti, and Raul who are great players.'

The French footballing legend was asked to pick out his favourite. 'The most skilful is Thierry Henry; he has impressed me the most. He's played a great tournament. He has the pace of Anelka, and the sense of Trezeguet. He's got something that no French player has ever had. He can do everything: from scoring goals, to giving assists, crossing and creating space for other players, and he fights for every ball. I've never seen a player in France like him.'

With praise like that, Henry had a lot to live up to in the final in Rotterdam, and he was determined not to disappoint. Henry had extra motivation for the final after his unsuccessful spell in Serie A. 'Playing Italy in Euro 2000 was kind of special for me because I didn't do well in Italy and wanted to make a point,' Henry says.

Henry was again selected as the lone striker as Lemerre reverted to 4-5-1 to combat the Italian 3-5-2 formation, and he was a constant threat to the experienced *Azzurri* back line – both Luigi Di Biagio and Fabio Cannavaro received yellow cards for fouls on the mercurial striker. With Zidane being skilfully shadowed by Demetrio Albertini, Henry was responsible for creating most of the chances for France, but none of them found a way past Francesco Toldo in the Italian goal.

It was the 55th minute before either side found the back of the net, and it was the *Azzurri* who drew first blood. Alessandro Delvecchio met Gianluca Pessotto's right-wing cross with a left-footed finish into the roof of the net from six yards to put Italy ahead. The goal prompted a change from Lemerre, and he sent on Wiltord in place of Dugarry. The substitution eventually brought a reward for France and it was a bitter blow to the tough Italian defence, as Wiltord sped on to a long clearance from Barthez and shot past Toldo in the fourth minute of injury-time at the end of the game.

With such a late goal, the Italians had no chance of restoring their lead before the whistle and the game went into Golden Goal extra-time. After grabbing such a dramatic equaliser, the momentum was clearly with France and they completed a remarkable comeback when the other two substitutes combined in the 103rd minute. Pires got away down the left-hand side and cut back a perfect ball for Trezeguet to rifle home.

Trezeguet's Golden Goal meant that France became the first team to add the European Championship to the World Cup and, while Henry and his compatriots were happy lifting the Henri Delaunay Cup in turn and celebrating in Rotterdam, the Champs Elysees turned into party central once more. Jacques Chirac again got in on the act, appearing on live television to congratulate the nation. 'Tonight, I am proud of France and I am proud of the French. The French team has kept its genius,' the French President said.

Les Bleus needed everything they had to get through a tough final against such a well-organised defence as the Italians, and they were only seconds from failure before Wiltord's intervention. Henry was, as ever, full of praise for his opponents. 'They were compact and it was difficult to break them down,' he said. 'I had to try running from the centre to the wings because it was the only way I could get the ball at my feet. The Italians tend to always concentrate on the game, but they must have taken their eyes off for some amount of time during the game because we managed to score right at the end of the game.' They couldn't have left it much later.

Having won the two biggest international football tournaments in the world, there must have been something special about *les Bleus*, but Henry found it hard to say what made that side so good. 'I can't explain to you about the France team. We have a great mentality as you saw in the final and the semi-final. All the time we were losing 1–0 to the Italians and to the Portuguese, we attacked again and again. Coming back is usually difficult but of course we have a lot of quality and we have our mentality. We had to enjoy that final and then go and enjoy it with our fans in Paris.' Back in Paris the French squad was again met by thousands of ecstatic football fans, as the crowds swamped the Place de la Concorde less than 12 hours after the final and Trezeguet's Golden Goal.

Henry had finished both the World Cup in 1998 and the European Championship in 2000 as France's highest goal-scorer, with three goals in each competition. He had also been selected for the UEFA Technical Committee's 16-man

All-Star Teams in both of the tournaments. But as a key player in the two successful French sides, he refused to be drawn as to which of the sides was the better. 'I think it is difficult to compare the two. People will say that we are better now because we won away from home and because we played many great teams. But in football, a game is always a fight. For example, in qualifying we scored a goal in the last minute against Andorra to win 1–0 so that wasn't that easy. You can't compare the two since we won both the competitions.'

By leading the line in France's successful European Championship campaign, Henry had continued his development as a striker and he was certain of how to maintain his progress as a forward. 'Right now I need to have a good rest and then I really want to win something with the Arsenal next season,' he said. 'I signed for them to win some trophies and I was so disappointed with the end of the season for Arsenal because we finished far behind Manchester United and then we lost the UEFA Cup final too. Next season I want to make up for it. But for now I am happy to have won the European Championship with France.'

After the busiest season of his career, Henry had played 58 games for club and country, notching up 31 goals, and it's fair to say he deserved a break.

Chapter seven
Jacques in the Box

'We need a player who will be a fox in the box and on the pitch,' said Henry. 'We need a player like Owen is for Liverpool. I make a lot of runs and get wide a lot, but Owen is always in the box and we need someone like that. When I make wide runs and put in crosses, there is often no one there to put the ball in the net. Owen was the hero because he is always in the right place. We need a goal-scorer like that.'

Speaking after the FA Cup Final defeat at the hands of Michael Owen's Liverpool, Thierry Henry was understandably upset as he finished his second season at Highbury without a trophy. Having spent a great part of the year destroying full-backs and putting the ball into an 18-yard box devoid of Arsenal players, he felt the signing of a natural goal-scorer would complement his fantastic abilities, and bring some silverware back to north London.

The season started poorly as Arsenal crashed 1–0 away to Sunderland in their first game. Talismanic midfielder Patrick Vieira was sent off late in the game in the Stadium of Light and then received his marching orders for the second time in a week during Arsenal's first home game, a rare victory over Liverpool. The opening goal in a 2–0 win came from one of Henry's new team-mates Lauren, a Cameroon international signed from Spanish side Real Mallorca. Midfielder Lauren – full name Laureano Bisan-Etame Mayer – had been signed by Arsene Wenger, along with Henry's international team-mate winger Robert Pires from Olympique Marseille, to replace the Barcelona-bound pair Manu Petit and Marc Overmars.

Henry also got his first goal of the season in the last minute against the Scousers as he raced through in what was becoming typical Henry fashion. He had been held in high regard throughout Europe since he burst on to the scene as a winger with Monaco, but after his transformation into an attacker of real quality at Arsenal, and following his European Championship success with France, Henry was now regarded as one of the top three strikers in Europe. With the extra attention this was sure to bring him from Premiership defenders, Henry had a tough task ahead of him to live up to his prolific first season at Highbury, but he maintained his excellent scoring rate in the next game with a pair of goals against plucky Charlton Athletic.

Vieira was in determined form in the last game before his five-game ban, and he also grabbed a brace. The Senegal-born midfielder opened the scoring in the first half before

Charlton hit back to take a 2–1 lead into the break. Half-time provided a chance for the Gunners to regroup and, shortly after the restart, Henry lashed in a Tony Adams pass on the turn to equalise. But the Addicks would not lie down and they hit back within a minute through Graham Stuart. Arsenal dug deeper, however, and a further goal from Vieira levelled the scores, before Henry gave the north London side the lead, collecting a Pires cross with a fantastic first touch to take the defender out of the game, then beating the keeper with ease before Silvinho completed the scoring late on to make it 5–3.

Arsenal had to come from behind again a week later as they trailed 2–0 late into the game against Chelsea at Stamford Bridge. After 76 minutes, Henry pulled Arsenal back into the contest with a simple finish following good work by Silvinho down the left. The Brazilian full-back had also started the season well and he completed the comeback with five minutes to play, lashing in a loose ball from the edge of the Blues' box.

An impressive comeback against a valiant Charlton side, followed by another improbable turnaround at the Bridge, showed the team spirit that was developing among Wenger's multi-national squad. The English players, all remnants of George Graham's reign at the club, had always displayed true grit, as typified by the resolute defending of Adams, Lee Dixon and Martin Keown. But now the 'Old Guard' were passing that British fighting quality on to the likes of Ljungberg and Bergkamp, Henry and Vieira. And the amiable young Frenchmen were making it a relaxed, open and welcoming environment in the dressing room to help create what Monsieur Wenger often refers to as the special 'Arsenal spirit'.

Another Frenchman to be welcomed in to the Arsenal fold was striker Sylvain Wiltord, who signed from Bordeaux. After making a substitute appearance in the comeback in west London, the French striker made his first start partnering his compatriot Henry up front in the next game away to Bradford City. The West Yorkshire side made life tough for the Gunners for a second successive season and the points were shared as Arsenal again came from behind to draw 1–1. The goal came when young left-back Ashley Cole, deputising for the injured Silvinho, converted a cross from Henry.

The fine goal-scoring form from Arsenal's left-backs continued in the next game away to Sparta Prague. After crashing out of the Champions League at the first hurdle the previous year and finishing second best in the UEFA Cup final, Henry and his team-mates were determined to make an impression back in the upper echelon of European competition. Drawn in Group B with Shakhtar Donetsk of the Ukraine, Lazio from the Italian capital and the Czech champions, it was important to get off to a good start in Prague. And Arsenal did just that as they took all three points in eastern Europe, with Silvinho's goal securing a 1–0 win.

With games coming thick and fast due to participation in the Champions League, and the fact that Wenger now had four attackers of proven international class at his disposal following the acquisition of Wiltord, Henry found himself rotated out of the starting line-up for the first time since his rebirth as a striker. Coventry City were the visitors to

Highbury as the fresh legs were given a run out and Wiltord justified his selection with the opening goal, his first for Arsenal. But no second goal was forthcoming, and it took the introduction of Henry from the bench to make the game safe as he crafted a second goal for Paolo Vernazza.

Being a substitute was a far cry from the previous season when Henry had become the mainstay of the Arsenal attack. At the start of the season, before the signing of Wiltord, Henry had been asked if he felt under pressure as Arsenal's number one striker: 'Not really,' he said. 'I prefer to be in that position than sitting on the bench. Sometimes it's strange because you have players who can't seem to manage and can't accept the pressure. I like to be under pressure; it's good when you go to shoot or take a penalty, it makes me play better. But it doesn't mean I'm going to score all the time.'

But Henry took relegation to the bench, which would be unthinkable today, with the good grace expected of such a model professional and, following the Coventry game, he was back leading the line as Shakhtar Donetsk came to north London. The Ukrainians proved much tougher opponents than expected after losing their first game at home to Lazio 3–0 and they managed to get themselves into a commanding position, leading 2–0 in the final minutes of the first half despite relentless Arsenal pressure. The Gunners' constant attacking menace finally got its reward late in the half as Wiltord followed up Henry's saved penalty attempt. It was the first time Henry had failed to score from the spot in an Arsenal shirt and this may have had something to do with the fact that he had failed to score in the previous three and a half games despite numerous attempts.

In the second half, Henry and his fellow attackers continued to lay siege to the Donetsk goal, but it took an unlikely hero to get Arsenal the 3 points their play deserved as Martin Keown first bundled in Silvinho's corner with 85 minutes on the clock and then, in stoppage time, the uncompromising centre-back converted Kanu's pull-back to make it 3–2 to the Gunners.

Henry's barren spell continued in the next match, although he still managed to influence the outcome of the game as Dennis Bergkamp followed up one of his shots to make it 1–1 away to Ipswich Town. The Dutchman took his good form into the next game where he created both goals for Fredrik Ljungberg at home against Lazio. Arsenal won 2–0 and took control of Group B.

Henry had now gone six games without a goal and Arsenal fans could have wished for their main offensive weapon to be in better form for the visit of the league leaders. But the only goal of the game when Manchester United visited Highbury on 1 October 2000 came from the boot of Thierry Henry and it was well worth waiting for. With Dennis Irwin in close attendance, Henry received the ball with his back to the goal on the corner of the visitors' box. He flicked the ball up with his right foot, swivelled and struck the ball, again with his right, all in one movement with such pace and precision that the ball arrowed into the top corner of Fabien Barthez's goal, leaving the French goalkeeper with no chance of a save.

It was a goal of such breathtaking brilliance that it will live long in the memory of all those who saw it. Arsene Wenger was unequivocal in his praise of his star pupil and the strike that won the game. 'I don't think I've seen many better,' the manager said. 'It was a goal from nothing. It has been playing on his mind that he hasn't scored so it was important for him. I think sometimes it is easier when you do something crazy like that because you don't have time to think about what you are doing. He is a fantastic finisher and has frightening pace; he is probably now the best around.'

Henry had scored 16 goals in 15 games in an Arsenal shirt on either side of Euro 2000 before hitting his dry patch, and he admits that it was starting to depress him. 'I was down because I hadn't scored recently,' Henry said. 'Barthez was my team-mate for Monaco and France, so it was strange to get a goal against him, but we needed it.'

Henry needed it more than anyone, as his manager testified. 'It was important for Thierry because he has never gone through a patch like this where he hasn't scored. It's part of the learning process for him,' Wenger said. 'But I kept confidence in him because he can provide chances as well as score them; it's just that sometimes his team-mates are not quick enough to get into the box.'

Even if his team-mates are not always fast enough to convert some of the chances that the mercurial Frenchman creates, they were very quick to praise his spectacular strike. 'Go and check out that Henry goal, it's a very special effort,' wrote Bergkamp on his personal website only days after the game. 'What a joy it is to have him at the club.'

Henry scored another, somewhat simpler goal in his next game for the club when Aston Villa came to Highbury. He ran on to a Pires ball and shot through a defender's legs and past David James to win the match 1–0. Arsenal followed up their two Premier League victories by qualifying for the next stage of the Champions League with a 1–1 draw in Rome against Lazio and a 4–2 home win against Sparta Prague, either side of a London derby away to West Ham United. Against the Hammers, Henry again found himself on the bench as Arsenal registered their first Premier League away win of the season at the fifth attempt. Arsenal's number 14 was restored to the first XI in the next match when Arsenal bettered their four-goal haul against Prague with a 5–0 demolition of Manchester City at Highbury. Henry was the hero as he scored two goals and created another for his compatriot Sylvain Wiltord.

After City's visit to north London, Arsenal found themselves second in the table behind the other team from Manchester, if only on goal difference, but despite getting a second away victory of the season – a 1–0 win against Middlesbrough through a penalty from Henry – the Gunners gave up valuable ground in the title race with just one point coming from a possible nine as Wenger's strikers hit three consecutive blanks.

The month of November wasn't just bad for Arsenal on the domestic front as they lost their last Group B match away to Shakhtar Donetsk 3–0 and, although that didn't stop them from progressing to the next group stage, their first game in the second group stage saw them crash 4–1 to Spartak Moscow in bitterly cold, arctic temperatures.

December started better for Henry and his colleagues as they added another win to their impressive home form, beating Southampton 1–0, before the visit of Bayern Munich in the Champions League. Group C of the second stage consisted of Arsenal, Spartak Moscow, Bayern Munich and Olympique Lyonnais and, after losing so heavily away in Moscow, it was vital that the Gunners got a good result against the Germans before the winter break.

Arsenal got off to a great start when Henry scored his first European goal of the season in his eighth game – a very poor return considering he had notched eight in twelve games the previous season – reflecting the extra respect and attention he was getting throughout the continent. There were only four minutes on the clock when Henry ran on to a Kanu pass to open the scoring and, when Henry returned the favour, setting up Kanu ten minutes into the second half, it seemed the Gooners' dreams were coming true. But Bayern Munich rapidly responded through a Michael Tarnat free-kick, before fighting back to 2–2 with a goal from Mehmet Scholl.

The visitors' comeback meant that Arsenal would be bottom of the group until the competition resumed in mid-February. After securing just one point from their first two matches, there was going to have to be a dramatic improvement in the last four games for the north London side to progress from Group C. But the Arsenal players quickly put this disappointment behind them and trounced Newcastle United in the next game.

Henry opened the scoring after 13 minutes, latching on to an Adams ball over the top, and he created another goal for Ray Parlour. The Romford Pele was in inspired form and notched his second-ever Arsenal hat-trick as the Geordies were put to the sword 5–0.

A big win was the perfect tonic for the Gunners just before the north London derby at White Hart Lane, but the under-achieving Lilywhites lifted their game to secure a draw against their bitter rivals, who had to wait until the last minute for Vieira to head in a corner to make it 1–1. If Arsenal had won the game against their neighbours, they could have closed the gap behind Manchester United at the top of the table to just three points. Henry, however, refused to give up the fight for silverware. 'Of course it's still possible for us to win the title,' Henry said. 'Manchester United had a long break when they went to Brazil last season and were fresh when they came back. I want to see if they are going to be fresh this time as well.'

Henry then conceded that he feels some teams are beaten before the game starts against the Gunners' championship rivals. 'Sometimes I think that when Manchester United play away, they are allowed to play. Not even from the start do some teams try like Charlton [who battled back from 3–1 down to draw with the champions] recently did. They didn't give up and showed everyone what is possible.'

Looking ahead to Arsenal's next game away to Liverpool, points were vital to keep Wenger's side in the title race, but Henry was taking nothing for granted. 'It's never easy there but I hope we will take at least one point.'

It would be one point more than their Mancunian rivals achieved on Merseyside. 'Manchester United do sometimes drop points against big teams,' Henry went on. 'Liverpool drew there [at Old Trafford] last season, Chelsea drew there this season and we always get points there. So it's not a surprise.'

Liverpool manager Gerard Houllier was determined that his defenders wouldn't be caught unawares by the pace and the skill of the young Frenchman he had coached many years before. 'Thierry is a very dangerous and quick striker,' the former National Technical Director of French football said. 'He is very mobile and has plenty of movement up front. He can score goals, right foot, left foot, and he has improved a lot, I think, in the past two years. He's a world champion, a European champion and, as everyone knows, I have known him for a very long time and he's a very gifted player.'

Unfortunately for Arsenal, Henry failed to find the target as the Gunner's terrible away form hit a new low the following Saturday when they lost 4–0 at Anfield, two days before Christmas. But a trend was developing in Wenger's Arsenal – affecting Henry in particular – and that was the way in which they responded to setbacks. On Boxing Day, just three days after the loss to Liverpool, Arsenal beat Leicester City 6–1 and Henry scored his first Arsenal hat-trick.

It was a game that showcased all the exceptional attributes that mark Henry out as one of the best footballers of a generation. His first goal came ten minutes before half-time as he half volleyed a Pires corner straight into the back of the net from the edge of the area. It was a sublime piece of skill. Henry then demonstrated his passing ability as he set up Vieira for Arsenal's second before Ade Akinbiyi gave the Foxes a glimmer of hope.

Henry wiped that out soon after, however, as he restored the two-goal advantage with a display of his strength, holding off Matt Elliott before slotting home. Arsenal's fourth came courtesy of Ljungberg, before Henry showed his pace and close control, racing on to a Nelson Vivas pass, then standing up Tim Flowers in the Leicester goal, rounding the keeper and stroking the ball into an empty net. Having scored three for the first time in his professional career, Henry still had time to whip in a perfect cross for Adams to complete the scoring at the far post.

Henry was delighted to have finally got three goals in one game, but typical of a man who is never prepared to rest on his laurels, he spoke of his disappointment that he hadn't done it sooner, 'It was a very special day for me because it was my first hat-trick for Arsenal,' he said. 'But it should have come before now. Even last week I could have scored three against Tottenham.'

Wenger was very happy with Henry's performance and that of the team, but he was finding it hard to understand why a side that had only dropped 4 points in 14 games at home was so poor on their travels. Of 14 away games in the Premier League and Champions League, Arsenal had lost twice as many as they'd won and only 2 of Henry's 14 goals came away from Highbury – and one of those was from the penalty spot. 'Thierry was outstanding, but he and everybody else have to show we can be consistent away from home as well,' the manager said. 'We are strong at Highbury, unbeaten here in the Premiership, but frankly I don't know why we cannot seem to do it away, because we try to play the same way everywhere. Whether we rely too much on Henry for the goals or whether he relies too much on the team playing well is a question for which I have to find an answer.

Until I do, there is no point in trying to catch Manchester United and win the Championship.'

Such a defeatist attitude may have undermined his players, since in the next match at home against Sunderland Arsenal threw away a 2–0 half-time lead, after Henry had provided crosses for both Vieira and Dixon to score, to draw 2–2. This meant that, going into the New Year, Arsenal were eight points behind Manchester United in a seemingly lost title race.

But the efforts of Henry for Arsenal and France throughout 2000 saw him rewarded with the French Footballer of the Year award. In a poll of journalists by *France Football* magazine, Henry came out on top and he was happy his good form was being noticed. 'This was my best year, for sure,' Henry said. 'But it was not easy at first and people forget that, when I arrived at Arsenal, I was living on the bench. With the Gunners, my game improved in all its aspects, headers, controlling the ball and especially tackling. In England, even if you're technically gifted, you're nobody if you're not aggressive.'

But individual awards meant little to Henry and he was far more interested in getting his hands on some silverware with his club. 'Of course I am quite happy with being voted the French Player of the Year, but the main thing in my head now is to win something with Arsenal.'

On New Year's Day, Henry's trophy ambitions took a further setback as Arsenal lost to Charlton Athletic at the Valley. Henry was missing with a knock he had picked up against Sunderland two days before and the Gunners failed to find a way through the Addicks defence without him. The home side came out on top 1–0. Henry had a chance to rest his injury again the following weekend as Arsenal began their FA Cup campaign away to lowly Carlisle United. Wiltord filled Henry's boots well, scoring the only goal in a tough trip to the North-East.

After sitting out a couple of games Henry was fit to reclaim his position in the Arsenal attack for the visit of Chelsea, but Wenger's side's stuttering form continued as they dropped two home points against the Blues in a 1–1 draw, and followed that with a 0–0 draw away to Leicester City. The only redeeming feature of the game at Filbert Street for Arsenal fans was the first appearance of a new left-footed midfield player, who was there to add balance to the centre of the park, something that had been missing since Petit's departure for Barcelona. After problems with his passport had delayed his arrival in England, Edu – or Eduardo Cesar Gaspar, to give him his full name – had taken a long time from signing for the Gunners to kicking his first ball in a red-and-white shirt. But he only lasted 15 minutes against the Foxes before a broken leg meant he had to make way in a dull game in the Midlands.

Henry found himself surplus to requirements again in the FA Cup, as Wenger preferred to rest his star striker and give Wiltord the opportunity to lead the line. Which he did to great effect against Queens Park Rangers in a 6–0 win, which meant Henry could rest easy on the bench. On the back of their effortless Cup win, Arsenal put together a run of three straight league victories before the recommencement of the Champions League, culminating in Henry's first goal for a month and a half against Ipswich Town. After coming off the bench, Henry put the finishing touch to a fantastic passing move down Arsenal's right-hand side and secured the points for the Gunners in a 1–0 win at Highbury.

Having emerged from another barren spell, Henry went so far as to score a header in his next game away in Lyon, to make it three from three games in his home country since his transfer out of Monaco. He met a perfect cross from the left-hand side by the rampaging Cole with a textbook header to leave the keeper well beaten and the three points on their way to London. They were much needed points for Arsenal, as they lifted them off the bottom of Group C and into second place.

Buoyed by getting their Champions League campaign back on track, the Gunners headed into an FA Cup fifth-round showdown with Chelsea. After two draws in the league, it was always going to be a close game between the two London sides and, after a goalless first half, Henry gave Arsenal the lead from the penalty-spot early into the second. The perennial scourge of Highbury, Jimmy Floyd Hasselbaink, struck back before two late goals from Wiltord sent Wenger's men into the quarter-finals.

With games coming thick and fast, Arsenal had to entertain Lyon at Highbury three days later and the busy schedule may have been starting to affect the Gunners as they let a 1–0 lead slip to draw the game and leave the group wide open, with only two points separating second and fourth with two games to play. The hectic run of games had definitely left Wenger short of experienced cover at the back and Arsenal went into their next game away at Old Trafford without Adams, Keown or Dixon.

Henry managed to equalise an early goal, sidefooting home a Pires pull-back after good interplay with Wiltord down the right flank. But the lack of leadership in defence cost the Gunners and, after Henry's goal, it was one-way traffic as the reigning champions humiliated Arsenal 6–1. The loss left Arsenal 16 points behind Manchester United with only 10 league games remaining, and with this in mind Wenger rested Henry for the visit of West Ham 3 days before Spartak Moscow's journey to north London. Henry was not missed as Arsenal bounced back with Wiltord hitting a first-half hat-trick in a 3–0 win over the Hammers.

Arsenal managed to get some revenge for their mauling at the hands of the Muscovites in a 1–0 win. Henry again linked up with Ashley Cole, this time heading in a corner from the young full-back. It wasn't Henry's best game for the club and there was some controversy as Wenger decided to replace Bergkamp rather than Henry, much to the dismay of the Arsenal fans. But it was the Frenchman who kept the Gooners' hopes of progressing alive with his header eight minutes from time.

Always one to acknowledge his faults, Henry admitted liability for a poor performance. 'I should have been the one taken off as I was so bad. I didn't deserve to be there, I felt guilty. Sometimes you have to be honest with yourself and I wasn't playing well. I should have had to go off,' the striker said with refreshing candour. 'But in the end I wanted to prove the manager right and give something to him, to Dennis and the crowd. I wanted to score for Dennis.'

Bergkamp was having a good game and was not happy to

come off, but Wenger explained the thoughts behind his substitution after the game. 'Dennis played well and I can understand that he was not pleased to come off, but I was in a position where I needed fresh legs and had to make a decision,' the manager said. 'We needed physical power more than anything else in the last 20 minutes and I thought Henry could provide that. We had got to a situation where it didn't look like we could create any more. Henry did not have one of his best games but he is strong and powerful and in the end it got us a goal. I thought it was justice.'

With Arsenal winning and Lyon beating Bayern Munich 3–0, the result meant that, with one round left, any two of the top three sides could go through from Group C. Arsenal would top the Group by beating Bayern in Munich, but would go through, no matter what, if Lyon failed to win in Moscow. 'We will definitely go there [to Munich] to win,' Henry said. 'But it will be a strange game, and people will be listening to the other score-lines. It's a proper Champions League game, either us or Bayern can go out, or both of us can go through.'

Henry's manager echoed his opinion. 'It is one of the most competitive groups in the tournament,' said Wenger. 'All we know is that, with one game to go, Moscow are out. Anything else is possible.'

Before the conclusion of the second group stage of the Champions League, Arsenal had an FA Cup appointment with Blackburn Rovers at Highbury. Wenger again took the opportunity to rest Henry against lower-league opposition as Rovers were then in the First Division. With the then Blackburn manager, Graeme Souness, more focused on promotion back to the Premier League, Arsenal made short work of the Ewood Park outfit with two goals in the first five minutes and another before half-time in a 3–0 win.

A nice easy victory achieved with minimum exertion should have set Arsenal up nicely for their crucial European match in Munich but the Gunners put in one of their most woeful performances of the season as they lost 1–0 to the German champions. Lady luck was wearing an Arsenal shirt that day, however, and Wenger's side still managed to get through to the Champions League quarter-finals as Spartak Moscow held Lyon to a draw, meaning Arsenal finished level on points with the French side and went through because of the results between the two sides – an Arsenal win and a draw.

Henry was on the bench again for Arsenal's next game away to Aston Villa in a dull game that highlighted the tired state of Wenger's men. By rotating his attackers, the Frenchman had hoped his players would be sharp whenever called upon, but when the replacements weren't fresh, it gave the impression that the team lacked the cohesion and understanding that comes from playing together regularly. This was most noticeable at the business end of the season when players often begin to rely on instinct as their bodies tire. Villa Park bore witness to this in a drab 0–0 draw, which was, along with the game against Munich, one of the worst Arsenal games of the season.

Henry had the chance to put Arsenal's indifferent form behind him for a few days as he joined up with the French national squad. As World Cup-holders and European Champions, *les Bleus* only had friendlies to keep them busy until the next World Cup. Henry remained a vital member of Roger Lemerre's team and, in his sixth friendly since Euro 2000, he managed to add to his international tally with the second goal in a 5–0 rout of Japan.

Back at Highbury after the international break, Arsenal had to entertain Tottenham Hotspur in a game that was overshadowed by the news of the death of Arsenal legend David 'Rocky' Rocastle at the tender age of 33. The minute's silence before the game was impeccably observed by both sets of fans, making a mockery of Bill Shankly's now infamous quote about football, life and death. When the game finally started, it was obvious that the Lilywhites had come for the point that they started the game with as David Pleat took charge of Arsenal's neighbours following the sacking of former Highbury hero George Graham.

Pleat's negative game plan worked well for over an hour but, when the breakthrough came, it was fitting that it should be Arsenal's number seven who scored on the day Rocky lost his battle with cancer. Pires beat two defenders to score with a curling shot past Neil Sullivan in the visitors' goal. With only three minutes left on the clock, Sullivan was beaten again as Henry turned Chris Perry inside out before sidefooting past the keeper.

The 2–0 win in the north London derby got a tough week off to a good start for the Gunners, and it got better four days later as they won their Champions League quarter-final first leg against Valencia 2–1. It was Arsenal's first-ever game in the final eight of Europe's premier club competition and they acquitted themselves well. Battling back from Robert Ayala's first-half strike to dominate the second 45 minutes,

Wenger's side got back on level terms when a brilliant bit of awareness left Henry one-on-one with the goalkeeper. Kanu laid a Wiltord cross off to Pires with his back to goal and, as the Valencia defence tried to clear the box, Pires back-heeled the ball straight to Henry who stroked it home.

While Highbury was still rocking from the celebrations of Henry's equaliser, Parlour seized on a loose ball and drove forward into the Valencia half and unleashed a venomous shot from the edge of the box, which arrowed into the top corner to put the Gunners ahead after 60 minutes. In the final half-hour, Henry and his team-mates produced numerous chances but failed to add to their lead, so Arsenal would travel to the Mestalla with a slender one-goal advantage.

In the two weeks between the first and second legs of the quarter-final, Arsenal had some serious domestic business to attend to before flying to Spain. Next up for the Gunners was an all-north London FA Cup semi-final at Old Trafford. Tottenham had found a permanent replacement for Graham in the days after Arsenal's 2–0 Highbury win but, even with new manager Glenn Hoddle in charge at White Hart Lane, Henry was supremely confident when asked his thoughts on the big game by the BBC. 'I don't want to be arrogant or anything,' Henry said. 'But they have to be scared of us, not us scared of them, because it is going to be like the final of the World Cup for them.'

It is true that Tottenham were the underdogs as they were heading for another season of mid-table mediocrity in the league, but reinforced by the superstition about 'years that end in a one', they clung to the hope of an FA Cup

Top: Henry, back row far right, in his early days at Clairefontaine.

Right: 'L'attaquant De Demain': Henry made an instant impression at Monaco.

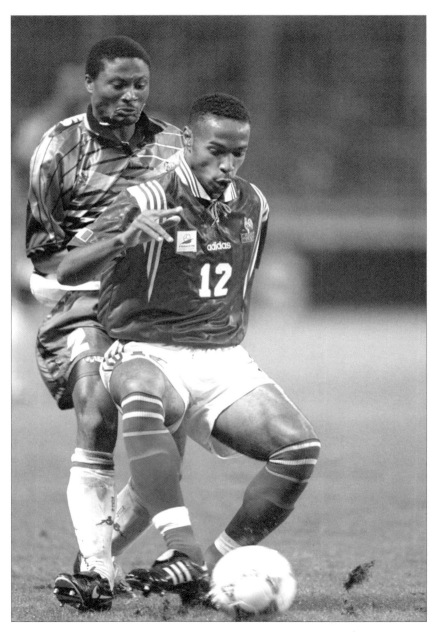

With his socks characteristically high, Henry made his international debut against South Africa.

Top: Celebrating World Cup victory with, from left, Marcel Desailly, Robert Pires, and Aime Jacquet in 1998.

Bottom: At Juventus, Henry didn't always see eye-to-eye with manager Marcello Lippi.

Top: Henry was delighted to join up with Arsene Wenger at Arsenal.

Bottom: Giovanni van Bronckhorst congratulates Henry, as his goal against Schalke 04 in 2001 makes him Arsenal's leading scorer in European competition.

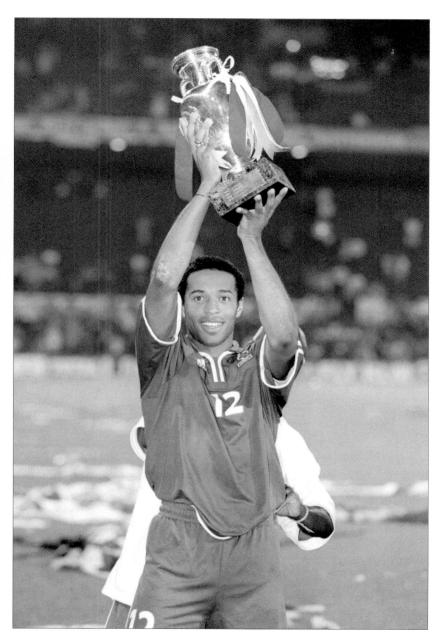

After a successful first year at Highbury, Henry was a key figure in France's Euro 2000 triumph.

Henry celebrated his first Arsenal trophy with his team-mates on a parade through the streets of north London.

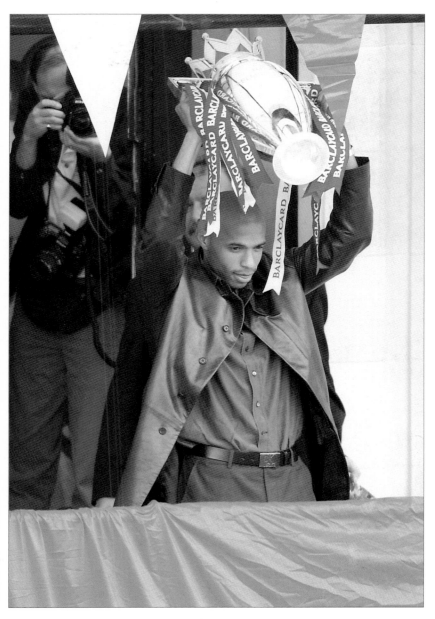

Days after the FA Cup success, Arsenal won the 'Double' at Old Trafford. Here Henry lifts the Premiership trophy at Islington Town Hall.

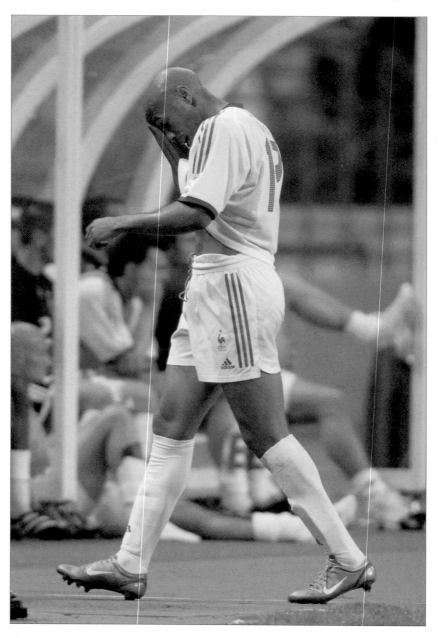

Henry was sent-off against Uruguay to compound his misery at the 2002 World Cup, in Japan and South Korea.

triumph. But Arsenal were once again enjoying a far more successful season than their neighbours with genuine if somewhat diminished title aspirations; they were also in the semi-finals of the FA Cup and the quarter-finals of the Champions League. But the beauty of sport lies in the uncertainty and the unpredictability of it all; just ask a bookmaker.

In the event, able to call on an almost fully fit squad, Arsenal had the better of the early exchanges and it was totally against the run of play when Gary Doherty scored the opening goal to put Tottenham ahead against their fiercest rivals. Football is a game full of superstitious people and for a while it seemed that there might be something behind the regularity of Tottenham cup wins in 'years that end with a one'. However, Vieira was having none of it and, with a performance that typified his contributions for the season, he won the game almost single-handed.

Henry put in a solid performance but Vieira, his compatriot and long-time friend, was colossal as first he headed in the Arsenal equaliser and then continued to drive his team-mates forward until the job was done. A Pires strike with 15 minutes to go meant that Arsenal would be going to the Millennium Stadium in Cardiff and Thierry Henry would be appearing in his first FA Cup Final.

Arsenal travelled back up to Manchester in high spirits three days later to face City at Maine Road. Henry was on the bench again as the manager rotated his strike force to good effect, the Gunners running out 4–0 winners with goals from Ljungberg twice, Wiltord and Kanu. Wenger's side were in great form after winning 4 games in 12 days and scoring 10 goals, but this was all undone in the next game as Arsenal finally conceded the title to Manchester United, losing 3–0 to Middlesbrough at Highbury.

It really was a bizarre game as the Gunners lost their first home game of the season apart from a Worthington Cup tie. Two–nil down at half-time by virtue of two own goals conceded by Brazilian duo Edu and Silvinho, Arsenal ended up losing the game 3–0 and they were left sixteen points behind Fergie's men with only five games to play. It wasn't the ideal preparation for the journey to Spain and the European showdown with Valencia, and maybe some of the Arsenal players had ignored the footballing mantra of 'taking one game at a time'.

If some players already had their minds on Valencia before the game against Boro, it didn't help them when they got out to Spain. With a one-goal advantage from the first leg, it seemed the team were caught in two minds as to whether to attack in search of the away goal that would leave the Spaniards needing two, or whether it was best to defend the lead for 90 minutes. In the end, neither option worked out for the Gunners and, with John Carew's late header, Valencia went through to the semi-finals. Arsenal were left with only the FA Cup to play for if they wanted to win silverware.

Henry and his team-mates continued to show their resilience the following weekend as they recovered from another setback to beat Everton 4–1. Henry slid a ball through to Ljungberg to open the scoring in the first half at Highbury and, despite the Toffees equalising through former Gunner Kevin Campbell, 3 goals in the second 45 saw Arsenal come out on top. Grimandi and Wiltord both scored before Henry added a late fourth as the ball broke to him from a Vieira tackle.

Following another international break, during which Henry scored in a friendly against Portugal, Wenger named his leading scorer among the substitutes for the trip to Derby County the following weekend. He hoped to keep Henry fresh for Cardiff. It didn't affect the outcome, however, as Arsenal came out 2–1 winners with goals from Kanu and Pires.

The Gunners won by the same 2–1 score-line in their last game before the FA Cup Final when Leeds United were the visitors at Highbury. Ljungberg played a one-two with Henry before opening the scoring, and Wiltord made it 2–0 before Ian Harte got a consolation goal for the visitors with a vicious free-kick.

Arsenal travelled to Cardiff with a full complement of fit players for a clash with Liverpool. In the two meetings between the sides in the league, it was one win apiece and, although Arsenal had suffered in the game at Anfield, everyone was predicting a close and exciting Cup Final. In a fitting tribute to the sadly departed Rocastle, the Arsenal mascot for the day was Ryan Rocastle, Rocky's nine-year-old son.

The Gunners had the better of the game from the start with Henry a constant menace down the Arsenal left, regularly speeding past the Liverpool right-back, Jamie Carragher, as if he were standing in treacle. But Arsenal were unable to beat Sander Westerveld between the sticks, and the one time Henry did get the ball past the keeper his shot was stopped on the line by Stephane Henchoz, whose clear use of an arm somehow went unnoticed by both the referee and his linesman.

In the second half, Arsenal continued to dominate the game and finally got the reward their play deserved after 72 minutes when Ljungberg's run into the box was perfectly picked out by Pires. The Swedish midfielder took one touch to go round the keeper and then finished brilliantly from a narrow angle. Wary of the way games had been lost earlier in the season, Arsenal refused to sit back and defend their lead. They continued to carve out chances, the best of which fell to Henry almost immediately after Ljungberg's goal, but Westerveld pulled off a brilliant point-blank save to keep the score at 1–0.

It was not to be the Gunners' day, however, and Liverpool equalised from nowhere when Owen seized on a loose ball after a free-kick to rifle home on the turn after 82 minutes. The diminutive England striker still wasn't finished and, with just three minutes left to play, he ran at the Arsenal defence and shot across David Seaman with his weaker, left foot. The Liverpool contingent were in raptures as they claimed the FA Cup like a phoenix from the flames. For their part, the Arsenal players and fans were inconsolable.

The game encapsulated Arsenal's season as they dominated the game almost from start to finish, creating plenty of chances with Henry at the heart of most of them. But they were away from Highbury and somehow they ended up with nothing to show for their efforts.

Henry was very hard on himself in the aftermath of the Final, saying, 'I messed up the chance to finish the game for us after Freddie put us in front. I missed a big, big opportunity for 2–0 and they would not have come back from that.

'I have had a fine season again, I think, and I wanted to finish it off by scoring and winning the FA Cup with Arsenal, but I missed my chances and Michael Owen took his. I have to admit it.'

But the Cup Final defeat and the agonising way in which it was inflicted only gave Henry and his team-mates more motivation and determination looking ahead to the following campaign. 'I want to come back next season and fight and do something for Arsenal. We want to have another chance to win the FA Cup and we want to win other competitions as well, but most of all we need to make a stronger challenge to Manchester United because the title race has been boring again.'

The season was not yet over, however, as the FA had rescheduled the Cup Final, moving it forward from its traditional place at the end of the league season to the weekend before the conclusion of the Premier League. The idea was to give successful sides more time to rearrange fixtures at a vital time of the season. With nothing left to play for in the league, the Gunners laboured to a 0–0 draw away to Newcastle United three days after the Cup Final, before heading for the south coast to face Southampton in their final game of the season.

The game against the Saints was a typical end-of-season affair with plenty of goals and chances at both ends. Arsenal took the lead twice, first through Cole and then through Ljungberg, with a final assist of the season going to Henry after he unselfishly laid the ball square following a good run. But in the last-ever league game at the Dell, it seemed appropriate when Saints legend Matthew Le Tissier scored a late goal on the turn to inflict another away defeat on the Gunners.

Arsenal finished the season in 2nd place, 10 points behind Manchester United, and Henry scored 17 league goals, one FA Cup goal and 4 in Europe, making a grand total of 22. Arsenal and Henry's dismal away form seemed intertwined as highlighted by the fact that only four of his goals were scored on his travels. But it would be somewhat harsh to lay the blame for a whole team's travel sickness on one player, even one as talented as Henry. Unquestionably though, the Arsenal squad as a whole under-performed on the road and they would need to improve the following season.

Despite his troubles away from home, Henry still managed to take some positives out of the season, pointing to his levels of fitness throughout the campaign. 'I feel lucky I didn't have a big injury or anything else and I've been able to play in all the games. That is definitely one of my satisfactions this season,' he said, before ironically missing his country's participation in the Confederations Cup that summer through injury. At least it gave him two whole months to recharge his batteries for the next long season when Henry and Arsenal would be looking to improve.

'You want to do well for your personal ambition, but you can't always think of that because success is within the team,' Henry said. 'I scored 26 goals last season and I have 22 this time, but I know I have missed many others. I am not the only one, but I hold my hand up and everybody has to do the same because we certainly don't want to feel so down like this again at the end of next season.'

With the determination that had hallmarked his Highbury career, it was fair to say that, if he put his mind to it, the chances were that Henry and Arsenal would be feeling a lot better 12 months down the line.

Chapter eight
Double the Fun

'I love life at Arsenal; there is no better place in the world at the moment. And if the board wanted me to sign away my life to the club, I'd probably do it at the moment. I'm only in my third season with Arsenal. But you get a feel for a place and a sense of belonging, and life couldn't be better,' said Thierry Henry. The Gunners had just won the Premiership and FA Cup Double and it was a good time to be an Arsenal player.

The 2001–02 season began with an influx of players at Highbury, Wenger had been very busy over the summer and signed five new recruits, including a potential 'fox in the box' of the kind Henry had wished for at the end of the previous season. Francis Jeffers was the youngster signed from Everton with a good scoring record at a mid-table club and it was hoped that his nose for goal would see him build a formidable strike partnership with Henry at Highbury.

Other new team-mates for Henry included Dutch midfielder Giovanni van Bronckhorst from Rangers and goalkeeper Richard Wright from Ipswich Town, but by far the most controversial signing of the close season was Sol Campbell from Tottenham Hotspur. After defensive injuries had undermined Arsenal's challenge for honours the previous season, the England centre-back brought valuable experience to the back line and would hopefully make the Gunners harder to beat especially on their travels. Henry was delighted with the signing of the tough-tackling defender, as he said, 'First of all I was thinking I wouldn't have to play against him any more, so I was happy.'

With Campbell in the line-up, Arsenal made a much better start to their new campaign than they had done their last, winning 4-0 at Middlesbrough to get the season up and running away from home. Henry also seemed to have put his travel sickness behind him and grabbed the first Arsenal goal of 2001–02, chesting down and volleying home a deflected Wiltord cross just before half-time. Ray Parlour's dismissal early in the second half reined the Gunners in somewhat before Ugo Ehiogu's late red card gave Pires a chance to add a second from the spot. Henry, the usual penalty-taker, had made way for Bergkamp who put the gloss on the win with two late goals.

With more points from one game than in the first three away games the year before, it was ironic that Arsenal should lose their next game at home to Leeds United. Wenger's side put the early season home defeat behind them in the next game as they racked up a second 4–0 score-line when Leicester City came to Highbury. Henry came off the bench at 2–0 to have a hand in the last two goals, clipping home a Kanu lay-off from the edge of the box and having a late header saved which Kanu followed up.

Having helped Arsenal to third in the league, three points behind early leaders Bolton Wanderers, Henry played in his second international of the season, yet another friendly, this time against Chile. With a chance to defend the World Cup just months away, it was important for coach Roger Lemerre to keep an eye on his players and, after playing the second half during a 2–1 defeat in Santiago, Henry flew back to the English capital for his first London derby of the season.

Henry maintained his new improved away form with the opening goal at Stamford Bridge, following up a shot by Pires which Ed de Goey pushed into his path. But Chelsea fought back and Jimmy Floyd Hasselbaink got his customary goal against Arsenal in a 1–1 draw. The next game for Henry was away in the Mediterranean as Arsenal began their Champions League campaign against Real Mallorca. The other teams in Group C were Schalke 04 and Panathinaikos, which made the Gunners clear favourites to progress to the second group stage.

But the Arsenal way is never the easy way and, after going a goal behind and down to ten men in the eleventh minute, Henry and his team-mates failed to find a way through the Spanish defence and lost the game 1–0.

Arsenal refused to be affected by this setback though and won their next game 3–1 away to Fulham. Ljungberg got the first goal after Henry's shot was deflected straight to him unmarked in front of Edwin Van Der Sar and the Swede made no mistake from five yards. After Steed Malbranque had equalised for the Cottagers, Henry himself restored the Arsenal lead with less than ten minutes remaining as he put the finishing touch to a beautiful move after Ljungberg picked out his run into the box. Bergkamp completed the scoring in the final minute and Arsenal won 3–1.

Back in the Champions League, Arsenal overcame a difficult German side at Highbury as they ran out 3–2 winners over Schalke 04 with Henry grabbing a brace. Henry's first goal was his 13th in Europe for the Gunners and it made him Arsenal's joint top scorer in European competition along with Ian Wright. It was an honour the two great strikers shared for less than half an hour, however, as Henry made the record his alone with a penalty two minutes into the second-half.

After writing himself into the Arsenal history books, Henry helped create a first goal for new boy Franny Jeffers in his next game against Bolton Wanderers at Highbury. It was a wonderful two-touch passing move that left the goal at the Scouser's mercy and the Gunners one-nil up. But a Michael Ricketts' equaliser meant the points were shared and the Trotters went home happy as Arsenal got ready for another long European journey, this time to Athens.

Panathinaikos had started their Champions League campaign very well with two wins and were sitting pretty on top of the group. Arsenal were third with three points from their first two games and they were desperate for some Greek gifts. Panathinaikos were not feeling generous, however, and after grabbing an early goal, they spent the rest of the match employing spoiling tactics, timewasting and feigning injury, to preserve their lead.

At the final whistle, Henry decided to let the referee, Portugal's Manuelo Melo Pereira, know what he thought of the home side's behaviour and he didn't stop when the Greek police tried to get involved. Henry had lost the plot, but, fortunately for him and Arsenal, UEFA didn't take any action against the fiery Frenchman. Henry, however, had let his easygoing mask slip and shown the world just how much he cared about his football.

The next Arsenal match was away at Pride Park and Henry made Derby County suffer for the ignominy of defeat in Athens by scoring an unstoppable free-kick as well as a penalty to give the Gunners a 2–0 win. The victory in Derbyshire was marred for Arsenal by a serious injury to young Jeffers after he had made only two starts, which meant that Henry would have to take more of the 'fox in the box' responsibility on himself. The win lifted Arsenal into second place in the league, three points behind Leeds, and Henry returned to France for a game against Algeria for *les Bleus*. He grabbed his 11th international goal in a 4–1 victory as the sequence of French friendlies continued.

Back in competitive football, Henry scored in a fifth consecutive league away game as Arsenal beat Southampton 2–0 at the St Mary's Stadium. It was one of his more fortunate goals – his shot from distance took a hefty deflection past keeper Paul Jones – but it guaranteed three more points for the Gunners after Pires's early strike.

Henry's many goals and exhilarating performances were getting him plenty of attention from all the big clubs in Spain and Italy, but Henry was very happy at Highbury and had no intention of moving on. 'People have been saying I am leaving, but I still have a contract at Arsenal,' Henry told the BBC. 'I have never said I am leaving Arsenal. You can see when I'm playing that I am trying 100 per cent. The way I'm playing is not that of a player who wants to leave. When I was down in my career Arsenal and Arsene Wenger got me ahead and I will never forget that. I am not the kind of player to leave after one or two years without giving anything back.'

It was very heartening for all the Arsenal fans to hear Henry pledging his future to the club as the Frenchman outlined his number-one priority for the season. 'The biggest thing is to triumph in your country first of all. You have to work well all season and that's the thing with us,' Henry said. 'Sometimes we play well for one or two months, then for one month we're not playing well and dropping points everywhere. Manchester United are playing well all season and even if they lose once or twice they keep the same style and keep winning the titles.'

The Champions League may not have been top of Henry's wish list but he still put in a match-winning performance when Panathinaikos came to Highbury, scoring both the Gunners' goals in a 2–1 win to gain revenge for all the histrionics in the Greek capital. However, Arsenal let two points slip against Blackburn Rovers at home in their next game, twice squandering the lead after fighting back from a goal down to draw 3–3. Henry got the third Arsenal goal as the Gunners' home form continued to suffer.

It was a different story in the Champions League where Highbury continued to be the fortress it had been in previous seasons, and Arsenal wrapped up their qualification from

Group C with a 3–1 win over Real Mallorca. Henry put in another fantastic European performance and grabbed the third goal to leave his manager purring.

In the post-match press conference, Wenger responded to claims from Sir Alex Ferguson that Manchester United's new Dutch striker Ruud Van Nistelrooy was the best hitman in Europe. 'I don't agree with Ferguson,' Wenger said to the surprise of none of the gathered journalists. 'They are two great strikers but Thierry is top, top class. I would not swap him for anybody and I want to keep this whole squad together. We'll gain a lot from getting through to the second round in the Champions League again, because this has been a much tougher group than many people thought.'

After his European exertions, Henry was among the substitutes for the journey to Sunderland and his absence was felt as Arsenal dropped two points in the North-East. Kanu opened the scoring for the Gunners, but former Arsenal player Stefan Schwarz hit back for the Black Cats, before Vieira's skied penalty meant the points would be shared. With Arsenal's European progress assured, Henry was also rested for the final game of Group C, a 3–1 loss away to Schalke in Gelsenkirchen.

Having been rested for two consecutive games, Henry was firing on all cylinders when Charlton Athletic came to Highbury. The famous Clock End clock had only reached seven minutes past three, when Henry latched on to a Pires pass to shoot early across Dean Kiely in the Charlton goal and open the scoring. Arsenal continued to create chances and dominated the first half, so it was a bit of a shock when the visitors first equalised through Steve Brown and then took the lead when Richard Wright punched a cross into his own net.

Things didn't get any better for the Gunners after the break as the Addicks continued to attack and found themselves 4–1 up after Claus Jensen's sublime chip and a goal from Jason Euell. Henry got Arsenal back into the contest with a penalty on the hour mark but the visitors held on for a famous 4–2 victory. Henry missed Arsenal's next game through injury as Wenger's side defended much better against Tottenham Hotspur at White Hart Lane. But a last-minute Gustavo Poyet goal cancelled out a fine Pires strike and honours were even in the season's first north London derby.

Henry had not been risked for the short trip down the Seven Sisters Road, as it came just four days before the journey to northern Spain for Arsenal's game against Deportivo La Coruna. The Gunners had been drawn in a very tough Group D, with Depor, Bayer Leverkusen and Henry's former club Juventus. The second group stage of the Champions League got off to a very bad start for Henry and his team-mates as they crashed 2–0 in El Riazor. It wasn't the best preparation for the visit of Manchester United to Highbury but the Gunners again showed their ability to recover from bad results as they put in a fantastic performance to beat the Champions.

Arsenal were trailing to a Paul Scholes goal at the break, but the Gunners claimed all the points with a dominant second-half display. Some of the Highbury crowd were still returning to their seats when Ljungberg levelled matters with a deft chip from the edge of the box. The score remained at 1–1 until ten minutes from time, when exactly one month before Christmas Day Santa Claus came early for Henry and Arsenal. Barthez was under no pressure when he went to kick the ball upfield, but an error by the French keeper sent the ball straight to Henry, unmarked right in front of goal. The Gunners' striker made no mistake from 18 yards and simply sidefooted the ball into the bottom corner to make it 2–1.

The Arsenal crowd were delighted to have come back from a goal down against their biggest rivals, and five minutes later things got even better for the home side as Barthez failed to gather a long pass from Vieira with Henry in close attendance. As the ball squeezed under the goalkeeper, Henry was on to it in a flash to roll it into the unguarded net. Coming back to win 3–1 against Manchester United four days after losing to Deportivo la Coruna showed remarkable resilience from Wenger's side and, later looking back at the season, the manager certainly wasn't underestimating the importance of result. 'It was one of the turning points of the season,' Wenger said. 'Because we had just lost in the Champions League and we were 1–0 down at half-time to Manchester United, we could have easily gone down again but we went up. We showed the mental strength that was typical in our season.'

It definitely was a key result and, although Ferguson's men were struggling a little in the league at the time, it took Arsenal into third place after a poor run of form, and left them just three points behind Liverpool at the top of the table. Henry's impressive away form continued in the next game as he set up Ljungberg for the first goal with a lovely reverse pass, before maintaining his 100 per cent record from the penalty-spot in the Premier League as Arsenal beat Ipswich 2–0 at Portman Road.

The next game was one Henry had been looking forward to, and it was his chance to show his former employers what they were missing first hand. Juventus came to Highbury as the early leaders of Group D, having destroyed Bayer Leverkusen 4–1 the previous week in Turin. Arsenal were not to be intimidated, however, and the Gunners took the lead when Ljungberg followed up Vieira's shot after 21 minutes. Henry scored Arsenal's second with a free-kick struck to perfection to give the Gunners a 2–0 lead at half-time. Trezeguet got one back for Juve, but Henry's schoolfriend failed to do any more damage to the Arsenal defence and Ljungberg's late second, after fantastic work by Bergkamp, gave the Gunners a 3–1 win to keep them in touch in Group D as the Champions League entered its period of winter hibernation.

The day after the European victory, Henry was the victim of the darker side of big city life as his north London home was burgled while he was out. A Metropolitan Police spokesman later revealed that the burglar broke into the star's house in Hampstead and tied up his cleaner, before ransacking the property and escaping with 'a quantity' of Henry's possessions believed to be leather coats and jewellery to the value of £25,000. The cleaner suffered bruises but fortunately did not require hospital treatment.

Henry didn't let the episode affect him on the pitch though and was fully focused on his next match when Arsenal were again forced to dig deep into their reserves of mental strength to overcome Aston Villa at Highbury. In a first half which resembled the visit of Charlton earlier in the season, the Gunners dominated for 45 minutes and yet found themselves 2–0 behind at the break. Yet another former Arsenal player had found it within himself to score against the Gunners as Paul Merson grabbed Villa's first.

Arsenal came out fired-up for the second half and were back in the game almost immediately when Wiltord volleyed home from inside the area. The Gunners laid siege to the Villa goal and after 72 minutes they got some reward as Henry flicked Vieira's pass into the corner of the goal to level the scores. Arsenal were keen to grab all the points though and continued to press forward. After a couple of close offside calls, Arsenal finally grabbed a winner in the 90th minute when Pires threaded a ball through to put Henry one-on-one with Peter Enckelman. Arsenal's leading scorer made no mistake as he stroked the ball into the bottom corner to complete a remarkable comeback.

There was more good news for Gooners days later as Arsene Wenger finally put pen to paper on an extension to his contract as manager of Arsenal. Henry was in no mood to go anywhere else either. 'I hope that I shall be here for a long while,' Henry told the French sports newspaper *L'Equipe*. 'I'm starting my third season at Arsenal. Sylvain Wiltord and Robert Pires are in their second, along with Lauren. We are creating a togetherness here. Arsenal are beginning to have spirit within the team and it's important that the manager stays. There has been the same base for players for about five years now and the club, like all clubs, must work on continuity.'

Henry also revealed that Arsenal had been the club for him even when he left Monaco for Serie A. 'I always wanted to come to Arsenal, even when I was transferred to Juventus,' he went on. 'I love the English championship and also the fans over here. The first Cup Final that I saw on television was Manchester United versus Crystal Palace [in 1990] and Ian Wright was playing for Palace. I admired this player straight away, and then I saw that he had signed for Arsenal. Also Arsene was there, along with quite a few French players. That also inspired me.'

Henry's goal-scoring form was inspired and he had bagged 21 goals before Christmas which even amazed him. 'Fifteen goals in fourteen league games, and six goals in seven Champions League games, it's frightening. Last year I scored 22 goals all season.' And there were memories of the previous season that still haunted him seven months on. 'The Cup Final is still stuck in my throat. After that game I was badly criticised, but it is something that you have to get used to when you play in my position. As a centre-forward you are either a hero or nothing. When you have a bad game, you often make your team lose. It's true that after the final I concentrated more on my role as a centre-forward, I wanted to be more of what the English people call a "fox in the box".'

Henry was certainly scoring more goals with his new approach to the game, but no matter how many goals he scored in the future he would always look to others for ways to improve, to players such as Real Madrid's Raul. 'I will never consider myself as the best; I've always admired Raul. I get the impression that he never gets the credit he deserves.

He is 26 and has already scored 130 goals for Real. I have respect for him, he is always there and gets on with his job.'

Against West Ham at Upton Park, Henry got on with his job of leading the Arsenal line as the Gunners again came from behind, this time to draw 1–1, with Henry flicking a Lauren cross to the far post for Ashley Cole to equalise. Newcastle United were the next opponents for Arsenal and travelled south having failed to win a single game in London in their previous 29 attempts. With Arsenal's indifferent home form, there was always a chance the Magpies would break their capital curse at Highbury but nobody could have expected the scenes that were to unfold after the game.

Arsenal were in dominant mood, creating plenty of chances in the first 45 minutes and they took a deserved lead through Pires who tucked away a Cole knock-back after Henry's juggled cross went past everybody in the six-yard box. But in the final minute of the first half, the referee Graham Poll somewhat harshly sent off Parlour for a second bookable offence after a foul on Alan Shearer. Andy O'Brien then equalised for the Geordies before the incident that really upset Arsenal and Henry in particular.

Arsenal were defending high up the pitch as they pressed for the goal that would put them back in front when a Kieron Dyer pass set Laurent Robert free in the Arsenal half. The French winger raced away and, as he pulled his foot back to shoot, Campbell slid in with as good a tackle as you ever will see to put the ball out for a corner. But Mr Poll saw things differently and it's the referee's opinion that matters, so Newcastle were awarded a penalty and Campbell received a yellow card for his troubles.

Shearer claimed his first-ever Highbury goal with the disputed penalty and, although Robert broke away to score a third, totally legitimate goal late on, the damage had already been done. At the final whistle, Henry ran to Mr Poll to ask him why he had sent off Parlour and penalised Campbell, but a number of the Arsenal coaching staff and substitutes saw him charging at the referee and tried to hold him back. Desperate to make his point to the person he saw as the cause of the defeat, Henry started shouting at the official and wrestled himself clear of his club-mates to continue his protest.

Henry was clearly incensed by the result and the way in which it had been inflicted, but it would have been best for all involved if he had waited until he and Mr Poll were within the sanctity of the dressing rooms before asking him his questions. As it was, Mr Poll was very upset at being reprimanded so dramatically in public and reported the striker to the FA. Henry wasn't helped by the fact that the Newcastle match had gone out live on television and, as he approached the referee, a cameraman had been perfectly positioned to transmit pictures of the striker struggling with his team-mates as he tried to make his point. The footage was shown almost continuously on the sports news channels for days as the media milked the story for all it was worth.

It must be said the pictures weren't pretty – the usually gallant Frenchman in a fit of rage – but Henry came out to defend himself in the *Daily Telegraph*. His explanation was simple. 'Injustice makes me unhappy. If a player kicks me, I don't react. I don't scream,' Henry said. 'The only time I open my mouth is if there's an injustice. I don't regret what

I did at the end of the Newcastle game. I didn't swear at the ref. I didn't touch him. I didn't do anything wrong. I just wanted to ask him something. It looked bad because my team-mates were holding me back.

'What is worse: to punch someone as some players have done or to try to talk to the ref as I did? I have heard a lot of people saying foreign players don't care, that we come just to take the money, but I love Arsenal. I really care about the people here.' And seeing the star striker with his heart on his sleeve for the club meant that the fans loved him even more.

And a little indiscretion like that wasn't going to stop Wenger from standing by his man. 'We will defend him as vigorously as we have done everybody at this club,' the manager said. 'I have seen his [Graham Poll's] report and I think he has called it "aggressive attitude". But Henry did not touch the referee or insult him and we do not expect him to be charged. Players insult referees every week and yet nothing happens to them. Henry is a winner. He gets kicked 99 per cent of the time on the pitch and never reacts. I have spoken to him about it and he knows he overreacted. In an ideal world, he would not have reacted at all but, overall, his behaviour is very fair.'

Henry's team-mate and compatriot Vieira also came out in support of his friend, saying he was simply 'an emotional and passionate person, the kind of guy who does not like injustice'. But the FA did charge Henry and an FA spokesman came out to explain exactly what was involved. 'The charge is very open-ended,' said the spokesman. 'It is not like a violent conduct charge where there is a set penalty but the usual punishment for a charge like this is a one-match ban. The disciplinary committee will take into account the player's usual conduct on the pitch.'

So Henry was called to the FA headquarters at Soho Square. 'We will defend him to the hilt as always,' the manager said. 'We will go there to explain what happened. We will explain that Thierry is not usually a bad player and that he overreacted. Then the FA will make a decision and we will accept that. We know the maximum is a three-game ban, but it could be less than that as well. I don't say he has done nothing. He overreacted and he is the first to concede that. I don't believe that it is his intention to do it again. Sometimes people trying to stop you make it look worse than it actually is as it upsets you even more.'

Because the incident happened one week before Christmas, the FA took their time in charging Henry and, having been charged, Henry was given the standard 14 days to respond. When Arsenal announced they would defend Henry, a date had to be set for his disciplinary hearing. The date was finally set for 6 March, more than two and a half months after the event.

So Henry had plenty of games to play before worrying about any possible ban. These matches began with a trip to Anfield, a year to the day after the 4–0 defeat there. The Gunners were a different proposition on their travels this year, however, and even after Van Bronckhorst had been sent off after just 36 minutes Arsenal ran out 2–1 winners. It was another somewhat dubious red card as the Dutchman received a second yellow card for diving when he clumsily tripped over his own feet in the Liverpool box. This time Arsenal channelled their sense of injustice into a match-winning performance, as Henry's penalty on the stroke of half-time and a Ljungberg goal eight minutes into the second half ensured the points would be heading back to London despite Jari Litmanen's header.

On Boxing Day, Wenger's troops battled back successfully from being a goal down, yet again, to beat Chelsea at Highbury. Campbell's first goal for Arsenal cancelled out Frank Lampard's opener, and Wiltord settled things 20 minutes from time. Arsenal seemed to be enjoying coming from behind and Noel Whelan put Middlesbrough ahead in north London three days later, only for Pires and Cole to score, giving the Gunners another 2–1 win to take them to the top of the Premiership table at the end of 2001.

Arsenal's first game in 2002 was an FA Cup tie away against Watford. In the build-up to the game, Hornets boss Gianluca Vialli was asked how his side could stop Henry. 'I don't really know. With a gun?' came the reply. But wisely not resorting to such tactics, Vialli's side had little answer to the Frenchman and he opened the scoring after just eight minutes, taking Kanu's pass around Alec Chamberlain in the home goal. Two minutes later, Henry turned provider as he laid the ball square to Ljungberg for 2–0. With further goals from Kanu and Bergkamp and Watford fighting to the bitter end, the game finished 4–2.

Two league draws followed for the Gunners, 1–1 at home to Liverpool and the same score-line away to Leeds, before normal service was resumed with a 3–1 win over Leicester City. Henry got Arsenal's second at Filbert Street, tucking away a loose ball from the edge of the Foxes' box. Next up for the Gunners was another game against Liverpool as the two Premiership giants had been drawn together in the Fourth Round of the FA Cup.

Henry crossed from the left for Bergkamp to head home Arsenal's opener after half an hour. But the Gunners couldn't beat Jerzy Dudek again and, after Keown and Bergkamp received their marching orders in the second half, they had to hold on for the final 20 minutes with 9 men. The Gunners were getting very adept at winning with a numerical disadvantage and they did so again in the next match away to Blackburn Rovers.

Arsenal raced into a 2–0 lead after 20 minutes through Bergkamp and Henry who slotted the ball past Brad Friedel after being released by a long pass from Pires. Blackburn fought back to go in with the scores even at 2–2, but playing the final half an hour with ten men after Oleg Luzhny's red card, the Gunners still managed to create a winner as Pires slipped Bergkamp in to score Arsenal's third. The win left Arsenal second in the table, one point behind a resurgent Manchester United side.

With Henry and his compatriot Pires both enjoying excellent seasons, there was persistent press speculation linking them with moves away from Highbury. But Arsenal were optimistic they wouldn't be tempted away from north London, as chairman Peter Hill-Wood told the *Sun* newspaper. 'Thierry is a world-class player and, obviously, we don't want to lose him. Both he and Pires seem very happy and we hope they will be at Arsenal for many years to come.'

Fortunately for Hill-Wood and all at Highbury, Henry was more than content where he was. 'I am so happy at Arsenal,' Henry said. 'I have a real love for that club, and I am very happy with them. I found true happiness with Arsenal, and it is great for a player to have settled down in a club where he is happy.'

Henry admitted that Wenger's decision to extend his personal contract helped shape his own plans for the future. 'I am not going to lie,' said Henry. 'The fact Arsene decided to stay is very important for me because it allows us to follow a certain continuity with all the players he recruited. His record at the club is very positive: all the players feel free. Knowing he is staying triggers the desire to stay too.'

Back on the field, Arsenal drew the next game 1–1 against Southampton at Highbury, with Wiltord scoring for the Gunners. Wiltord was the scorer in the next game as well as Arsenal kept the pressure on Manchester United with another three points, beating Everton 1–0 at Goodison Park. After a further international break, with Henry playing for *les Bleus* in a 2–1 win over Romania, Arsenal's number 14 found himself on the bench for the FA Cup fifth-round tie against Gillingham.

The Gills weren't the pushovers many were expecting, however, and with the scores tied at 2–2, Wenger sent on his big guns, with Henry and Arsenal skipper Adams entering the fray. The double substitution had the desired effect and the Kent side were soon put to the sword, with the Gunners winning 5–2. The manager had been trying to rest his key men for the resumption of the Champions League three days later, but after his hand was forced he had rushed his skipper back from injury and Adams would now miss the next game, in Germany.

The absence of the inspirational centre-back cost the

Gunners as Bayer Leverkusen got a last-minute equaliser to cancel out Arsenal's goal from Pires. A real case of two points dropped, this draw stopped Arsenal from taking control of Group D and they were left in second place, two points behind their Galician conquerors Deportivo La Coruna.

Fulham were the side to suffer at Highbury days later as Wenger's side took their Champions League frustrations out on the Cottagers in their next game.

Henry was in irrepressible form as he linked with Wiltord to create the first for Lauren with five minutes gone and, after Steve Marlet had beaten David Seaman to a cross to level the scores, Henry set up Vieira for Arsenal's second with a reverse pass that beat the entire Fulham defence. Henry claimed the Gunners' third goal for himself as he caught Andy Melville in possession and rifled past Van Der Sar. The French striker was fortunate with his second, though, as Lauren's header rebounded off the post and hit Henry's shin before nestling in the back of the net to make it 4–1.

Wenger was more than happy with his leading scorer and took him off to rapturous applause, but Henry wasn't best pleased as he sought his second Arsenal hat-trick. 'Thierry wanted to score one more but he understands,' Wenger said. 'He loves the game so much and he had an outstanding game and made another step forward as a team player.'

The whole team took a step forward in the next game as Arsenal destroyed Bayer Leverkusen 4–1. The Gunners started the game at an exhilarating pace that was just too much for the Germans to handle. Arsenal were 2–0 up inside eight minutes as first Pires then Henry struck to put the north Londoners in control. Vieira got Arsenal's third shortly after half-time and Bergkamp completed the scoring late on with the pick of the bunch. It was a breathtaking performance from the Gunners that made the whole of Europe sit up and take notice, and left them with their Champions League future firmly in their own hands.

Henry was missing in Arsenal's next game but watched in amazement, like many football fans, as Bergkamp scored a sublime goal against Newcastle at St James's Park. There were 11 minutes gone when the ball was played in to Bergkamp on the edge of the Geordies box with Nikos Dabizas behind him blocking his route to goal. The Dutchman flicked the ball round the Greek centre-back with his left foot, while spinning the other way to pick the ball up behind the defender and coolly slot it past keeper Shay Given.

Campbell completed the scoring for a 2–0 win, but there was no mistaking which goal Henry was talking about after the match. 'We all know he can do it, but for me it's one of the greatest goals I've ever seen,' Henry said, overcome with praise for his team-mate.

Henry would have to get used to his place in the stands for a while. When his disciplinary hearing finally came round, the FA handed him a three-match ban. It seemed somewhat harsh that he should receive the same-length suspension handed out for violent conduct – given when someone, for example, elbowed an opponent in the face, broke their nose or fractured their cheekbone – but that was his punishment and it would begin with the FA Cup quarter-final against Newcastle United at St James's Park.

In the last game before his mid-season hiatus, Henry helped his team-mates to a fourth straight league win, 1–0 at home to Derby County. The goal came from Pires who was enjoying a fantastic spell of form and Henry, ever on hand with a compliment, was enjoying his compatriot's game. 'You dream to play with someone like that,' Henry said of his team-mate. 'He has to be on his own to score. If he sees someone else in front of goal on his own, he will pass, because that is Robert; that's the way he is, he just wants to make everyone happy.'

The form of the two French forwards was making Arsenal fans very happy, but with Henry suspended and Pires playing only the last half-hour as a substitute, Wenger's team could only draw against the Magpies in their cup-tie in Newcastle. With a replay rapidly arranged for a fortnight later, the good news for Gunners was that Henry would only miss one League match through his ban, the away game against Aston Villa.

But before that, there was a game against Deportivo La Coruna, which Henry could play in as his suspension only applied in domestic football. Henry made little impression in a match that showed exactly how far Arsenal had to go before they could win the biggest trophy in club football. The Spaniards came into the game with a major advantage as they had been able to rest many of their key players the weekend before the big match while Arsenal had their tough cup-tie.

But La Coruna played what could be considered a perfect European game, conserving their energy and striking with two beautifully crafted goals against the run of play to win

2–0. That result, combined with Bayer Leverkusen's home win over Juventus, meant that, no matter what Arsenal did in their last game, they would be out of the Champions League if the Germans won in Spain, due to the complexities of UEFA group standings.

After the Aston Villa away game which Arsenal won 2–1 in Henry's absence, the Gunners' European season was finished with the news that Depor were resting half of their first team for the visit of Leverkusen. Henry and his team-mates were devastated by the news and found it difficult to pick themselves up for their game against Juventus knowing that it almost certainly wouldn't affect their fortunes and lost 1–0 in Turin. La Coruna's depleted side were no match for the Germans and Bayer Leverkusen won 3–1 to ensure they went through to the Champions League quarter-finals along with their Spanish hosts.

Dumped out of Europe and in the middle of a domestic ban, Henry's mood was improved slightly by some new boots from his sponsors Nike. The American sportswear giants had managed to make their innovative Mercurial Vapours weigh just 196g each, making them 50g lighter than the track spikes worn by their top sprinters. Tests with the new boots saw Henry's lightning pace increase by an impressive 2 per cent over 50 metres and the Frenchman was duly amazed. 'I knew these boots were going to be light, but not this light,' Henry said. 'They are also very comfortable. I'm really looking forward to playing a match in these boots. All the time you are looking to be quicker then the defender.'

But Henry would have to wait a little bit longer to try out his new footwear as he completed his ban with a watching brief at Highbury for the FA Cup quarter-final replay against Newcastle. The Gunners made light of the absence of their leading scorer and the game was dead in the water after ten minutes as Pires and Bergkamp combined twice to score a goal apiece. Arsenal were once again displaying their spirit as they bounced back from their Champions League exit with a sterling display against the Geordies. Then disaster struck and Pires was carried off on a stretcher after 25 minutes.

The French winger hurdled a challenge from Dabizas and landed awkwardly, twisting his right knee. Henry was concerned for his friend and went to see him at the end of the first half. 'I felt the injury from the stands,' the striker said. 'I went to see Robert in the dressing room at half-time and he told me that the knee was all right and that he didn't feel so much pain.' Arsenal weren't disrupted by the injury and went on to win the game 3–0, booking their passage into the semi-finals.

A scan the following day revealed the damage was much worse than first feared: Pires had badly damaged his cruciate ligaments. It meant that he would have to undergo surgery and wouldn't play again until the next season, missing the climax of the season along with France's World Cup defence in Japan and South Korea. Henry found the news tough to bear. 'I was shocked about this news, it is very hard. I am very disappointed; it's very hard to find the words to express myself. Robert was experiencing a fantastic season. He was very happy at Arsenal after a difficult season in Marseille. I wouldn't want to be in his place at the moment.

'We are going to miss him a lot at Arsenal, and we will try to win something for him,' Henry said. He was speaking from the French national training camp in Clairefontaine ahead of France's game with Scotland. The French won 5–0, with Henry grabbing a glorious third goal after latching on to a cut-back from Wiltord and shooting into the top corner of the net from the edge of the penalty area. It was a great boost to the French team with the World Cup only two months away.

Back in the Premier League, the Gunners were also in fine form and they made it six league wins on the bounce in Henry's first game back after his suspension, at home to Sunderland. Arsenal were 3–0 up inside half an hour and the win put them third in the league, two points behind Liverpool with two games in hand.

Happy to be back playing rather than watching, Henry spoke of how he was enjoying his time in 'The Home of Football'. 'On the field the team beat like a single heart and, though you don't want to tempt fate, there is no reason why this team cannot go on and win plenty of trophies. Off the field I enjoy privacy I never thought was possible as a professional footballer. In other countries you're treated like a possession and taken for granted,' Henry said, thinking back to his time in Italy. 'But in England the fans are adorable, especially the Arsenal fans. They don't give the team stick; they don't pick on individual players. They just want the best for their team and back them.'

Henry always gave his best for the Gunners and he put in another masterful display against Charlton, winning the game in a ten-minute spell midway through the first half. Campbell's long clearance put Henry in the clear after 16 minutes and, with Richard Rufus in tow, he made no mistake, slotting past Kiely to open the scoring. Five minutes later, Henry put Bergkamp into space to deliver a sweet ball across the box for Ljungberg to tap home and Henry put the game to bed four minutes after that, finishing off some good work by Ljungberg and Wiltord.

Monsieur Wenger's men were on a roll and not even the visit of the old enemy could slow the Gunners' march to the title. Arsenal got another early lead as Ljungberg tucked away an Edu pass after 24 minutes, but when Tottenham equalised from the penalty-spot 10 minutes from time, the Highbury crowd thought they might have to settle for a draw. But less than five minutes later, Kasey Keller brought down Henry in the penalty area and the referee pointed to the spot. The French striker was off the pitch receiving treatment, so Lauren stepped up to roll the ball calmly down the middle of the goal as Keller dived away to his left, sending the crowd wild.

The Gunners were top of the table with six games left to play and, having wrestled three points from their north London neighbours, the league run-in was starting to look a lot better. Still in with a chance of a Premier League and FA Cup Double, Arsenal's next game was an FA Cup semi-final against Middlesbrough at Old Trafford. In a tense game in Manchester, the only goal came from Henry's corner as Gianluca Festa put the ball past his own keeper after it deflected off his knee and into the back of the net.

In France's last international before the end of the season, Henry and his team-mate's failed to find a way past the Russian keeper Ruslan Nigmatullin and the game finished goalless. But in the Premier League, nobody could stop Arsenal from scoring or winning and, after three more victories, it was time to go back to Wales to try and mend the damage done 12 months previously in the Millennium Stadium.

Henry was being increasingly heavily marked towards the end of the season, but with defenders concentrating their efforts on him, spaces opened up for his team-mates to exploit in games at the business end of the season. The main beneficiary in 2002 was Ljungberg. In Arsenal's six games heading into the Cup Final the Swedish midfielder scored six times, proving the Gunners were no longer reliant on any one man to provide their goals.

Against Chelsea in Cardiff, Henry was well marked by Marcel Desailly but that did not stop Arsenal winning, as first Parlour and then super Swede Ljungberg made good use of the extra space that comes from playing with one of the world's best strikers. After 70 minutes, Wiltord laid the ball off to Parlour and, as the defenders backed away from the England midfielder following the runs of Henry and Wiltord, Romford Ray unleashed a fantastic shot which had Carlo Cudicini beaten all ends up.

Ten minutes later, Ljungberg ran through a small hole in the Chelsea defence, holding off John Terry before curling home beautifully from the edge of the box. The Blues were beaten and Henry finally had the chance to get his hands on some silverware for the first time in his Arsenal career. But Henry and his team-mates couldn't celebrate too hard, as they still had a league title to win.

Four days later, Arsenal travelled to Old Trafford, five points ahead of Manchester United with two games to play and knowing that a draw would be good enough to claim the title. Henry missed the journey though, as an injury picked up late on in the Cup Final kept him out of what was to be a memorable night for everyone associated with Arsenal Football Club.

After 57 minutes, Wiltord scored the only goal when a Ljungberg shot was pushed into his path by Barthez, and the travelling supporters went mad. The Old Trafford 'Champions Section', as the Arsenal fans had renamed the small area set aside for away fans in the mighty stadium, broke into song and began a jubilant celebration that continued throughout the remainder of the game and all the way back to London.

It was fitting that the Gunners should win the title in their final away game as they completed a league season unbeaten on the road. It was especially good to do it at Old Trafford, exorcising the demons of the embarrassing defeat on the same ground the previous season. It also helped cheer up Arsenal fans that they had won the title in the backyard of their biggest rivals, and it was no surprise that everybody was still in party mood when Everton came to town for Arsenal's last game of the season.

Henry was fit to play against the Toffees and was straight into the spirit of things with plenty of flicks and tricks, but that still didn't stop him from scoring two goals. Bergkamp had opened the scoring for the Gunners, seizing on a loose ball in the Everton six-yard box, before the visitors hit back with two goals to take the lead. Henry's first came when he sidefooted home a Bergkamp pass from the edge of the box; the second arrived after 72 minutes when he chested down a cross-field pass from Edu and slotted the ball into the bottom corner.

Having put Arsenal ahead and grabbed a couple of goals for himself, Henry spent the last 20 minutes of the game in benevolent style, trying to create a goal for 'fox in the box' Jeffers against his old club. The Frenchman finally got his wish seven minutes from time as his far-post cross was well met by the young Liverpudlian to make it 4–2. The game finished 4–3 but with the final whistle came the trophy ceremony and a jubilant end to the club season.

Henry had a fantastic season with Arsenal and, after scoring a brace against Everton, he had the Premier League Golden Boot to go with his Premier League and FA Cup winner's medals. His manager thought it was a remarkable achievement. 'For someone who was initially convinced that he is not a typical goal-scorer, that is amazing,' Wenger said. 'Some strikers who have not scored for a while make you play as if you have 10 men but with Thierry it's always as if you have 11 as he provides so much. That's why I never put him under any pressure when he's not scoring.'

With Henry leading the line, Arsenal always looked like scoring and, even in the games he didn't play, the Gunners had managed to score at least once in every one of their 38 league games, a top-flight first. Henry scored 24 in the League and 32 goals in all competitions for Arsenal as they marched to the 3rd League and Cup Double in their history. All in all, he was very happy with his year.

'It seems like it's the perfect season,' Henry said. 'We don't usually do well at Anfield; we went there and won, despite playing with ten men for an hour. We don't usually do well at

Villa and we won there. All the time we were getting a good result after a bad one, so that shows a lot of character.'

The 2001–02 campaign was great for Henry and his Highbury team-mates, but the flying French forward saw no reason to stop there. 'I won the Golden Boot and Arsenal won the Double, and I just want to keep on winning with this team. I just want to keep on going for these people.'

And still just 24 years of age, there was plenty more to come for Henry.

Chapter nine
Va-Va-Voom

'I'm very happy that the company asked me to front the campaign, especially when I realised that I would be continuing one of the best-loved advertising campaigns ever to run in this country,' Henry said. 'Estelle Skornik [Nicole, of Papa and Nicole fame] wished me luck when she dropped by the film set. I hope this advert turns out to be as popular as hers was.'

At the end of the Double-winning season Thierry Henry had been chosen as the new face of Renault Clio, and with it came a slogan that would become synonymous with the striker maybe even more than the car it was used to advertise.

The phrase had been used in a previous Renault commercial, but when Gerry Moira and Ira Joseph, two Arsenal fans in the creative team behind the ad, watched Henry they saw 'va-va-voom' made flesh. Joseph told *The Observer* what drew them to the striker. 'It was just this contemporary French-ness, this effortless style and pace and a kind of detached self-confidence.'

Working with a very loose script, Henry seemed a natural in front of the camera. 'It was odd,' Joseph added. 'Football fans like to think footballers are as inspired and intelligent off the field as they are on it. Rarely is that the case. But it did seem so with Henry. You go to most clients and say we've got a footballer we'd like to use to sell your crown jewels and they might be hesitant, but as soon as the people at Renault met Thierry they could see he was perfect.'

Back to the day job, things were suddenly going less well for Henry and his international team-mates. Henry was missing from the French line-up with a knee strain when *les Bleus* crashed to their first home defeat for three years against Belgium. With less than two weeks to go before the World Cup, it wasn't the ideal preparation for their trophy defence and the manager was concerned as to the effect the defeat would have on his troops. 'When you lose you don't look at yourself the way you did before,' said Roger Lemerre. 'Defeat produces doubt and now it's up to us to provide the right answers. The result has left me a little unsure but it might help to put everyone back on the right track.'

In their first game in the Far East, France played a friendly against co-hosts South Korea and got a morale-boosting 3–2 victory. Henry played the first 45 minutes with no signs of the injury that had kept him out the week before, but there was more bad news for *les Bleus* as Zidane left the pitch midway through the first half clutching his thigh.

With only five days to go before their World Cup opener, the loss of their playmaker and inspiration was a particularly tough blow to bear. Having lost Pires and Zidane to injury, Lemerre shuffled his pack in midfield and started with Henry on the left wing for the tournament's opening match – France versus Senegal. The unknown Africans were making their World Cup debut in Japan and South Korea and few people could have predicted how they would announce their arrival on football's biggest stage.

The Cup holders struggled to break down the Dakar Lions' well-organised defence and, after half an hour, Senegal took the lead as El Hadji Diouf's hard work up front brought its reward. The French defence failed to deal with a cross from the African Footballer of the Year and Papa Bouba Diop stole in at the far post to score the first goal of the 2002 World Cup.

The goal failed to spur the French side into action and, although Henry had some good efforts in the second half, they couldn't beat the Senegal keeper Tony Sylva. The game finished 1–0 and *les Bleus* were under immediate pressure as they would have to win their next two games to qualify for the knock-out stages.

That task proved too difficult for the French, though, and against Uruguay in Busan they again failed to score – the game was a 0–0 draw – but the real story of the match was the sending-off of Thierry Henry. The Arsenal striker was enjoying a lively game as he endeavoured to get France's World Cup campaign back on track. That all ended in the 25th minute, however, as he was shown a straight red card for going in studs-up on Uruguayan captain Paolo Montero.

That draw didn't put the French out of the tournament. A win in their final Group A game against Denmark could still see them progress to the last 16. But without Henry and with Zidane rushed back from injury, heavily strapped, *les Bleus* fell to a 2–0 defeat at the hands of Denmark. Their reign as World Champions was over.

Rather than emerging as one of the tournament's stars as many had predicted, Henry had played in a struggling side, out of position and carrying an injury. His frustrations had got the better of·him causing him to mis-time a tackle against the South Americans and now the French team were on the first plane home.

After a couple of months spent dwelling on the World Cup failure, Henry was itching to get back to playing football by the time the new season came around. But speaking ahead of the Community Shield clash with Liverpool, Henry was still upset at being played out of position in Korea. 'The problem I had in the World Cup was the position I was asked to play,' the striker said. 'In three years with France and for Arsenal, I had played in the middle of the attack.'

The other factor in France's fall from grace was the tiredness of players, according to Henry. 'Sometimes your body tells you, you are not a robot.' But the Gunners' goal-scoring machine would soon be back in action as Arsenal headed to Cardiff for the traditional curtain-raiser to the season. As League and Cup Double winners, Arsenal had to play the team that had finished second in the league earlier in the year, so Liverpool would be the opposition in the Welsh capital.

Arsenal won the game 1–0 with goal coming from Gilberto, the new boy getting his Gunners career off to a good start with the winner at the Millennium Stadium.

Gilberto Aparecido da Silva had been signed from Atletico Mineiro after impressing playing for Brazil in Japan and Korea. The midfielder played every minute of the South Americans' World Cup-winning campaign and it was hoped that he would lighten the load of newly appointed Gunners skipper Patrick Vieira in the middle of the park.

Wenger had handed the captain's armband to Vieira following Adams's retirement. Since Mr Arsenal's long-time colleague Lee Dixon had also hung up his boots, Wenger's other summer signing was a defender, 2001 French Footballer of the Year Pascal Cygan from Lille.

In the first Highbury game of the new season, it was as if the Gunners had never been away. They extended their Premier League record to 14 consecutive wins, beating Birmingham City 2–0. It took Henry just nine minutes to open his account for the season as his free-kick squeezed under Nico Vaesen and into the back of the net. Wiltord got Arsenal's second 15 minutes later as the Premiership new boys were exposed to the speed of counter-attacking at the Champions' disposal.

After only one league match, it was time for Henry to return to France duty for his first game under new boss Jacques Santini; Lemerre had been sacked after the World Cup. *Les Bleus* got off to a poor start under their new manager with a 1–1 friendly draw in Tunisia, and the international break seemed to disrupt the rhythm of Wenger's men as Arsenal found themselves 2–0 down with half an hour left to play in their next game against West Ham at the Boleyn.

In a comeback that displayed all the grit that had taken

them to the title the previous season, the Gunners struck back with a fantastic goal hammered home by Henry. The Frenchman received the ball from Vieira, spun round Christian Dailly and, as the ball bounced, he controlled it on his knee before smashing a half-volley past David James from 25 yards. Seaman saved a weak penalty from Fredi Kanoute, before Wiltord completed the comeback at the death to preserve the Arsenal unbeaten run with a 2–2 draw.

Henry was delighted to be back, playing and scoring in the red and white of the Gunners and revealed to the *Sunday Mirror* just how happy he was at Highbury. 'As long as Arsenal want me, I want them,' the Frenchman said. 'The fans love me here and the people have so much confidence in me, so I can never walk away from these people. They have given me everything – love, honesty and belief – ever since I arrived here.'

The people at Arsenal had good reason to put their confidence in Henry and he continued to deliver in the next game at Highbury against West Bromwich Albion. The Baggies were already 2–0 down thanks to goals from each of the Arsenal full-backs, Lauren and Ashley Cole, before Henry weighed in with his first assist of the season. After 24 minutes, Henry spotted Wiltord's run down the right flank and picked him out with a measured pass that Arsenal's record signing chipped over the advancing keeper to make the score 3–0. Henry made another goal in the final minute for his young fellow countryman Jeremie Aliadiere as the Gunners ran out 5–2 winners.

A toe injury kept Henry out of Arsenal's next game away to Chelsea, and remarkably it proved to be the only league game he missed all season. The Gunners put in a battling performance without him, though, as they played almost the whole second half with ten men. Again they managed to come from behind to draw 1–1 with Kolo Toure grabbing his first Arsenal goal.

Henry was fit to play in the next Arsenal game and he was joined on the pitch at Highbury by his old schoolfriend Anelka. The former Gunners' hitman returned to north London with Kevin Keegan's Manchester City and even managed to beat Seaman to level things after Wiltord's opener. But Henry was not to be outdone by his buddy and scored what turned out to be the winner three minutes before half-time.

Cole picked out the Highbury hero on the edge of the box and he rolled the ball into the bottom corner of the net. After bagging his goal, Henry lifted up his shirt to reveal a message on his T-shirt, 'For the new-born Kyd', which at first confused some people in the media, but it turned out simply to be a congratulatory message for his friend Sharleen Spiteri, the lead singer of Texas and a celebrity Gooner, on the birth of her child Misty Kyd.

The vest message was not only Henry's most memorable but also his last since FIFA regulations had banned such displays from the start of the season. The French striker received a slap on the wrist and was told never to do it again. Fortunately for the Gunners, that didn't stop him scoring and, in his next game, he broke the deadlock just before half-time at the Valley, driving home a Bergkamp pass from the edge of the area. It was the 45th consecutive top-flight game in which the Gunners had found the target, setting a new record and giving Henry and his team-mates another small piece of history. Two more goals followed in the second half as Arsenal beat Charlton 3–0 with Wiltord and Edu, who headed home a cross from Henry, completing the scoring.

Now that Arsenal were off to a flying start in the Premiership, it was time for them to turn their attention back once more towards European action. In the first group stage of the Champions League, the Gunners had a tough draw, being pitched against Borussia Dortmund, PSV Eindhoven and Auxerre. But Monsieur Wenger's men made a fine start to the competition, beating Dortmund 2–0 at Highbury with two second-half goals to go clear at the top of Group A after match-day one.

Having taken their domestic form into Europe, the Gunners had to fight to the end to claim all three points at home to Bolton the following Saturday. Arsenal had created chances throughout the first half but only took a 1–0 lead into the break after Henry took a Bergkamp through ball around Jussi Jaaskelainen. Only seconds into the second-half, the Trotters equalised out of the blue as a Gareth Farrelly cross floated over Seaman's head from an improbable angle, and Arsenal struggled to reclaim their lead throughout the second half.

With time running out and the visitors reduced to ten men, Kanu got a very late winner to maintain Arsenal's 100 per cent record at Highbury. It seemed that no one could stop the Gunners with their creativity and pace cutting through every defence that got in their way. And away in Eindhoven, Arsenal set another new record for speed.

There were just 20.07 seconds on the clock when the ball

crossed the line for Gilberto's opener against PSV, making it the fastest-ever goal in the Champions League. More importantly for Arsenal, it helped get them off to the perfect start in their bid to put some wretched European away form behind them. They had gone eight games on the road without a win on the continent; in fact, you had to go back to February 2001 for their last victory, a 1–0 win over Lyon.

Having made such a good start and with Bergkamp starting his first-ever away game in the Champions League, Arsenal held their nerve and added three goals in the second half to beat the Dutch side 4–0.

Henry was impressive once again as he created the first for Gilberto and, after Ljungberg got the second, the Frenchman scored two goals, linking well with Kanu and then Wiltord. One of the most notable things about Henry is that it doesn't matter who he is playing with, he is always able to score a goal or create one for someone else, a fact which had not escaped his manager's attention. 'Thierry can marry his style with anyone,' Wenger said. 'He can play wide, behind the strikers or as the main man. He's creative, enjoys the freedom of movement and is difficult for opponents to fix. Thierry has not been educated to be a striker; he was brought up a winger. He likes to feed team-mates just as much as he enjoys scoring goals. I don't like selfish players. I like guys who enjoy playing for the team.'

The whole team seemed to enjoy themselves against PSV and they continued to have fun against Leeds four days later. Terry Venables' team were unfortunate to be playing against an Arsenal side that was on top of its game and it only took nine minutes for Kanu to find the back of the net and put the

Gunners on their way to another win. When Henry poked home a pass from Kanu in the 47th minute it was 3–0 and, when the game finished 4–1, Arsenal were top of the table and being lauded as one of the best teams of all time.

Auxerre were the next victims of Henry and co, as Arsenal made it three from three in the Champions League. Gilberto's goal gave the Gunners a 1–0 away win, the first club game Henry had played in France without scoring since he left Monaco three and a half years before.

With Arsenal top of both of their leagues and Henry at the heart of all their best moves, the Frenchman's agent, Jerome Anderson brokered a deal which saw Henry move into the top flight of football earners. He would rake in an estimated £2 million a year for the next five years from Nike. 'Considering Thierry's still just 25 and the fact he speaks English and Italian as well as French, he is a serious player both on and off the pitch, the most complete player on the planet,' Anderson said. 'That is why Nike want to keep him on their books. Thierry has been with them for some time, but they wanted to extend his contract and we have done so.'

On that kind of money, Henry could afford to be generous and in the next game he continued his new habit of creating goals for others, as he set up Kanu twice in a 3–1 Highbury win over Sunderland. It was Arsenal's 12th consecutive home win, and people were beginning to ask if anyone could or would ever stop the Gunners.

Wenger's men were forced to take a break, though, as the multi-national side swapped their red-and-white shirts for their country's colours. Henry reported for duty with France for their European Championship qualifying games against

Slovenia and Malta as a UEFA rule change meant that the holders would still have to qualify. This may not have been a bad thing after the World Cup debacle, where some said the two years of friendly matches had worn away at France's competitive edge.

The two games were easy for a French side with a point to prove and they followed up a 5–0 home win against the eastern Europeans with a 4–0 win in Malta as Henry grabbed two more goals for *les Bleus*. Having racked up a few air miles for the sake of national pride, Henry and his Highbury home boys got on the Arsenal team bus for a trip to Goodison Park.

Unbeaten in their last 30 Premiership games, Arsenal were 1–0 up after 8 minutes when Ljungberg tucked away a loose ball in the Everton box, and it looked like it was going to be 31. But the Toffees had other ideas and they also had Wayne Rooney. Thomas Radzinski got the home side back on level terms, but 19 October 2002 will always be remembered in football as the day Rooney, aged just 16, announced himself to the Premiership with the last-minute wonder goal that broke the Gunners' unbeaten run.

After falling from a horse, it's best to get back on it as soon as possible, and so it is in football. Arsenal were lucky to have another game three days later to put the defeat behind them. Auxerre came to north London wary of an Arsenal backlash and with a perfect game plan. Guy Roux's men defended in numbers from the start, but with a team full of young players willing to run all night long, they hit the masters of the counter-attack on the break. The French side were 2–0 up at half time and it could have been more.

Arsenal put in a gritty, fighting display in the second half and managed to get one goal back through Kanu, but even the introduction of Pires as a substitute, on his comeback from injury, was not enough to stop the Gunners crashing to a second consecutive defeat. The side that had been the best thing since sliced bread one week before were suddenly looking a bit off colour. Having played his 4th game in 11 days, against Auxerre, Henry put the back-to-back defeats down to fatigue. 'At the moment myself and some of the others are exhausted,' the striker protested.

Looking ahead to putting things right, Henry went on, 'I think one thing that I have to find really quickly is my fitness. That is the main thing because usually I am running around and lively. I am honest when I say at Everton it was like I wasn't even on the pitch and [against Auxerre] it would have been the same. But we started to play because we have pride and, when we were 2–0 down, it was more like anger than the way we normally play.'

And Henry didn't think it was just the Gunners whose players were suffering from the tough schedule that comes with playing a lot of games for your country, adding, 'If you look at the weekend and all the players who were on international duty and were in the starting line-up of their team; have a look at how they performed. Real Madrid lost and I heard that it was one of the poorest games they played; Barcelona lost; Dortmund drew and Inter drew with Juve. A lot of teams struggled. We are all human. I am not complaining, I am just saying that sometimes it is hard.'

The Frenchman always finds defeat tough and paid credit to Auxerre but refused to call two losses in a row a crisis, saying, 'I am more than upset, don't get me wrong, but you do lose games. Some people are talking about maybe a crisis and I just say that I think some teams would like to be in the same position as us at the moment.' Arsenal were still top of Group A and second in the Premiership, just one point behind Liverpool. It was hardly the end of the world.

Against Blackburn Rovers at Highbury, Arsenal were unlucky to come across an inspired goalkeeper in Brad Friedel as they lost 2–1 and, four days later, a free-kick from Henry couldn't stop the Gunners losing 2–1 again, this time in Dortmund. The Gunners had followed the loss of their 30-game unbeaten league run with four defeats on the spin, a record under Wenger. But Arsenal did receive some good news in Germany, as PSV beat Auxerre, to ensure Arsenal's progress to the second group stage with one game remaining.

Having got lucky in Europe, Wenger's team got just the slice of good fortune they needed to turn their form around against Fulham at Loftus Road. Henry curled in a corner from the left and, under no pressure, the unfortunate Steve Marlet sliced the ball past Edwin van der Sar to put the Gunners in front. Arsenal held on to their 1–0 lead for the remaining hour of the game and they could happily say their losing sequence was behind them.

Newcastle were beaten 1–0 at Highbury before the Gunners completed the first round of the Champions League with a 0–0 draw at home to PSV. Arsenal had got their season back on track and not before time since the next visitors to Highbury were the old enemy, Tottenham. This turned out to be a very entertaining game for Arsenal fans as the Gunners ran out 3–0 winners, but there is one special reason why this game was so memorable and that was the goal that Henry scored after 13 minutes.

Wiltord had already had one goal ruled out for offside when Vieira headed clear from the Arsenal box to Henry, who seemed far from danger, midway inside his own half. Then, after shielding the ball from Tottenham's Matthew Etherington, he headed upfield. Tottenham defenders backed off and in a matter of seconds the flying Frenchman was approaching the edge of the visitors' box. When a tackler finally approached, Henry shaped to shoot before moving the ball to his left foot and curling home from 18 yards. Sensational.

Henry was so ecstatic with his goal that ran the length of the pitch in celebration, ending up right in front of the away fans and somewhat out of breath. When the Frenchman describes his goal he doesn't do it or himself justice. Words can only go so far. 'With the Tottenham goal, I first of all just wanted to keep the danger out of our box but then I ran towards their net,' he says matter-of-factly. 'I saw Stephen Carr coming so I feigned to shoot. Then I saw Ledley King coming, so I pushed the ball on and finished it with my left foot.'

Television viewers later voted it the Goal of the Season. It had everything: pace, power, control and skill. Even the then Tottenham captain was full of praise for Henry and his goal. 'Henry is immense,' Teddy Sheringham said, 'he's got incredible pace and it just seems he has different gears and when he gets into that third gear it's just end of story for anyone chasing him. His pace scares defenders and I just wish I'd had half of it. But it's not just about pace; he's got great skill. The goal he scored against us, he used his pace then shaped to shoot before curling a great shot into the top corner. It's no good just being quick without the ability to match it.'

Henry's ability was there for all to see in the second half as he ran at King and cut back inside, dumping the England defender on his rear before setting up Ljungberg for Arsenal's second. Wiltord completed the scoring, and it looked like Henry and the Gunners were back on form after their 'tired spell'. But after another international break, when Henry played in France's 3–0 friendly win over Yugoslavia, all eyes turned to the St Mary's Stadium to see how Arsenal would fare against Southampton.

Time away from Wenger's coaching again had a disruptive effect on the Gunners as they lost 3–2 on the south coast. With Arsenal always playing at such a high pace, it was essential for success that the players remained sharp and in harmony with each other.

Whether Henry's team-mates struggled to get on the same wavelength without as much of Wenger's fine-tuning as normal, or just that the players were run down after travelling as far as they had to in international weeks, it was fair to say that the Gunners fans were always somewhat restless after their heroes came back after playing for their various countries.

Thankfully, Arsenal managed to get back to winning ways in the next game as Henry once again demonstrated his worth to the Gunners. In Italy's Eternal City, Arsenal overcame AS Roma with a certain Frenchman scoring all his side's goals. Roma took the lead after just four minutes, but that just stirred Henry into action and, just over a minute later, the scores were level as he tucked away a cross-field ball from Gilberto. In the second half, Henry scored two more to bring up his first European hat-trick and give Arsenal a fantastic 3–1 start to the second group stage.

Afterwards Henry was typically focused on the team when asked about his superb display. 'It is wonderful to score a hat-trick, but the main thing is that we won the game,' the Frenchman insisted. 'We have to keep our feet on the ground as this victory will mean nothing if we don't beat Valencia at Highbury in a fortnight.'

Henry's third in Rome was a beautifully taken free-kick which curled sumptuously into the top corner and there was a case of déjà vu at Highbury three days later when another lethal Henry dead-ball left Aston Villa grasping for air. 'I have been practising free-kicks,' Henry told the *Daily Telegraph*. 'It's a bit difficult to do after training because there are so many games the boss doesn't want us to put extra pressure on our thighs. If I do "shot, shot, shot" in training, the day after the body is tense. But sometimes with Sylvain, Robert Pires and Dennis, we stay and do some free-kicks. I was feeling confident against Roma. Sylvain and Robert came over and I said to them, "I feel like this one, let me do it."'

He was still in confident mood against the Villa and even had the audacity to chip a late penalty straight down the middle of the goal as Peter Enckelman dived away to his left. With his many goals and fantastic all-round play, Henry was receiving plenty of praise, but he would take none of it for himself and insisted the compliments be shared around.

'I am nothing without my team-mates,' Henry mused. 'I cannot score a goal by myself. When I see Patrick Vieira, Gilberto, Freddie Ljungberg, Sylvain Wiltord and Dennis Bergkamp even, running their hearts out to get the ball for me to go on a quick counter-attack, I say to myself, "I must do something for them." People ask me why I look down on the pitch sometimes and it is when I haven't helped my team. When I don't score, I feel upset for the midfielders and defenders. It was as if I hadn't turned up. I am only there to finish the job of the team. You can't have the individual ahead of the collective. Never.'

Obviously there are the occasional exceptions to prove the rule as Henry pointed out. 'Maradona could carry the team on his shoulders with his attacking ability and his attitude but did you see the way the other Argentina players were fighting for him? Did you see the way Argentina defended? They were quite dirty, quite tough. When Maradona was delivering, if you had asked any Argentine player, "Would you die for Maradona?" they would all say, "Yes, as long as he keeps scoring."'

Possibly a little overdramatic, but the same sense of camaraderie was obviously in effect at Arsenal. 'Our team is a family,' Henry said. 'Against Roma, we were all fighting for each other. We are close off the pitch. Some players have children; we are not always over at each other's homes. But sometimes we hang out, meet and eat. The spirit is really great. We laugh all the time. Everyone takes the mickey out of me, Patrick and Dennis. If we are in training and someone misses a pass, we give him a real look!'

Playing against Roma in Italy, Henry insisted there had

been no extra motivation to give his former Italian employers a taste of what they'd given away. 'People like to give Juve stick because historically they are the best team in Italy. When I do something against an Italian side, they say, "Why did Juve let him go?" I wasn't there for revenge; I was there to get Arsenal three points.'

The Gunners next chance to get three points was away at Old Trafford and, ahead of the game, some of the Manchester United players were talking about Henry and they were full of admiration. Ruud Van Nistelrooy compared himself unfavourably to the Frenchman, saying, 'You see Thierry and it's beautiful; you see me, it's not classic. He is fantastic.' The Netherlands international forward added, 'He is the complete striker. Such a combination of speed, control and skill is so rare. You see quick players but a lot of the time they do not have the control or the great touch and feeling in their feet like he does. If I could take something from him, it would be his speed. He is the quickest in the Premiership.'

The Old Trafford front man wasn't alone in thinking he was second best to Henry, as French defender Mikael Silvestre gave his opinion with the added benefit of having seen both in action in the same team. 'I would take Henry [over Ruud] because he is a lot faster, and he gives a team more attacking options.'

Ferguson's men were very generous before the game, but on the pitch they were far less charitable as they beat Arsenal 2–0. It was the first time in 55 Premiership games that the Gunners had failed to trouble the scorers and they were unable to find the target in their next game either as they drew 0–0 with Valencia.

One point against a well-organised Spanish side, with defender Robert Ayala particularly impressive, left Arsenal with a very respectable four points in Group B, as the Champions League took its Christmas holiday. Able once more to concentrate on domestic business, Arsenal made the small trip down the Seven Sisters Road for the second game of the season against their neighbours.

Stung at having been so comprehensively beaten at Highbury a month earlier, Tottenham managed to put in a much-improved performance in front of their own fans and they even took the lead and held Arsenal to 1–1 at the break. But despite the opposition's extra resilience, Henry still managed to create a wonderful chance in the second half that would have rivalled his previous derby effort. Henry broke from deep inside his own half to beat four defenders and lay square to Bergkamp, but Stephen Carr managed to block the Dutchman's shot and Henry's fantastic run will disappear into the archives with all the other 'nearly' great goals.

Deep into December and the year was drawing to a close as Arsenal beat Middlesbrough and West Brom. All the talk was of Henry's chances of winning the *Ballon d'Or*, the award for the European Footballer of the Year. 'Thierry has had an outstanding performance again and an outstanding week,' Wenger said. 'He should certainly be Footballer of the Year in this country. As for footballer of the season, we will have to be patient and see. European Footballer of the Year? I'd say he's in contention certainly.'

Arsenal's skipper, Patrick Vieira, was less reserved in his judgement. 'To be honest with you, I think Thierry is the best striker in the world because he can score the goals that make a difference. Even if he's not having a good day, he can give a pass or can still help us. I think by far he's one of the best at the moment and he's a strong character. The only way he isn't going to win the European Footballer of the Year, maybe, is that France didn't do really well at the World Cup. But if you base it on what he has done with his club, then he should win it.'

Henry himself was not particularly concerned by all the trophy talk, though as he said, 'In a personal way, it's always nice to have that [award]. But I don't really look at that for myself when I play for Arsenal or France. I just want to play and do well. I'm happier than ever about the way I feel at the moment. You can see that on the pitch. Obviously I had a bad spell recently and wasn't scoring a lot. But I was still helping the team to score goals and that's one of the things about me. I said after the game against Auxerre at home that I was a bit tired and couldn't perform. I am only a human being and you always go through some periods when you can't deliver. But now that I have my legs back, I can run. It's as simple as that.'

With his laid-back attitude, Henry wasn't bothered by not topping the poll for 2002 European Footballer of the Year as Ronaldo claimed his third *Ballon d'Or*, but Henry's manager didn't feel the performances of the Brazilian over the previous 12 months merited the award. 'Ronaldo was the player of the World Cup but has not played much before or after,' Wenger said. 'The World Cup is 3 weeks and the year is 52 weeks.'

Henry may not have got the trophy, but he got the winner against West Brom at the Hawthorns and followed that up with the equaliser against Liverpool at Highbury. He also bagged Arsenal's 3rd goal at home to Chelsea to take him to 98 goals for the Gunners. Any concerns that Henry might suffer in what cricketers call the 'nervous 90s' were quickly dispelled in his next game as he scored the first and last goals in Arsenal's 4–0 win away to Birmingham to bring up his century.

'To score a hundred goals at Arsenal means a lot to me. When I first arrived, it didn't look like I was going to do that,' he said and, always thinking of the team, quickly adding, 'but more important is the three points today.'

The game at St Andrews was Henry's 181st for the Gunners, a phenomenal strike rate that made the man responsible for encouraging his goal-scoring success very happy. As Wenger said, 'Henry was exceptional today, I think he is a fantastic striker – the exception becomes the norm with him. He's only 25 and has played just three years in this position. But what I like about him is that he is not only a goal-scorer but also a team player who provides chances for other players as well.'

The result moved Arsenal five points clear of Manchester United at the top of the table and Wenger was happy. His side seemed to be rediscovering their awesome autumn form. 'I enjoyed the team performance,' the manager said. 'There was a good passing game and sharp movement. Maybe we were fortunate to score first and we suffered a few moments of anxiety with the long ball but we always looked in control. I am very pleased because it looks like our fluent game is coming back and that can only be good for us.'

The Gunners, and Henry in particular, looked very fluent

in their next game, a 3–0 win at home against West Ham. Henry scored all three goals, a mixed bag of a hat-trick with a penalty, a header and a typical Arsenal breakaway goal. The header came from a deep Bergkamp cross and the two men, whose talents seem perfectly matched on the pitch, were highly complimentary about each other off the park. Bergkamp, who completed his Arsenal century one week before the Frenchman, spoke fondly of his strike partner.

'If you're a striker, you'd love to have the skills he's got,' said the equally blessed Dutchman. 'He has so much pace, skill and strength. You can't wish for anything more from a striker. The goals he scored at Birmingham summed Thierry up. It's important that you have confidence in your team-mates that they will make the passes. With Thierry in this sort of form, once we make those passes the question is who can stop him? With his pace there's not a defender in the world who will be able to stop him.'

Henry was equally grateful for the passing ability of the man who has set up so many of his Arsenal goals. 'It seems like you can make a run, any run, and somehow, even though there are lots of players in between, Dennis will see you,' Henry said. 'He makes things look so easy. We all know it's not, but you have to play with him to understand. It is instinct. He's played with me, Ian Wright, Nicolas Anelka, Kanu and adapted to them all. There are not many Bergkamps around.'

Indeed, there is only one Dennis Bergkamp and the non-flying Dutchman put in a fantastic cameo against Farnborough Town after he and Henry had shared a special award ceremony on the Highbury pitch to mark their respective centuries of

Arsenal goals. Henry was enjoying a well-earned rest in the FA Cup as his colleagues guided the Gunners into the Sixth Round with a 5–1 win over the Cup minnows.

Henry and Bergkamp received their centurion trophies to rapturous applause from the crowd along with the Arsenal team and staff. Afterwards, the Frenchman told the *Daily Telegraph* how much everyone's encouragement meant to him. 'The thing that most gives me strength is that I know what my team-mates and boss think about me and that the fans support me. That's an English thing. If you lose one or two games in Spain, Italy or France, then you are in trouble. In England, fans support you more when you lose.

'When I didn't score for five games in the league I got some stick in the media but people didn't mention I had six assists. I bend my runs out to the left and defenders follow me which leaves a massive hole in the centre for people to go into and score.'

As an attacker who provides as many chances for others as he takes himself, Henry thought it a shame that forwards are only judged by their strike rates. As he put it, 'People only rate strikers by goals and that is a shame. Of course, Ronaldo can score goals by himself. I like strikers who can create goals as well. The best player I have ever seen is Marco van Basten. He was a proper player; he used his skills to be effective for the team. Van Basten had an arrogance about him, not in a bad way, but in a way that said, "Just give me the ball." He was good in the air, was quick, could hold the ball up, could score and give assists. What more do you want?'

Henry also admires those players who battle for the team, without necessarily grabbing any of the praise. 'Take Emile

Heskey. I feel for him sometimes because he is the one who jumps in the air, gets the elbow in his face and makes all those runs for other people. No one sees that. All people say is, "Heskey is not scoring." But he is helping his team.'

Henry could never be accused of not helping his team and, in his next game against Heskey's Liverpool, it was his shot that Pires followed up to open the scoring. But having talked about how Heskey didn't get the praise he deserved, Henry found himself being upstaged by the often-lampooned England striker when the big centre-forward's late header grabbed the headlines at Anfield.

Arsenal recovered from that blow in their next game by beating Fulham 2–1 at Highbury, before heading to St James's Park for a big game against Newcastle and Alan Shearer. The Geordie striker was another member of the Henry fan club. 'Henry is a world-class player and his goals record is fantastic too. It is so much more difficult to name a weakness. His pace is frightening,' Shearer said. 'People say he doesn't score many goals with his head! But does he really have to with the ability he has in his feet? He makes spectacular goals look so easy but I assure you they certainly aren't. His technique is fantastic: he can score goals with either foot, he can run in behind you, he can come short too. He takes people on, he can dribble and is simply superb. His record proves that he is so consistent.'

Henry proved just how consistent he could be by picking up his 18th Premiership goal of the season against the Magpies as he took Wiltord's pass round Shay Given to score, but it wasn't enough to win as the Toon Army roared their men on to grab a 1–1 draw.

February was a busy month for Henry as he had 7 games in 26 days and the next one was for France against the Czech Republic. France lost 2–0 and carried their dodgy 2002 form into 2003. Wary of the number of games Henry was playing and always willing to rest his star striker in the FA Cup, Wenger named the number 14 on the bench for the trip to Manchester United.

Old Trafford had been a happy hunting ground for the Gunners in the Cup with semi-final wins there in the two preceding seasons and the sequence continued as Arsenal ran out 2–0 winners. Arsenal dominated the game from start to finish and, although Ryan Giggs had a chance to open the scoring, he somehow failed with the goal at his mercy. Ferguson wasn't happy with his side's capitulation – so angry was the Scot, in fact, that he felt the need to kick a stray boot in the direction of England skipper David Beckham, splitting his eyebrow and damaging their relationship beyond repair.

Back at Highbury, however, Henry had a Champions League match against Ajax to win and the Gunners got off to a flying start. Wiltord grabbed a goal after just five minutes and it looked to be only a question of how many Arsenal would win by as chance after chance went begging. But as if from nowhere, the Amsterdam team were level through Nigel de Jong. Ronald Koeman's young side took huge confidence from their equaliser, became very difficult to break down and the game finished 1–1.

The Gunners' next game was a relative walk in the park as they won their second game in Manchester in the space of seven days, destroying City 5–1 at Maine Road with four goals in the first nineteen minutes. Henry scored one and made two as his fantastic season continued, but even he couldn't find a way to goal in his next game.

In Amsterdam, Arsenal drew a blank as the team made famous by Johan Cruyff's 'total football' turned their back on flair and kept 10 men behind the ball for almost the entire 90 minutes. But the Gunners still topped Group B after four games and in the Premier League they extended their lead at the top to eight points with a win over Charlton at Highbury.

Henry created yet another goal against Alan Curbishley's side, rolling a perfect ball across the six-yard box with the outside of his right foot for Jeffers to sidefoot home. And Henry couldn't recall ever playing better. 'I have never had form like this before,' he said. 'Everyone here at Arsenal believes in me and that helps. The thing is, when you're playing like this, the hardest thing is to stay at this level. We all know as footballers that it's not easy to go on the pitch and produce every weekend. I know everyone expects that from me but it's not easy to do it.'

Henry was happy with his team-mates and the rapport they had developed in their years in North London. 'Look at Patrick Vieira's commitment and how long he's been here. Then there's Dennis Bergkamp, Freddie Ljungberg, Robert Pires, me and Sylvain Wiltord. You don't hear anyone saying they want to leave. There's a great spirit here and that's what it's all about.'

The Gunners' spirit saw them come back from being a goal down against Chelsea in their next game, an FA Cup quarter-final at Highbury. John Terry opened the scoring for the Blues before Henry had a controversial penalty saved, but Jeffers levelled things for Arsenal. Then Henry put the Gunners ahead with another of those moments of genius that were so abundant in his season.

Vieira played a ball over the top of the Chelsea defence and, as Carlo Cudicini rushed to the edge of his area to claim the ball, Henry brought it down with perfect control before spinning around the keeper and rolling the ball into the empty net.

Chelsea struck back to take the game to a replay, further crowding the Gunners' busy calendar. But after the game the questions had nothing to do with football or the fantastic goal the Frenchman scored. Instead Henry was asked about the coin that hit him during the match, hurled by a Chelsea yob in the crowd. 'I think it is sad. But what is the point in getting upset?' Henry told the *Sun* newspaper. 'I just want to concentrate on playing football. It would have been stupid to react in some way, particularly when I should be saving energy for the team rather than getting stressed by those sorts of things. I don't remember being hit by a coin. I was more concerned about my shin after a clash with Carlo Cudicini. As I stood up, I noticed the objects lying on the floor.'

Some of the Chelsea followers may not have been big fans of Henry, but their manager certainly was. 'Henry has every possible weapon which a striker should possess in his armoury,' said Claudio Ranieri. 'He plays with speed, class and a light-footed elegance, which makes him beautiful to watch. To me he is a brilliant footballer who keeps everyone, fans and opposition supporters, on the edge of their seats with excitement throughout a game. Henry is an artist and players like him are the reasons people get involved in football.'

Henry was glad that some people were appreciative of his game, but stayed focused on the job in hand and that was winning games with Arsenal. Unfortunately for the Gunners, Henry and his team-mates failed to create a winner in any of their next three games as Champions League football sailed over the horizon for another year.

Things got off to a good start against Roma at Highbury as Vieira's header put them 1–0 up after 12 minutes, but they couldn't get the second goal that would kill off the game. The Italians equalised in the last minute of the first half and held on for a 1–1 draw and a share of the points. The Gunners followed that up with defeat in the league at Highbury as Blackburn once again came to London with an inspired Brad Friedel in goal to beat the Champions 2–0.

So Arsenal weren't in their best form for the trip to Valencia and, despite knowing a draw would take them through to the knock-out stages, they failed to stop John Carew as the big Norwegian striker put the Gunners out of Europe for the 2nd time in 24 months with 2 goals in a 2–1 win. Henry had got Arsenal back on level terms four minutes into the second half with a fine curling shot after a one-two with Pires, but they fell behind again seven minutes later and could find no way back into the game.

Henry and his team-mates were down after again failing to impose themselves on the Champions League, but they had no time for moping around – not with their hectic schedule! Everton came to Highbury hoping to inflict more misery on the Gunners, but the Rooney-inspired Toffees weren't able to do the League Double over a gritty Arsenal side. It was strange but comforting to see the Gunners grinding out a result, as Henry admitted afterwards. 'When you can do it in style, you do it in style. Sometimes the goals flow, and it looks easy. But if we could win every game until the end of the season playing like we did against Everton I'd take that. We didn't play well individually but we did play well as a team. We showed our mentality because, to be honest, we didn't play the way we normally do. We all fought for each other and showed something people don't always notice about us. The Everton game was about fighting and working to win. It was about passion and desire. It was about who wanted it most – and we dug in and got a result.'

After digging in against Liverpool's Blues at Highbury, Arsenal had to travel across London for their Cup replay against London Blues Chelsea. Stamford Bridge was packed as the home fans tried to cheer their team to victory, but Arsenal were in determined mood and, with Vieira again inspirational, they beat Chelsea 3–1 with Henry playing only the last 15 minutes. Wenger was wise to rest his front man ahead of another international break and, playing for France, Henry kept their World Cup qualifying effort on track with two wins – at home to Malta where Henry scored twice and away against Israel.

The disruption of international week affected the Gunners once again as they dropped two points away to Aston Villa, letting a one-goal lead slip to finish 1–1. Henry had another chance to rest the following week as Wenger continued his FA Cup selection policy. Arsenal's leading scorer only played as a substitute as the Gunners beat Sheffield United 1–0 at Old Trafford, with Seaman turning back the years to produce an incredible one-handed save from Paul Peschisolido.

Seaman picked up a knock and would miss the next game, but Henry was back in the starting line-up for the visit of Manchester United in the Premier League. Arsenal were three points behind the Red Devils with a game in hand and, although not as vital as the showdown of the previous season, the result could still play a large part in deciding the destination of the title. In the end, the points were shared as Van Nistelrooy opened the scoring before Arsenal hit back with two goals from Henry. Unfortunately, barely a minute after taking the lead, Wenger's men were pulled back by a Giggs header which made the score 2–2.

Come the end of the season, however, it was not the result that affected the Gunners but the circumstances in which it arrived. Vieira hobbled off with the injury that was to bring his season to a premature end after half an hour and, with only five minutes left to play, Campbell was sent off for violent conduct as Ole Gunnar Solskjaer ran into his slightly raised arm. The loss of two of Arsenal's most experienced and determined performers proved fatal in the final weeks of the season and Henry and his team-mates could only finish second behind Ferguson's men.

Arsenal put the result behind them in the knowledge that, if they won their remaining five games, the title could still be theirs. And so the Gunners went away to Middlesbrough and won 2–0. Henry scored another free-kick and created the other goal for Wiltord, but next up was a game away to Bolton Wanderers. This was the game that would encapsulate the Gunners' season.

Henry was again in masterful form as he led the home defence a merry dance at the Reebok Stadium and, although a goal proved elusive in the first half, the Gunners were 2–0 up ten minutes into the second as Henry created goals for Wiltord and Pires. Shortly after the second goal, Ljungberg was taken off after being taken out by Jay-Jay Okocha. More outrageous challenges followed and the Gunners soon lost Pascal Cygan and Lauren to injury. Arsenal's rhythm was disrupted after making 3 enforced substitutions in 15 minutes and Bolton poured forward to take advantage of uncertainty in the new back line.

The Trotters managed to get back on level terms from two set-pieces as Youri Djorkaeff and then a Martin Keown own goal seriously dented Arsenal's hopes of back-to-back Premiership titles. Looking back at the season, Henry was asked by the *Guardian* to describe the Gunners' season in three words. Almost straight off, he came up with 'Dominating. Injury,' before thinking a bit longer and adding, 'Lost it. "Lost it" is two words. But, yeah, "Lost it".'

It only took him seconds to come up with what he thought had been the nadir of the campaign. 'Bolton, no doubt about it,' Henry said. 'The game against Bolton was exactly what I said about our season. We were dominating. Injuries. Lost it. Our season was against Bolton.'

It certainly wasn't the Gunners' best performance of the year, but having gone into a 2–0 lead, it is a game they should have won. 'That's the thing that made the difference last season: when we were not on our day we were still winning,' he continued. 'We did manage to do that at the beginning of this season – I remember we drew at West Ham; they could have been 3 or 4–0 up. David [Seaman] saved a penalty and we came back to 2–2 from nowhere. I don't know how. At West Brom we were shocking but we won 2–1. That's important.

'But at the end – even worse – we were on top of a team and we were conceding goals. It is about character. When you can pass the ball as we can, that's normal. But when you don't – when it's not as easy as normal – you have to force yourself somewhere else, you have to do it mentally.'

But as the season drew to a close, Arsenal failed to rekindle the necessary mental resilience and it was that which cost them.

Henry's fine form throughout the season had brought him a great deal of praise from a great number of footballing people. It also brought him the PFA Player of the Year award. In a poll conducted by the Professional Footballers' Association, Henry finished top to ensure he would at least have some personal silverware with which to end the season.

The PFA dinner came the day after the Bolton match and, although Henry was still visibly upset about the result, he was pleased with the award. 'This means a lot to me because the other players have voted for me,' the Frenchman said. 'They all know better than anyone else because they play against me and they must have noticed something, so I'm happy they have noticed something.

'It's never easy when you come from another country to get people to like you but, at the end of the day, the most important thing is football, no matter which country you are from. We are all trying to play the same and to do well on the pitch, so nationality doesn't really matter.'

Internationally Henry continued his good season with a

brace against Egypt, taking his total to six goals in eight games for Santini's side since the World Cup.

On his return to England, Henry's Arsenal lost 3–2 to Leeds United at Highbury, sending the title north to Manchester. Without Vieira and Campbell, the Gunners were exposed defensively and fell behind three times to the Yorkshire side who were fighting for their Premier League survival. Henry and Bergkamp twice brought Arsenal level, but needing a win to keep their title dreams alive, they had no reply to Leeds' third goal. Defeat left an insurmountable gap between first and second at the top of the table.

Unable to repeat their League and Cup Double of the previous season, one Gunner was still a double-winner as Henry won the Football Writers' Association Footballer of the Year award to go with his PFA trophy. Happy as he was with his achievement, there was no way he could hide his frustration at the way Arsenal had surrendered an eight-point lead at the top of the Premiership. 'It's a great pleasure to win this trophy but I would rather have won the league,' Henry said. 'You suffer all year for the title and there's no greater pleasure than to win a major trophy with your team. But I don't really know what to say about this award. I've been so happy in England although sometimes I know it doesn't look like that on the pitch. I know how much football means to the fans and that's why I yell and shout on the field.'

Voted for by the men in the know, the football writers themselves, the award was a close-run thing as Ruud Van Nistelrooy's goals propelled Manchester United to the Premier League trophy, but Henry's all-round contribution had seen him edge out the Dutchman.

In his next game he was again at the centre of everything again as Arsenal won 6–1 against Southampton at Highbury. Henry didn't score a goal himself, but created three as Pires and Jermaine Pennant both grabbed hat-tricks.

The game showed just how unselfish Henry is – at this point, he trailed Van Nistelrooy by one goal in the race for the Golden Boot and yet he spent the whole game putting goals on a plate for his team-mates.

'People always see the goals, and for me strikers are not only about scoring goals,' Henry told the *Guardian*. 'Before the Southampton game, I said to myself it would be quite nice to catch Van Nistelrooy. But in the game I found myself setting up other people. I am not greedy, but I could have been greedy in that game. It's quite important for me to respect the game.'

Henry continued to gain more and more respect within the game with another hat-trick of assists in the Gunners' last league match of the season. He scored one himself and made three for Ljungberg in a 4–0 win in Sunderland. 'I'm not only a goal-scorer. Sometimes people put me in the same league as [Michael] Owen or Van Nistelrooy but I'm not at all like this type. I'm not trying to be better than Ruud, but the one thing I was pleased with this season was the goals I gave. I think it's pretty rare to see a striker with that amount of assists.'

Indeed Henry set a new Premiership record of 23 assists in the 2002–03 season; he also scored 24 league goals as the Gunners finished in second place. Despite this excellent marksmanship, Henry was second in the race for the Golden Boot as Van Nistelrooy grabbed one in his last game to edge out the Frenchman.

The Dutchman was still full of praise for his rival. 'To play in partnership with Thierry Henry would be amazing,' Van Nistelrooy said. 'If we were a duo, it would be fantastic. With his pace and vision, his scoring ability and his ability to let others play well, it would be fantastic to play with him. Thierry is a player who is much more involved all over the pitch.'

Great strikers continued to pay tribute to Henry and one of them was Alan Shearer who spoke up before the FA Cup Final. 'The Frenchman didn't beat Ruud Van Nistelrooy to the Golden Boot this season – but he has swept almost everything else before him,' said the former England captain. 'The respect his fellow pros have for Thierry is shown by all the awards he has picked up recently. He is the Players' Player and Football Writers' Footballer of the Year. He's a fantastic footballer – with skill, pace and the ability to make finishing easy. Give Henry one chance and you are one down. Some of his goals have been outstanding – he is a world-class player. Some of his play has been simply breathtaking and I don't doubt he could pick up all the plaudits after this afternoon's final.'

Henry turned in a starring display again in Cardiff and picked up the official Man of the Match award for his brilliant attacking play as the Gunners beat Southampton 1–0 through a Pires goal. After the disappointment of missing out on what had looked like a possible Treble just two months before, it took a resolute performance from Henry and Arsenal to make sure that the Highbury trophy cabinet wouldn't be bare for the next 12 months.

'When you lose key players at such a time, obviously it is

massive,' Henry told the *Guardian*. Being without Vieira, Campbell, Ljungberg and Lauren at important points in the season had been too much for the Gunners to contend with. 'Sometimes you can do it during the season, dig in for one or two games. But this was for quite a lot and at that time of the season when you need those players. I am not looking for excuses; all I'm saying is that it does change things a bit. But it doesn't mean you should lose a title.'

The title was gone for this year but Henry, FWA, PFA and PFA Fans' Footballer of the Year winner with another 32 goals in his 55 games for Arsenal, was already looking to the future. 'There is no anti-climax. At the end you have to give credit to Manchester United. They did well to come back and we didn't do enough to keep our lead. But life goes on. We have had worse seasons. We won the FA Cup and we were competing for the title. Maybe everyone was expecting us to retain the title but we didn't.

'Now we must come back even stronger. That's one of the things about a winner's mentality – you won't accept it. You have to say to the others, "Well done," but you don't have to accept it.'

And the important is that there was no way Henry was going to accept second best for long.

Chapter ten
Best in the World

'It's amazing to win the title and stay unbeaten. We're down in history and we're the first team to do it. I'm aware that Preston did it 115 years ago, but there were only 12 teams in the league then, so we'll really go down in history as the first team to do it.' These words from Thierry Henry came after he had helped guide his team through an entire league season without defeat, an incredible feat with so much strong competition around.

But it was not achieved without disappointment. 'The team deserves something special this season,' he said. 'We didn't go very far in the Champions League, we got knocked out of the FA Cup in the semi-finals, so we deserve this.'

Before embarking on his monumental season, Henry had had a very memorable summer. After the frustration of throwing away the league, the Frenchman masterminded his country's success at the FIFA Confederations Cup in his home country. With four goals in five games, Henry was the leading scorer in the competition and he was also named Player of the Tournament. The Cup was overshadowed by the tragic death of Cameroon's Marc-Vivien Foe in the semi-final against Colombia and Henry poignantly dedicated his winning goal in the final against Cameroon to the memory of his opponents' fallen team-mate.

Better news was to follow for Henry when, on 5 July 2003, he married his girlfriend of two years, Claire who models under the name Nicole Merry. The two starred together in Henry's Renault Clio advert, but despite popular belief that they had met on set, they were actually already an item before that.

In fact Henry is believed to have asked for his girlfriend to appear with him in the ad. Before stealing the scene from her fiancé, strolling around in one of his shirts, the Croydon model's most notable appearance was as a 'VIP Stewardess' in the film *The Fifth Element*. Fans of Luc Besson's futuristic flick will note that, on the flight to Fhloston Paradise, Merry's stewardess is not the one 'getting busy' with Ruby Rhod.

The wedding took place at Highclere Castle, a Victorian estate owned by the Earl of Carnavon. The Earl's home was closed to the public for the day as 200 people rolled up for the £40,000 ceremony in 2,000 acres of Berkshire countryside. The guests included Patrick Vieira, Emmanuel Petit, Arsene Wenger and a number of other Arsenal players, showing just what a tight-knit group they are.

Highlighting Henry's position as a fashionable male, he even asked Giorgio Armani to custom design his suit for the occasion.

GQ magazine reported the event in detail. 'Giorgio Armani designed a light beige suit and matching waistcoat in heavy cotton twill, and paired it with a crisp white cutaway collar shirt with double cuffs. He completed the look with a bronze tie and a matching handkerchief and brown shoes.'

Always thinking about football, Henry mused that settling down would improve his game. 'Getting married is part of the evolution of my career,' he said. 'Before on the pitch I was a bit crazy. Now I've calmed down. It's the same in my private life.'

Certain people in the media were amazed that Henry didn't sell his wedding photos to one of those magazines which are always willing to offer big money for an exclusive insight into the lives of the rich and famous, but anyone who knew the Frenchman was not at all surprised.

'I am just me. I don't want photos or articles in magazines, I don't know who would be interested in that. I want people to care about my performances on the pitch, not my haircut or dress sense,' Henry said. 'To each his own. My France team-mate Djibril Cisse dyes his hair blond, while David Beckham changes his hairstyle 10,000 times a year. But I'm not like that. I want people to talk about me, not for my clothes, my haircut or my cars. When fans come up to me, they prefer to talk about my game or my goals.'

Not long after his honeymoon, Henry went back to what he does best – scoring goals. His season kicked off with the Community Shield against Manchester United in Cardiff and, at his fifth attempt, Henry scored his first goal in the Millennium Stadium. The Frenchman's free-kick put the Gunners one up, but Ferguson's side hit back through

Henry's international colleague Mikael Silvestre as the Red Devils went on to win 4–3 on penalties after Henry had been substituted.

Arsenal's prolific front man had put the previous season behind him, and was looking to get the Gunners back to trophy-winning form. 'When you fall, the most important thing is how quickly you get back up,' Henry told *SKY* magazine. 'We lost the league but that is finished now. It's gone, over. I spent the summer with my national team. Now I'm back at Arsenal and I'm focused again.'

And this time, as he stressed, he was focused on Europe and the elusive Champions League. 'I want to build something with Arsenal and, if we can bring the trophy to London one day, it would mean making history. I'm obsessed by the idea of making my mark in history. And Arsenal is my paradise.'

Henry had indicated just how happy he was in his paradise by signing a contract extension before joining up with France at the end of May. He was to be joined at Highbury for years to come by Vieira and Pires who also put pen to paper in the close season. Those were the most notable of the Gunners signings of the summer as Wenger, with his newly awarded OBE, chose to work with a small squad in the forthcoming season.

The astute French manager had only signed Jens Lehmann from Borussia Dortmund to replace Seaman, who had joined Manchester City, and young full-back Gael Clichy from AS Cannes. With a summer outlay of less than £2 million, a lot of people were writing off the Gunners before the season started, saying they should have splashed the cash – like

Manchester United and Roman Abramovich's Chelsea had done – if they wanted to improve on the last campaign.

But Wenger knew better and was sure the heartbreaking end to the previous year would drive his men on to greater things.

The Gunners got off to a good start in the league as they beat Everton 2–1 at Highbury. Henry scored the first from the penalty-spot as he claimed Arsenal's first league goal for the third consecutive season. With their newfound resolve, Henry and his team-mates refused to let an international break disrupt their rhythm, as it had done so many times before, and demolished Middlesbrough 4–0 in the next match.

Four days after playing for *les Bleus* in Switzerland, Henry scored one and made another as the Gunners went 3–0 up against Boro in a little over 20 minutes. Arsenal maintained their 100 per cent start to the new season with wins over Aston Villa, 2–0 at Highbury, and a 2–1 score-line against Manchester City in the new City of Manchester Stadium.

The game against City was the first time the Gunners had been behind in a game since that day in May when they had surrendered the title, but trailing to a Lauren own goal at half-time, Wenger told them that, if they wanted to win the title, it started here. And in the second half, Arsenal grabbed the two goals they needed to win the game and leave themselves on top of the pile at the end of August.

In September, Henry helped France secure qualification for the 2004 European Championship with wins over Cyprus and Slovenia. France had dominated their group from the start and the six points they earned booked their tickets to Portugal to defend their trophy the following summer.

The month had started well for Henry with France but back in north London things didn't go quite so swimmingly. Against Premiership new boys Portsmouth, the Gunners dropped their first league points of the season as they came back from a goal down with a highly debatable penalty that Henry had to take twice. Referee Alan Wiley pointed to the spot after Pires appeared to be clipped in the box, but on further inspection Pompey seemed to have grounds for complaint.

Henry made no mistake from 12 yards, slamming the ball into the bottom left-hand corner of Shaka Hislop's goal. But Mr Wiley called for the kick to be retaken after encroachment by some of the Arsenal players; Henry was unfazed and simply put the second spot-kick past the keeper, this time to the right.

The next visitors to Highbury were Inter Milan as Arsenal were drawn in a an exhausting Group B that would require two trips to the former Soviet Union to play Lokomotiv Moscow and Dynamo Kiev. The Milan side inflicted a first defeat of the season on the Gunners as they hit the back of the net with their first three attacks to race into a 3–0 lead. Arsenal had been all over their guests, so it came as a bit of a shock when they found themselves so far behind at half-time, Henry even missed a penalty at 2–0, further compounding the misery for the Highbury faithful.

With the media already interpreting Wenger's modest summer spending as a lack of ambition for honours, there was a lot of pressure on the Gunners to perform after such a comprehensive beating – one that supposedly ended their Champions League hopes at the first hurdle. So Arsenal were doubly determined to prove their doubters wrong in their next match away to Manchester United.

'When everyone is doubting us, saying we are finished, we always bounce back. That's what we did at Old Trafford,' Henry said, looking back at the season. 'Some people were saying that the Champions League is all over for us, and they were mentioning about the way we lost the title last season, but when people say that we bounce back.'

Arsenal played probably their most defensive game of the season, proving themselves dogged and resilient at the back even without Sol Campbell. But following the controversial sending-off of Vieira, who picked up a second yellow card for waving a foot in the direction of Van Nistelrooy, the home side were awarded a debatable late penalty as Diego Forlan tussled with Keown.

Van Nistelrooy struck the bar with the spot-kick and the Arsenal celebrations were a little unsavoury as they mocked and jostled the tumbling Dutchman. At the final whistle shortly afterwards, Keown leaped in celebration, landing almost on top of Van Nistelrooy and catching the former PSV striker with his arm. Most of the players who were still on the pitch subsequently got involved in a bout of pushing and shoving, the kind that is always best described in the sporting arena as 'handbags'.

'Van Nistelrooy missed the penalty and, when I look back on that penalty award, I still think, "Whatever",' Henry said. 'It seems that, when someone goes down for us a little bit too easily, everyone goes mad, but when it's another team nobody says anything. But also remember the way we defended that day, the way we were ready to fight for each other – and in the right way! After that game, a lot happened here – a lot. The more you doubt us, the more we provide things – and we couldn't have been doubted any more after that game.'

The press had a field day with the scenes at the end of the game between England's two most successful sides. They even went so far as to rename the match 'The Battle of Old Trafford', but it just provided extra motivation for Henry and his team-mates. 'They wanted to put us down but we showed our character. We wanted to show that we were not the team that people were saying we were,' Henry said. 'Seriously though, with all that coverage after that game I thought that Martin must have killed someone. Then afterwards I saw the Blackburn versus Southampton game where there was proper fighting, real punches, but ours was just pushing. They talked about it as if someone had been killed.'

Like many of his team-mates, Henry had developed an 'us against the world' mentality under Wenger, probably the 'special Arsenal spirit' he so often mentions. 'They carried on for three months, they still talk about it. The picture of Martin jumping over Ruud Van Nistelrooy will go down in history. I've seen so many worse things this season, but you know – whatever.'

Having battled to a point in Manchester, the Gunners had a game against the Toon Army at Highbury. Arsenal showed they hadn't exhausted their reserves of spirit and they managed to beat Bobby Robson's Newcastle side despite letting the lead slip twice and losing Vieira to injury in the 25th minute. Henry opened the scoring, tapping in a Lauren cross that Titus Bramble failed to clear in monsoon conditions. But the Geordies conjured up an equaliser to that and then to Arsenal's second which came from Gilberto.

The Gunners got lucky, however, when Jermaine Jenas inexplicably handled a Pires corner and Henry displayed his confidence and skill, running up and chipping the resulting penalty straight down the middle of the goal.

Arsenal had used all three of their substitutions and Ljungberg was limping around the park, so the Gunners were effectively down to ten men in tough conditions when the penalty was awarded. Sensing it was the last chance to win the game, the pressure was on Henry as he later admitted. 'That was one of the toughest penalties I've ever taken.' You wouldn't have thought so watching it!

After showing their mettle in the Premiership, Arsenal had a chance to get their European campaign back on track in Russia. Desperate for points following the game against Inter, the Gunners put in another resolute away performance and kept a clean sheet against Lokomotiv Moscow. But the goal that would turn one point into three continued to elude Henry and his team-mates, and their Champions League future was beginning to look nearly as bleak as the Russian winter.

Things weren't looking great domestically either, when the Gunners travelled to Anfield and found themselves a goal down after 13 minutes but, displaying the character so fundamental to their season, Wenger's men battled back to win 2–1. Liverpool played some of their best football of the year in the first half and Arsenal were lucky to go in on level terms following Hyypia's own goal. But after the break, the Gunners showed it really is a game of two halves as they dominated throughout and claimed the points with a Pires wondergoal.

Two months into the season, the Gunners were once again looking like genuine title contenders, but so were the 'nouveau riche' Chelsea who were looking to break the duopoly of Manchester United and Arsenal in the Premiership. After a busy summer in the transfer market, Claudio Ranieri had dished out £100 million of Roman Abramovich's billions and the Blues came to Highbury with great expectations.

Chelski's hopes were dealt a blow early on, however, as Edu's free-kick deflected into the back of the net. The visitors hit back with a rare Hernan Crespo goal and for a long time it seemed likely that the score would finish 1–1. But Carlo Cudicini showed just how tough life is as a keeper; seconds after making a stunning save to foil Henry, the Italian let a low cross slip through his hands and Henry wasn't even looking at the ball as it struck his leg and rolled over the line.

The win put Arsenal top of the pile as they tried once again to take their league form into Europe. A trip to Kiev is never easy, and so it proved for the Gunners as they lost 2–1 despite Vieira's return from injury as a second-half substitute and Henry's goal ten minutes from time. With one point from three games, Arsenal were bottom of Group B at the halfway stage and they knew they would have to win their next three games to book themselves a place in the knock-out stages.

Given the great form of the Gunners in England with such a multinational side, it was odd that they were underperforming overseas. 'It's so strange,' Henry told the BBC's *Football Focus*. 'I remember when I first arrived here we were not doing so well in the League, and we were doing well in the European competitions. Now we're doing well in the league and we're not doing well in Europe. It is so strange. Trust me, we are trying to do well.'

Nobody had ever doubted the effort Henry and his team-mates were putting in, but the Frenchman had a point when he said Wenger's men might be trying to overplay it. 'Maybe, instead of playing how we know we can play, we're trying to play too well. We should maybe come back to the basics. But it is frustrating because we know what we can do. In England you can see the way we can play the ball, but when you see the Champions League games, to be honest, we are not doing it.'

Arsenal had failed to pick up all three points in a European match in the last eight attempts, and that would have to change. 'We need to win somewhere, somehow,' Henry added. 'But that's the thing – we don't know how many games that will be. But it's not finished yet. Last year we started so well in the Champions League and didn't qualify, so we'll see what happens.'

Henry was philosophical but still focused on putting the problems right. 'Sometimes you have some bad moments and sometimes you have good moments. We just have to bounce back from the bad moments. It is a big disappointment but at the end of the day that's not the first time and it won't be the last,' he continued. 'Sometimes things happen in football. With France, we lost in the World Cup and everyone was killing us. That's the way it is sometimes. You go through good and bad moments but you have to lift yourself up and try to show that was a mistake and try to perform.'

Henry refused to blame a lack of summer signings for the losses. 'It is too easy to look at excuses,' he said. 'It was 11 players against 11. We lost. It is too easy to say that we should have done this or we should have done that. We were on the pitch, no one else and no money. We don't have to hide.'

Arsenal could take hope from Newcastle United's performance the previous year, when the Magpies lost their first three group games and still went through. 'Maybe they will or maybe they won't say we are out of the Champions League. Last season we were going to win it. People can talk too quickly sometimes and maybe seeing what Newcastle did last season can be a good thing for us. They lost their first three games and people were saying they were out of it and then they went through and people were saying, "How amazing." I didn't want to lose on Tuesday but it is better that we lose now.'

Back in London, Arsenal avoided defeat against Charlton Athletic at the Valley after a trademark Henry free-kick flew past Dean Kiely to equalise a highly dubious penalty awarded against the Gunners for a trip by Lauren on Matt Holland.

But Arsenal were taking motivation from anything and everything that went against them. 'We were all fired up after that penalty we had conceded, that's why I celebrated like I did when I scored. I was wound up,' Henry told *Arsenal* magazine. 'I was wound up because I said to the referee, "What did you see for the penalty?" and he said, "Matt Holland's not that type of player," so I said, "And that makes it a pen?" That wasn't a good answer for me, but at least it fired us up.'

The Gunners came out firing on all cylinders in their next match and were 3–0 up against Leeds after 33 minutes. Henry scored two goals as Arsenal recorded back-to-back 4–1 wins at Elland Road in the league. It was the perfect way to prepare for their next game, the make-or-break Champions League game against Dynamo Kiev at Highbury.

Once again Wenger's side struggled in a European game and, with time running out, the game remained goalless. But fighting to the end brought reward for the Gunners as Henry flicked on Wiltord's cross at the near post and Cole's diving header brought Arsenal's first European win in nine attempts.

The late goal put the Gunners right back in contention in Group B, just three points behind leaders Inter Milan who they would play next. There were 20 days and 3 games for Henry to play in before the return trip to Italy, and the win over Kiev served as a great boost for the Gunners before they entertained Tottenham.

Arsenal were behind at half-time as Darren Anderton's goal gave Tottenham hope of a first win at Highbury since May 1993, but Monsieur Wenger's men showed tremendous spirit as they came back with goals from Ljungberg and Pires to win the first north London derby of the season. Henry then left the capital to join up with *les*

Bleus for a friendly against Germany and he scored one of the goals as France beat their hosts 3–0 in their first warm-up match for Euro 2004.

After the game, Germany's greatest-ever player Franz Beckenbauer revealed how impressed he was with Henry. 'We're light years away from producing an attacker of this quality.' This was a fitting compliment for the man with warp-speed legs as well as a pleasant ego boost for the Gunners striker from 'the Kaiser', a man who really knows his football.

With the big game in Milan looming, Arsenal travelled to St Andrew's seeking to consolidate their position at the top of the league. Birmingham failed to bring the Gunners down on the day England won the Rugby World Cup and Henry set up two of the goals as Arsenal ran out 3–0 winners. The City manager was unhappy to have been on the end of another Henry-inspired beating. 'Some people say he's not a prolific goal-scorer. But if 32 goals in 2 [consecutive] seasons isn't prolific, I don't know what is,' Steve Bruce said.

'Throw in all his "assists", the fact he plays week in, week out and that the rest of us are for ever going, "Bloody hell, not Henry again," and I would have to vote him the world's best at the moment,' Bruce went on. 'He's a fantastic talent and the complete footballer – probably the most coveted in the Premiership. It's a privilege for the rest of us to be on the same field. If I could have anything I wanted for Christmas, I'd take Thierry Henry.'

But with a month to go before the visit of Santa Claus, the chances of the Arsenal number 14 turning up in the former Manchester United defender's stocking were looking extremely slim.

Three days later, all eyes turned to the San Siro stadium to see if Wenger could finally get his men to perform in Europe. The Gunners were without Vieira and Lauren through injury and non-flying Dutchman Bergkamp because of the travel required, but Inter's experienced defender Javier Zanetti was certain of the man to watch in the Arsenal camp. 'Henry is a fantastic player and has shown it for a long time,' the Argentine said. 'He's been playing at the top level in Europe for years. It's difficult to mark him. We'll have to be very aware.'

In the end, it didn't matter how alert the Italian side intended to be. On that November evening in northern Italy, Thierry Henry was just unstoppable. The mercurial Frenchman scored two and made two as the Arsenal beat one of Serie A's best sides 5–1. Henry will remember it for ever. 'One of the best memories of my career,' he announced. 'Because of the stadium, the competition, against good players – it was special and I think it will go down in history.'

It will certainly stick in the minds of all those who watched it and the result meant that, if Arsenal finished level on points with the *Nerazzuri*, then the Gunners would be ahead by virtue of their head-to-head results. 'That was the result we needed as well to put Inter out of it because, even had they come back level with us, our goal difference was better,' Henry told *Arsenal* magazine. 'That was the score we had to do and we did it, nobody would have predicted that before.'

It was an incredible game. Henry opened the scoring after 25 minutes, sidefooting home from the edge of the area after playing a one-two with Cole. Christian Vieri's goal meant the scores were level at half-time, but Henry raced down the left and cut back to Ljungberg to restore the lead four minutes into the second half.

With five minutes to go, Henry scored the goal of the game. Breaking from inside his own half with Zanetti in close pursuit, Henry slowed to a standstill as he entered the home side's area before accelerating past the Inter captain and shooting across the keeper for 3–1.

Edu and Pires put the gloss on the win with their two late goals, but there was no mistaking who the Italian press were talking about when one of their papers ran with the back-page headline KNEEL DOWN BEFORE THE KING.

Even the England manager got in on the action. 'Henry has so much speed it is frightening. He is incredible. He could sell his pace, he has so much to spare,' Sven-Goran Eriksson said. 'He also scores goals and, if you give him half a yard, he is gone and you are in trouble. I've seen so many games when Henry has played well. But the match against Inter Milan was a good example of him at his best. He scored two, showed lots of pace and a great deal of intelligence.'

Henry's legendary team-mate Bergkamp was always willing to wax lyrical about the Frenchman and, after Arsenal's 'Italian Job', he heaped more praise on his strike partner's head. 'Henry received many individual honours last season. And this is right because now we are seeing a player at the top of his profession,' the Dutchman said. 'At 26, he is at that age when everything comes together for a footballer and this is happening for him.

'He is a joy to watch – and this is great news for Arsenal. You hear stories about great players from all over the world and about how they don't train as hard as they should. But you can't say this about Thierry. He is always giving 100 per cent on the training pitch. And if you think some of the tricks and moves during games are special, just imagine the kind of skills we are treated to in practice!'

It is hard to think that Henry's skills in practice could be any more impressive than those he displays so regularly in football grounds around the world, but 'the Iceman' is right to say there appear to be few, if any, chinks in the Frenchman's armour. 'It is hard to find any weaknesses. But if Thierry feels he can improve any area of his game, he will do just that.

'But I think Arsene Wenger and the players around him have been a factor. We have done our best to support and encourage him since he came to Highbury. The best thing about playing with him is he makes things easy for me. You feel he can do something extra. And by giving him the ball you think he can make a difference.'

Bergkamp may not have been in Italy to supply any of his killer passes to Henry, but he appreciated what he saw in the San Siro, as did many others.

Fulham manager Chris Coleman almost certainly watched the game and, wary of the way in which Arsenal demolished the seasoned campaigners of Internazionale, he brought his side to Highbury merely looking for a point. The young Welsh manager got his wish, too, as the Gunners drew a blank after their mid-week heroics with goalkeeper Edwin Van Der Sar playing a key role in the 0–0 result.

After dropping two home points, the Gunners found themselves one point behind Chelsea in the league and they headed for the Walkers Stadium without Henry. In another remarkable season, the journey to Leicester turned out to be the only game Arsenal's talismanic striker missed throughout the league campaign. It has since been revealed that, since joining the Gunners, Henry had played in 20 games more than any other Premiership player for club and country – a fitting testament to the stamina of the teetotal Frenchman and the way in which he leads his life.

With his damaged hamstring, Henry had to tune in to the game on the radio at home and he listened as his team-mates dropped two points in the last minute against the Foxes. But he was soon able to put his frustrations behind him as he returned to the starting XI for the visit of Lokomotiv Moscow.

The Russians had been enjoying their Champions League football and found themselves at the top of Group B after five games. This made it another game that the Gunners had to win to ensure their safe passage to the knock-out stage in the new format. Henry seemed to be carrying his injury and was less explosive off the mark, but he still managed to provide Pires and Ljungberg with incisive passes to complete a 2–0 win for the Gunners and send them through as group-winners.

Henry had been in devastating form throughout 2003 but had missed out on all the big awards. As another fine year drew to a close, there was a lot of talk about the illuminating play of Arsenal's star forward and how he would pick up the European and/or World Player of the Year gong. Michel Platini thought his countryman deserved some recognition. 'He can do everything, scoring goals, giving assists, crossing, and creating space for other player. And he fights for every ball. I've never seen a player in France like him.'

And Ashley Cole was in no doubt as to the number-one forward in football. 'To be honest, Thierry is different class. In my mind there is no better striker in the world at the moment,' the full-back said of his team-mate. 'I would hate to face him in a competitive game for fear he would make a complete mug out of me. He's so hard to defend against.

'I swear he takes it easy in training for fear we might all lose our confidence,' said the young defender. 'Marking him is near impossible. His pace is devastating – I don't think I've ever come up against a player with so many attributes. I don't envy anyone who has to defend against Thierry because he can destroy you. It would help if you could work out the way he plays, but it's impossible, believe me.'

Arsene Wenger was happy to see Henry named in the final three for the World Player of the Year award along with Real Madrid duo Ronaldo and Zidane. 'If you consider individual performances over the year, rather than the achievements of the clubs they play for, I'd say Thierry deserves to win,' the Highbury boss said. 'For me, the fact that he's in the top three, with Ronaldo and Zidane, is enough in itself. It says what he has achieved and for me there's nothing to choose between them.'

Henry's manager has always been impressed by his star pupil. 'Thierry is a complete player now,' Wenger said. 'I believe that if you are a winner, you are willing to do whatever it takes to win. Thierry does that. I'm convinced there's still more to come from him. I have seen improvements in every part of his game, especially in playing the final ball. You only have to look at the Lokomotiv Moscow game. They were organised not to give him room but he still found the space to make the goals for Robert Pires and Freddie Ljungberg. There are a lot of players who suffer from selfishness in front of goal. But the complete player is the one who knows when he has to make the pass.'

Henry's club skipper also thought his fellow countryman deserved the plaudits he was getting. 'Thierry is fabulous,' Vieira said. 'He likes to score goals but he likes to give goals as well and that is the difference between a good and a great player. If it was my choice, I would make him World Player of the Year because of what he has done in the national team and with Arsenal.'

There wasn't too much longer for everyone to wait before the winner was announced. After a 1–0 home win against Blackburn, Henry was named the second-best player in the world when he finished runner-up behind Zidane in the FIFA World Footballer of the Year vote. The Real Madrid playmaker was full of praise for his international colleague. 'There is not a word to sum up how good Thierry is. The things he is doing at his age are unbelievable,' Zizou said. 'He has so much ability and it is a pleasure to play alongside him in the French team.'

After dropping two points at the death against Bolton, a 1–1 draw at Highbury, Henry received more good news when he finished second behind Pavel Nedved in the voting for the *Ballon d'Or*, the European Footballer of the Year award.

Nedved was amazed at his success. 'I didn't even dream of this. For me, Thierry Henry is the best forward in the world now,' said the Juventus midfielder. 'I am very happy. I did not think I would beat Thierry Henry, Paolo Maldini or Zinedine Zidane and, if I had voted, I would have voted for Thierry and for the other players on the podium. I am very happy for myself, my wife, my children and country but I don't know how I beat Thierry Henry or Zinedine Zidane.'

It may seem strange that a man can be voted the second-best player in the world at the same time as being voted the second-best player in Europe and finish behind very different footballers in each. Of course the voting systems are very different. The FIFA 'World' award is voted for by the international managers of each of the teams in the world game, whereas the prestigious *Ballon d'Or* is awarded by *France Football* magazine after a survey of 52 football journalists from around Europe.

Henry may not have been officially the best player in Europe or the world, but he was in great demand. Roman Abramovich tried to make the Christmas wishes of a lot of Chelsea fans come true when he hand-delivered an offer for Henry, believed to have been £40 million. David Dein, the Arsenal Vice-Chairman, was not to be swayed by the money though. 'Henry is not for sale at any price – not to Real Madrid, not to Chelsea, not to any club,' Dein said. 'Money is only good if you can buy another player as good as Thierry, but there is no one in the world like him.'

The problem with great players is that all the big clubs want them and it is important to let them know where you stand should other teams come knocking. 'We know that Real Madrid are interested in our player and we know that

Chelsea also want him because last week Roman Abramovich himself came to Highbury to present a formal offer for him,' Dein continued. 'But we said the same thing we will say to Real Madrid if they present an offer, or to any other club for that matter, and that is that Henry is not for sale. He is the best. Henry is irreplaceable in every sense. If we sold him, we would weaken our team, strengthen the opposition and demoralise our manager, coaching staff and the rest of the team.'

The Gunners' leading scorer was not interested in moving to Chelsea or Madrid. 'I have heard the rumours linking me with Real Madrid but I take no notice,' Henry told the *News of the World*. 'I prefer building something with Arsenal. Winning the Champions League for the first time with the Gunners would mean making history. It's impossible that I could ever wear a Manchester United, Liverpool or Chelsea shirt, or anyone else's. And that's not just talk. I can't see myself coming back to Highbury with any other team because Arsenal is my paradise.'

Back in the Garden of Eden that most people call Highbury, Henry was again in scintillating form as he inspired Arsenal to a 3–0 win over Wolverhampton Wanderers with two goals; he also had a hand in the other. In the last game of 2003 away to Southampton, Henry continued to create for others as he played Pires in with a precision pass for the only goal of the game.

To celebrate his outstanding 12 months for Arsenal and France, Henry received more plaudits in his homeland at the end of December. First he won France's Sports Personality of the Year in a poll organised by *Ouest-France*, the country's

Henry with his girlfriend, now wife, the model Nicole Merry.

Henry doesn't always smile when he's playing, such is his concentration and focus, but goals often bring out a Gallic smile.

Top: Arsenal legend Ian Wright presents Henry and Dennis Bergkamp with trophies to celebrate them both scoring 100 goals for Arsenal. Henry would go on to become Arsenal's all-time leading goal-scorer, breaking Wright's 185-goal record.

Bottom: Henry scored two, and made two as Arsenal thrashed Inter Milan 5-1 at the San Siro.

Henry shows his appreciation to the Portsmouth fans, who were cheering his name throughout Arsenal's 1-1 draw at Fratton Park.

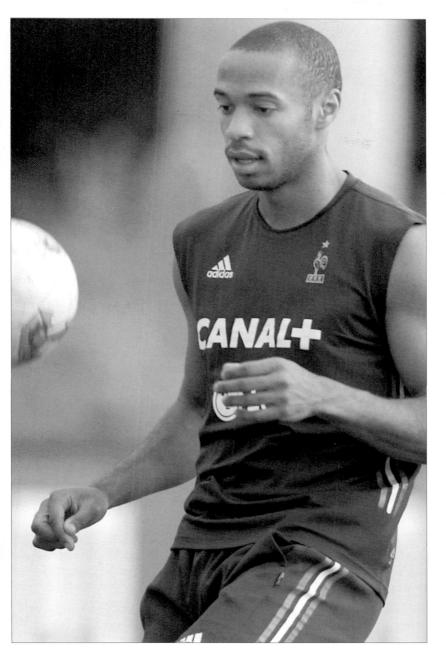

Training at Clairefontaine ahead of the 2003 Confederations Cup.

Top left: Henry won the PFA Player of the Year, and FWA Footballer of the Year in 2003, 2004 and 2006. Here he stands with the 2004 PFA trophy.

Top right: For FIFA's centennial, Pele chose the most outstanding 100 living players in World football. Here he presents Henry with his award.

Bottom: More disappointment came for *les Bleus* when they were beaten 1-0 by Greece in the quarter-finals of Euro 2004.

Top: Henry with his grandfather, enjoying a holiday at the family home on La Desirade, a small island off the coast of Guadeloupe.

Bottom: 'Don't leave us Thierry!' Arsenal fans beg their captain to stay prior to the Champions League Final in Paris.

Top: Henry goes agonisingly close to opening the scoring
against Barcelona…

Bottom: … But it is to end in disappointment for the Arsenal captain and
his manager Arsène Wenger. It wasn't all doom and gloom however, as
soon afterwards Henry agreed to stay and signed a new contract with the
Gunners. Premiership defences can look forward to locking horns with
him for years to come!

biggest newspaper. Then he was named French Footballer of the Year for the second time in his career, the first being in 2000, by *France Football* magazine.

Henry had beaten the FIFA World Player of the Year Zidane into second place and he was very happy with his trophy. 'It is nice to be ahead of Zizou,' Henry said. 'I have gained a lot of maturity and also brushed up my game tremendously this year. You cannot rely on talent alone any more unless you are a guy like Diego Maradona; in my opinion, it is mental strength and hard work that really make you progress.'

To open his account for 2004, Henry made a rare appearance in the Third Round of the FA Cup as the Gunners got their trophy defence off to a tough start with a trip to Leeds. With Henry at the helm, Arsenal clocked up a third successive 4–1 victory at Elland Road, even gifting their hosts a 1–0 lead after a Jens Lehmann error. Henry was determined to take his form into the New Year and did so magnificently, scoring the equaliser and creating the next two as the Gunners kept their impressive FA Cup run going.

And Henry was keen to keep it going for as long as possible. 'People say that players that come from a another country are not worried by the FA Cup,' said the foremost French Footballer of 2003. 'But we have shown we are interested in it because we have played three finals in a row – winning twice and losing one. So at Arsenal we will be trying to do something in the competition again this year.'

Back in the league, Arsenal dropped a couple more points away to Everton before Henry had another of those days where everything he touches turns to goals. Playing Middlesbrough at Highbury, Henry opened the scoring from the penalty-spot before hammering a free-kick into the visitors' area, where Franck Queudrue kindly applied the finishing touch, shinning it into the back of his own net. Pires and Ljungberg added further goals for the Gunners and a late Boro penalty saw the game finish 4–1.

Many strikers would have asked for an own goal like Queudrue's to be added on to their tally, but not Henry. 'How can you claim that?' the Frenchman said in disbelief. 'Nine out of ten times they would have cleared that so I thought they were a little unlucky.'

The Gunners dominated the game from start to finish and certainly deserved some luck. 'We know when teams come to Highbury they like to stay at the back and counter-attack,' Henry told *Arsenal.com*. 'If we don't score early, it can be tricky. We did score in the end, and after that we know we have players to capitalise on the situation. At the start, their back four were playing well and their midfield were staying just in front of them. It was difficult even though we were creating some chances. Then we got the penalty and, after that, it became a little more easy.'

Arsenal's victory put them on top of the table on alphabetical order with an identical league record to Manchester United and it was good to pick up all three points after letting some leads slip in the league recently. 'We did that against Leicester, Bolton and Everton,' Henry admitted. 'Even though we did not play that well, when you concede a goal in the last few minutes you feel a little frustrated. But sometimes we did not do enough to keep the result. You get what you deserve, that is why we were trying to play our best against Middlesbrough.

'We know it is never an easy game against them. I remember a couple of years ago they won 3–0. But, in the last couple of years, we have won without it being a pretty game. The own goal of Queudrue was unlucky for them but after that we scored some good ones.'

Henry's next goal for Arsenal certainly wasn't pretty but none of his team-mates were complaining. Away at Villa Park, Arsenal picked up the points with two Henry dead-balls; the first left the Villains feeling robbed.

The Gunners were awarded a free-kick just outside the home side's area and, with Thomas Sorensen standing next to his right-hand post still lining up his wall, Henry asked referee Mark Halsey if he was allowed to take the kick. The ref said yes, blew his whistle and the Frenchman struck the ball over the wall and into the net. The points were made safe with a penalty from Henry eight minutes into the second half and the Gunners' lead at the top of the table was fully merited.

Following the Aston Villa match, Wenger treated Henry to a two-week break in a bid to keep him sharp for the second half of the season. With Arsenal playing two cup games against Middlesbrough, the manager decided it was the perfect opportunity to give his star some 'R and R'. Arsenal's mixture of youths and reserves lost the first leg of their Carling Cup semi-final, but a much more familiar-looking side beat the Teessiders 4–1 in the FA Cup, even if Ljungberg had to partner Bergkamp up front in the absence of more recognised strikers.

After his mid-season rest, Henry was joined at Highbury by a new arrival. Days after telling the press that he wouldn't be conducting any business in the transfer window, Wenger signed promising young Spaniard Jose Antonio Reyes from Seville. Wenger decided to splash the cash on the versatile forward saying that, with six months to adjust to the English game, Reyes would be able to impose himself on the Premiership from the start of the 2004–05 season.

With Wenger's Arsenal playing such a fast game, it was hoped that the pacey winger-cum-striker would be able to integrate himself into an electrifying strike force that already included Henry, Pires, Ljungberg, Bergkamp and Wiltord, who admittedly was somewhat less effective after his early-season injury.

After a pre-game presentation to the retiring David Seaman, Manchester City were caught out by the speed of Arsenal's attacks and they fell behind to a Michael Tarnat own goal as the German international stretched in an attempt to stop a cross from Henry reaching Ljungberg. The Gunners' second was less about pace and more about skill and power as Henry hit a rising shot from the corner of the box that seemed to accelerate as it passed David James in the visitors' goal.

Reyes received an introduction to English football in the last 20 minutes and Henry was impressed by his new team-mate. 'I just think that he looked good,' Henry said. 'He was lively and wanted to play football. He looked like he was going to fit into our team. We want guys who can play football.'

City got a late consolation as Anelka enjoyed another

goal-scoring return to Highbury and, after the game, it turned out the City manager was another of Henry's admirers. 'He has confidence, he can score goals, he works hard and is equally happy out wide or in the middle – he's perfect,' Kevin Keegan said. 'The really frightening thing about Henry is that he is still young and learning his trade, so there is much more to come.'

The goal against Keegan's men was Henry's seventh in his last seven Arsenal games and he made it eight from eight in his next match against Wolves at Molineux. The Gunners won 3–1 and Henry's strike took him to 99 Premiership goals. Any thoughts that proximity to another goal-scoring milestone would be an albatross around the striker's neck quickly disappeared in the next game as Henry brought up his Premiership century against Southampton.

Henry was the 7th man to notch up 100 goals in the Premiership and, by completing his ton in his 160th game, he became the 2nd-fastest striker to reach such a total, admittedly well behind Alan Shearer who took 124 matches to achieve the feat. It also made Henry a more prolific Premiership striker than Arsenal's leading scorer Ian Wright who took 173 games to become a centurion.

With a one-goal lead, the game was far from over and Henry quickly got himself on the way to his second century with another goal in the last minute – by coincidence, he had also scored his first Premier League goal against Southampton.

Gordon Strachan was yet another opposing manager to be left in awe at the gifted striker. 'Arsene Wenger was talking about comparisons with Johan Cruyff,' the fiery Scot said.

'A player who only comes round every ten years – and Thierry Henry is definitely one of those.'

Himself a hugely talented individual, skipper Vieira was impressed by Henry's contribution to the team. 'At the moment he is the best in the world. He creates chances and he scores goals,' he said. 'He is not selfish at all in front of the goal; you see that in the number of assists he gives. He is a perfect example of how you have to work if you want to be successful. I have seen him from the start and he learned from the players we have had around here – Wrighty, Dennis Bergkamp. They are fantastic players to learn from. He is intelligent and his play is really clever.'

Along with making a little bit of history for the club that he loves, Henry was just happy to have secured another three points but rumours of him moving to Real Madrid or Chelsea wouldn't go away. 'I am the happiest man in the world here. I'm bored with it all,' Henry said of all the transfer talk. 'I'm happy here and it's about time that people put it in their brain. Why would I swap that? That's what I'm trying to explain to people.

'This is what I've always dreamed about. What else can you want than that? I'm playing for people that love me and doing well and the team is doing well. The fans sing my name all the time. When I was young that was all I wanted in life,' he continued. 'All I wanted was to be recognised as a footballer. As soon as the referee blows the whistle, I'm the happiest man in the world. I'm not happy when I'm outside the pitch. I'm happy on the pitch here playing for a good team.'

To have clocked up a hundred Premiership goals meant a lot to Henry. 'To do it with the same team is really special.

I have shown my loyalty to Arsenal. I always mention it and showing it on the pitch is something really important. You can always talk and talk, but you can see that I'm happy here and I'm doing everything all the time I can to make my team win.'

The next two games for Arsenal and Henry were both against Chelsea as the league's fixture computer and the Cup draw conspired to give the Gunners another chance to get intimately acquainted with an opponent – following their four games in a month against Boro. Arsenal proved to be FA Cup conquerors of Chelsea for the fourth successive season as they beat the Blues 2–1 at Highbury without even putting Henry on as a substitute.

Henry was back in the side for the league game at Stamford Bridge as Arsenal won by the same score-line, despite getting off to a terrible start and conceding after only 27 seconds. It was the Gunners' 26th League game of the season and they were yet to taste defeat as they sought to wrestle the title back from Manchester United. By beating Chelsea, Arsenal opened up a 7-point gap over Fergie's side with 12 games to go.

Having strengthened their domestic position with two wins over their London rivals, Arsenal travelled to Spain for the first leg of their knock-out stage game against Celta Vigo. Henry had the chance to reacquaint himself with his old team-mate Silvinho who was now playing in south-eastern Spain.

The former Arsenal left-back wasn't the only Brazilian playing for Celta and, in a nightmare for commentators, the Spaniards also had a midfielder by the name of Edu. This wouldn't normally have been too much of a problem but Arsenal's Edu was in a rich vein of form and managed to put the Londoners ahead twice. The first of his goals was equalised by his namesake in the other team, but in the end the Gunners claimed their first-ever win in Spain 3–2 – and with three away goals they were in a strong position for the second leg.

Back in north London, one of Henry's team-mates decided to get in on the act of reaching goal-scoring landmarks as Pires notched up his 50th Arsenal goal after 2 minutes of the match against Charlton at Highbury. Henry got the Gunners' second barely a hundred seconds later with his 20th league goal of the season – Arsenal were 2–0 up with only four minutes gone. With nine straight wins going into the game, Wenger's side may have thought the game was won, but Charlton fought back to 2–1 and came close to scoring another couple of times in the last five minutes. In the end, however, Arsenal held on for the win.

Things were a lot easier for the Gunners in the next game as they travelled to Fratton Park for an FA Cup quarter-final against Portsmouth. Harry Redknapp decided to take the game to Arsenal by selecting an attacking line-up, but the extra space at the back was well exploited by Arsenal and Henry in particular as he carved through the home defence almost at will, scoring two in a 5–1 victory.

The verve and skill which Henry displayed against Pompey earned him a standing ovation from the whole stadium when he was substituted with 20 minutes to go and it was not the first time the Gunners received applause away from home, showing just how well Wenger's side were playing their football.

Arsenal continued to play good football in their next game as they beat Celta Vigo 2–0 to go through to the Champions League quarter-finals. Henry scored both goals as he broke his two-year Highbury European goal drought – he had not scored in a home tie in the Champions League since the 4–1 demolition of Bayer Leverkusen in February 2002.

The Gunners were flying high now and not even a game against Blackburn and the ever-impressive Friedel could slow them down. Henry even had a goal disallowed for a foul on the American keeper as he stole the ball from under his nose just as the custodian was about to kick it upfield. The decision didn't affect Henry or Arsenal as they went on to win 2–0 in the wake of Henry's blistering free-kick and Pires' late opportunist strike.

Blackburn's Graeme Souness was another manager barely able to stop himself from praising our man. 'Henry is as quick as anyone playing today – and maybe anyone that has ever played. He also has a great technique and is a big strong lad,' the former Liverpool legend said. 'People would be surprised how big he is if they stood next to him. How do you stop him? No one has worked that out yet. Maybe you need a cannon to stop him.'

Perhaps because no one resorted to such violence, Henry was irrepressible and he helped the Gunners set another record in their next match as they became the first top-flight English side to remain unbeaten after 29 league games of a new season. The feat was achieved with a 2–1 home win over Bolton and victory helped Arsenal to open up a nine-point gap over Chelsea at the top of the table.

The Gunners were well placed as they went into a spell of six games in the space of 18 days that would define their season. In that time, Henry also had a game for France against Holland, which made for an energy-sapping one game in every two and half days. Tiring enough before you even think about travel!

The game-athon started with Arsenal's Champions League quarter-final first leg away to Chelsea. Given their repeated pairings in the FA Cup, there seemed to be a certain inevitability about the two sides being drawn together in the last eight of Europe's premier club competition, and so it proved.

The Gunners conceded the opener to their west London rivals for the 3rd time in the season, but the Blues failed to beat Arsenal at the 17th attempt. Pires responded quickly with a header from a Cole cross and the game finished 1–1. Arsenal's next game was in the league against Manchester United.

The press furore had just about died down from the Old Trafford match five months previously, but given a chance to bring it all out into the open once again the media built the rematch up as some kind of second skirmish in a fabled military campaign. Fortunately for any fan of football, there was no more ugliness in the Highbury game as Arsenal, sitting comfortably above their great rivals in the league, dominated the game from the start.

Henry scored Arsenal's goal, taking a Reyes pass and striking a ferocious swerving shot past Roy Carroll from 25 yards. Yet another landmark fell with the Frenchman's wonderful strike as he became Arsenal's joint leading Premiership scorer, sharing 104 goals in the English top flight with the legendary Ian Wright.

Louis Saha equalised for the visitors late on as Wenger and his men started looking forward to the other big games they had coming up. With the fixtures list again throwing an international friendly date in at the most inopportune moment, Henry played for France as they drew 0–0 in Holland.

Arsenal's next match was against Manchester United again, this time in the FA Cup semi-final at Villa Park. Away from their preferred semi-final location of Old Trafford and, with Henry named on the bench for the only time in the season, the Gunners lost 1–0. Arsenal had all the best chances but even with Henry's appearance as a second-half substitute they failed to hit the target and Manchester United scored with their only attack of the game.

Defeat stopped Arsenal from enjoying a fourth consecutive Cup Final and highlighted how the fortunes of the two sides had shifted since the previous year as Ferguson's team fought tooth and nail for their one remaining chance to lift silverware that season, while the Gunners rested their best player with an eye on the return game against Chelsea in Europe.

Arsenal had been unbeaten against Chelsea in their last 17 meetings and everyone was expecting it to become 18, which would see the Gunners through to the semi-finals. If football always did what was expected you would lose half the enjoyment, but it was tough for any Gooners to take pleasure from this game. In the first half, they dominated playing towards the Clock End and Reyes slotted home a knock-down from Henry in the 45th minute. Then they let a 1–0 half-time lead slip to a 2–1 deficit at full-time.

Chelsea played well, but after their winner arrived in the last minute, many critics thought that Arsenal's exhilarating play in the first half had left them a little jaded, especially during such a frantic spell of games. So for the second year in a row, Wenger's hopes of a Treble had been reduced to hope of a solitary trophy. And with a tough home game against Liverpool coming three days after the Champions League disappointment, there was a chance their week could get a lot, lot worse.

Highbury was still in shock when Sami Hyypia opened the scoring after five minutes, but Henry levelled things up after half an hour as he seized on to a Pires ball that had been hit over the top and nutmegged Jerzy Dudek.

Then Michael Owen hit back just before the break and there was concern among Arsenal fans that their players wouldn't be able to lift themselves in the second half – not after their cup exertions against Manchester United and Chelsea – but they could not have been more wrong.

'That was amazing. Anyone who loves Arsenal, watching that game at the stadium or wherever they were, even people who didn't like Arsenal at the time. [We were] 2–1 down at half-time. I bet a lot of people were thinking, "Oh, they've gone. Everything is gone,"' Henry told *Arsenal* magazine. 'In the dressing room at half-time, and you can ask Patrick about this, I was laughing. I don't know why, maybe it was nervousness, I don't know. But at one point I just looked at Patrick and starting laughing, and he was laughing back at me.

'As I always say, when I'm on the pitch I concentrate and try my best, but in the dressing room that day for some reason Patrick and me were laughing. But when we came back out for the second half, you could see that we were not laughing any more.'

Within five minutes of the break, Arsenal were ahead as first Pires and then Henry struck to maintain the Gunners' tilt for the title. 'The goal I scored to make it 3–2 was my favourite of the season. Not particularly for the way I scored it, but just the circumstances surrounding it.'

The goal was another memorable strike by the talented trophy-winner as he received the ball 50 yards from goal, ran around Didi Hamann, dropped his shoulder on the edge of the Liverpool box to such effect that Jamie Carragher fell over, ran through the space now vacated by the versatile England defender and curled his shot past Dudek. It was barely a minute after the equaliser and Highbury started to believe again. Henry even completed a hat-trick 12 minutes from time to put the cherry on top of the cake – sweet victory!

Such a rollercoaster ride of a week had to level out at some point and, away to Newcastle, it did just that as the Gunners fired blanks in a 0–0 draw. Even a stalemate couldn't take the fun out of playing football for Henry – he took a great deal of pleasure from running out with all his mates in the Arsenal team. 'Sometimes it reminds me of when I was playing for a non-league team because we all get on so well,' he said. 'It's like when you are kids, you have so much enthusiasm.'

The Frenchman's passion was there for all to see the following week as he scored back-to-back Friday Highbury hat-tricks against Leeds. The Yorkshire side's defence had no answers to the pace and running of Henry and he went one better than against Liverpool, grabbing four goals for the first time as a professional. In a momentous season, Henry racked up another notable achievement as he recorded his 150th Arsenal goal with his final strike against Leeds.

By surpassing John Radford's total of 149 in the famous red and white, Henry became Arsenal's 3rd-highest goal-scorer behind Cliff Bastin and Ian Wright. Wenger was impressed by the scoring rate of his prodigy. 'Everyone wants to break records,' Wenger said. 'Ian Wright was more obsessed with goals than Thierry but he is already very close and that is amazing considering the amount of time he has been at the club. He only joined us in 1999.'

The Arsenal manager was another man struggling to put Henry's brilliance into speech. 'Thierry is the best in the world. We are running out of words to describe him – and I prefer to watch him rather than talk about him,' Wenger added. 'His finishing was clinical and he will only get better. Thierry is coming in to his best years now and he is so clinical. But he is helped by playing with quality around him.'

The excellence of Arsenal's play had put them in a position where they could wrap the title up at the ground of their oldest adversaries. The Gunners had just finished warming up at White Hart Lane when they received the news that Newcastle had beaten Chelsea and that therefore a draw against Tottenham would secure the Premiership. Buoyed by the news, Arsenal came out firing on all cylinders and went one up after just three minutes as an opposition corner resulted in an Arsenal goal for the umpteenth time.

Henry ran the ball into the home side's half before playing Bergkamp in on the left flank. Seeing Vieira's run into the box, the Dutchman's cross was perfect and the skipper stuck out one of his telescopic legs to guide the ball home. Wary of crowd trouble, the Gunners downplayed their celebrations at that strike as well as their second goal. They were easily in control of the game.

With a 2–0 half-time lead and with riot police in attendance in case the Tottenham fans didn't take too kindly to the Gunners winning the league at White Hart Lane for the second time, Arsenal eased off a little in the second 45 minutes.

The Lilywhites pulled themselves level through a long-range effort from Jamie Redknapp and a controversial late penalty. When the equaliser went in, the Tottenham fans and players went so crazy with their celebrations that one of their players had to be substituted.

Only seconds from the final whistle, the home side's revelry caused any thoughts the Arsenal players had of not celebrating winning the League to go flying out of the window. When the whistle blew, the whole squad ran as one over to the visiting support to share the moment with their fans. Having wrapped up league titles at Old Trafford and White Hart Lane in the space of 24 months, Gunners fans were in heaven and the Arsenal players were just as happy. Later that day, things got even better for Henry as, hours after claiming the Premiership title at Tottenham, he was named PFA Player of the Year for the second successive season.

Henry was picked out by his fellow Professional Footballers as the best in the league and he was joined in the PFA Premiership Team of the Year by five of his Arsenal team-mates – Vieira, Pires, Campbell, Lauren and Cole – showing how Wenger's team had wowed pundits, fans and players alike with their incredible football. Henry was only the third player to win it twice and the first to claim back-to-back PFA awards.

Henry insisted he would be nothing without his team-mates. 'I am quite lucky to play in a special team. The strikers grab the headlines but I have special players around me,' the award-winner said. 'We play as a team and we are willing to fight for each other, and you need that ability. It's like we are a family, willing to do things together and fight for it.'

Arsenal had won the league without tasting defeat and, with four games to go, they could concentrate on attempting to become the first team to complete a whole campaign in the English top flight unbeaten since Preston North End did it in the inaugural season of the football league. With the pressure of the title race lifted off their shoulders, the Gunners paradoxically lacked inspiration in their next two games as they tried to preserve their incredible run.

A stalemate against Birmingham at Highbury was followed by a 1–1 draw at Fratton Park as the Pompey faithful took Henry to their hearts once more. Portsmouth opened the scoring, but their fans seemed more interested in the Gallic flair of Henry and started chanting his name in appreciation of his skills. And they followed that up with many others, including the rather optimistic,

'We're gonna sign Henry…

We're gonna sign Henry…'

To show the home fans how grateful he was for their support Henry donned the Pompey shirt that he had swapped with Lomano Lua Lua and applauded the crowd as he walked around the pitch at the final whistle.

'That was just amazing,' Henry later told *Arsenal* magazine. 'They were singing my name and saying I was a Pompey fan. It was almost too much. It was like I was playing at Highbury. Nothing will ever be comparable. Playing away yet everybody is singing your name – amazing. That's why I wore the shirt at the end to thank them. I doubt that I will ever play for Portsmouth so it was a thank-you to them to wear their shirt even if it was just for a moment.'

Henry was back in the red and white of Arsenal for the game against Fulham as the Gunners got back to winning ways with a 1–0 win at Loftus Road, and afterwards he received news of another historic accomplishment as he picked up the Football Writers' Association Footballer of the Year award for the second time.

It was another first as Henry became the seventh man to win the award twice and he joined an impressive cast consisting of Sir Stanley Matthews, Sir Tom Finney, Danny Blanchflower, Kenny Dalglish, John Barnes and Gary Lineker, but none of them had won it in successive years.

The astounding double-double award-winner was

delighted. 'I always said that I wanted to make history, winning it twice in a row is unique,' Henry said. 'It is very special, and compared to last season to have the award and to win the league is extra special, and the way we won the league as well.'

Henry's amazing form was recognised in the fact he won nearly 90 per cent of the votes and he was clearly enjoying himself more than ever. 'Things are happening for me at the moment, I don't want it to stop. I think sometimes it is good when you don't actually realise what is happening, and you just try to go with the flow. I'm more than pleased with the award as well, because it's something unique. The only thing I can add is *"merci beaucoup"* as they say.'

While the grateful Henry was mainly aiming to complete the season unbeaten in the final game against Leicester, he was also looking to become the first Gunners striker to score 30 league goals in a season since Ronnie Rooke bagged 33 goals in the 1947–48 campaign. The Foxes took the lead before Henry completed the big 'three-o' from the penalty-spot after Frank Sinclair had brought down Ashley Cole. In a fitting end to the season, Patrick Vieira scored the last goal of the Gunners' campaign to claim three points. Then he went up to lift the trophy.

So Arsenal finished the season as undefeated Premiership Champions with the most prolific attack and the meanest defence. Henry himself scored 30 league goals, 39 in all competitions, and he was named PFA, and FWA Footballer of the Year, while also finishing second in the World and European awards.

Truly it had been a remarkable season as Henry

acknowledged. 'After the game myself and Sol were in the centre-circle during the lap of honour and we were saying to each other, "Let's enjoy this,"' Henry said. 'You never know when it's going to happen again – it might be next year, it might be in five years. We had a busy summer coming up, so we just wanted five minutes to enjoy ourselves.'

And after his season, there was no doubt that Henry deserved it.

Chapter eleven
Va-Va Vroom for Improvement

'Thierry is amazing. A dream you want as a player,' said Arsène Wenger. 'He says, "Give me the ball and I can pass you because I have the acceleration to do that." It must be an amazing feeling to be able to do that. Such power. He is intelligent and understands everything. Sometimes you say that God has not given you everything, but with Thierry he has been given a lot. It is not only talent, it is motivation and intelligence.'

It is that self-motivation which drives Thierry Henry on to improve himself as a player at every opportunity and the Arsenal manager believes that his star pupil's best years are ahead of him and that he can still improve. It is a chilling thought.

The will to better himself, instilled in him by his father at an early age, is still there, and Henry says that he 'eats, sleeps and breathes football.' With his skills and his dedication, it seems that the stars are the limit for this incredible man and footballer. So why did it all go wrong at Euro 2004 in Portugal?

Before heading to the Iberian peninsula for the defence of France's European trophy, Henry and his team-mates held Brazil to a 0-0 draw and beat an obdurate Ukraine side 1–0, with Zinedine Zidane scoring the winner from Henry's knock-down in the last minute. Admittedly they were not exactly results that would have sent shock waves through the footballing world, but *les Bleus* seemed to be in good health, which was more than could be said for their abysmal performance in the 2002 World Cup.

Henry was asked if the failure in the Far East provided an extra motivation for the European Championship. 'Even if we had had an amazing World Cup people would still expect us to do something great,' the Arsenal striker said. 'You win or you lose. If you play for England, or France, or Germany, or Spain, or Portugal, or Italy – I can name all the squads in the world – they expect you to do well. For us, though, it is extra, as we had a poor World Cup – we didn't even score a goal. So even if we score a goal, at least then we will have done better! It won't be that difficult [to do better] but I hope...'

Henry was central to French hopes, but they were by no means a one-man team. France travelled to Portugal with the best player in the world, Real Madrid's Zinedine Zidane, and the world's best defensive midfielder, Patrick Vieira. Throw in Pires, Trezéguet, Bixente Lizarazu, Claude Makelele, Lilian Thuram and Fabien Barthez, and you're looking at a pretty decent side.

With such household names, and with plenty more quality

players besides, the questions as the tournament began were: who would *les Bleus* face in the final? Italy or England, Portugal or the Czech Republic? How many goals would Henry score? How would England be able to stop the Premiership's best player in their opening game?

France were in Group B, with Switzerland, Croatia, and England, and the first game in their bid to retain their title as 'the best team in Europe' was against Sven-Goran Eriksson's Lions. The build-up to the game was filled with interviews involving the various players who would be facing club-mates in the cross-Channel clash. Henry against Sol Campbell and Ashley Cole was at the forefront as the temporarily dispersed unbeaten champions were thrust back together on opposing teams.

Henry, though, was not taking anything for granted. 'I respect England. I know more than anyone that they're capable of winning this European Championship,' said the world's number one striker. 'One thing I like about the England team is that they play with their hearts. Sometimes they're going to lose, but they play with their hearts.'

The admiration was mutual. One of England's Lionhearts, Liverpool's Michael Owen, was quoted before the game as saying that Henry had 'taken striking on to a different level'.

Henry insisted he was just playing the game the only way he knew how. 'I admire what Michael Owen can do because I can't do it myself,' he said. 'I can't stay in the box or stay around waiting for someone to deliver. I just can't. I would die. I can't, I can't. I have to move. Even if I have to drop deep and get the ball off our goalkeeper I will do it, because I need to touch the ball.

'I need to move, run and be involved in everything. That's me. If people think that's another level, that's fine. I don't see it that way,' Henry continued. 'But I admire the likes of Michael Owen, David Trezéguet, Pippo Inzaghi and Pauleta. It doesn't matter to them if they don't touch the ball a lot. I would go even further than that. If I score, but I don't play well, then I'm not happy. OK, I enjoy scoring, but if I don't have any pleasure in the game, I won't be proud.'

Henry didn't score against England; in fact he had a bit of a quiet game, but he still managed to win the penalty that got France the three points in the second minute of injury time. But with the doubters ready to put the boot in on France and Henry after they trailed coming into the final minutes of the game – they only won through a Barthez penalty save and the brilliance of Zidane – the French manager, Jacques Santini, came out in defence of his star striker. 'Does he need to score in every match or dribble past everyone from the halfway line? He was decisive against England,' Santini said. 'The fact that he was alert enough to intercept a pass and win a penalty in the last minute of a match shows this.'

Henry was more lively in the next match, against Croatia, but still failed to find the target, as *les Bleus* surrendered a 1–0 and had to come back from 2–1 down to claim a point. With no goals in the first two games, the whole of France was wondering what had happened to the double award-winning striker and scourge of English defences. 'I'm exactly the same person and athlete I was when I finished the Premiership season,' Henry explained to the *Independent on Sunday*. 'I honestly don't feel any different. I am fresh physically and I am relaxed mentally. The only thing that has changed is the opposition I am facing.

'The defenders know exactly what they are doing here in Portugal,' he continued. 'As soon as matches kick off, you can see they are going to make sure there is no room to operate in, whatever it takes. It's proving difficult and I'm having to attempt different things to try to break the deadlock. People in England know that I'm not a fox in the box, but against Croatia, for example, I felt I had no choice but to push right up. It's very frustrating, but I have to keep going and remain positive.'

With his optimistic view on life that shouldn't have been a problem, but was all the criticism getting to him? 'No, because I've always said that being a good striker is not all about scoring goals,' Henry said. 'People need to realise that, without Emile Heskey, there is no Michael Owen. Even when I was banging them in last season, I was insisting that there were more important aspects to my game than just finding the back of the net. What people who question me need to look at are my overall performances. Have they noticed that I created the winner for Zizou against Ukraine or won the penalty against England? I am still having an impact.'

But no matter how many times Henry said that he wished to be judged on his all-round play rather than just his goal-scoring, people would still want to see him hitting the back of the net. 'That would be great,' Henry said about his chances of scoring against the Swiss, 'but it's not going to be a case of just turning up. They played well against England for the first thirty minutes and will make life tough for us, too, especially at the back.

'Teams have been careful against us since we won the World Cup in 1998,' Henry continued, 'but I think it's getting worse. Until the game against Ukraine, I can't remember sides setting their stall out to do nothing but defend right from the off. Even England seemed happy to let us have all the territory and possession. There were times when they would just hoof the ball up field and then not even chase it. What can you do in that situation?

'It's true that we need to pick up the pace and maybe play a bit more direct,' Henry admits. 'I think we are being slowed down by the lack of challenges. We all have loads of time on the ball, but there is nowhere really to go.'

With almost every France move coming through Zidane, people began saying *les Bleus* played too slowly to get the best out of Henry and his Arsenal team-mates, Pires and Wiltord. Henry was having none of it. 'You can't start trying to blame the best player in the world for our problems,' he said. 'Unlike at Arsenal, with France we operate with a playmaker. Zizou is our number ten, and that means he dictates the play. You can't suddenly change all that.'

But the French were still determined to qualify from their group and a win against Switzerland would achieve their aims, so there was no reason to lose heart. 'Of course we are upbeat,' Henry concluded. 'In fact, that is the one big positive that we can take out of the first two matches. Two years ago at the World Cup we felt sorry for ourselves when things didn't go our way. But this time we are continuing to work hard and that's why we're managing to get the results, despite the difficulties we're encountering. No one in this group is going to give up.'

No one was expecting the Swiss to roll over against the French and, in Coimbra, the underdogs gave the champions a scare, holding them to a 1–1 scoreline until Henry opened his Euro 2004 account fifteen minutes from time. It was a valuable goal for *les Bleus*, a clinical finish from Louis Saha's flick-on, and it lifted the Arsenal striker's confidence to such an extent that he produced a piece of typical Henry magic eight minutes later, weaving through the Swiss defence to make it 3–1.

Zidane was delighted with his compatriot's return to scoring form. 'You haven't seen the best of us yet. It will make a difference Thierry scoring, not just getting the goals, but the style of football he showed,' the World Player of the Year said. 'With Thierry finishing like that, people will now see the old France.'

Henry was just happy to have avoided the hosts in the next round. 'We have been criticised, sometimes with justification, but the most important thing is to finish first in the group,' Henry said. 'I have respect for Greece, but it's still better to avoid Portugal.'

The way in which *les Bleus* had dug deep to get their results in the opening round, gave Henry the belief that he could be on the way to some more success with his teammates. 'We could well be on our way to another miracle,' he told the *Daily Mirror*. 'Euro 2000 was a miraculous win for us and there is that same feeling of something special in the squad again. We may not have been at our best, but we still topped our group, and there is the feeling among the players that we are getting better with every game.

'Just like at Euro 2000, we haven't played well in the group stage this year, but we have the belief and spirit that could carry us all the way to the final.' Henry said, drawing comparisons with France's last successful campaign. 'In the final four years ago, Italy led until the very end of the ninety minutes, then Sylvain Wiltord equalised and David Trezéguet got the golden-goal winner. It's going the same way this time – we scored those two goals in injury time when England were leading 1–0, and if Trezéguet hadn't equalised against Croatia we would have lost there as well.'

Henry was getting good vibes from his team-mates and was confident about the future. 'I have the feeling history could repeat itself here in Portugal,' he said. 'There's no doubt we're happy to get to the last eight – but we're definitely not satisfied. We need to play better, but the good thing is we know we can and the Greece game is the time to prove it.'

The Arsenal striker was making all the right noises ahead of France's quarter-final against Group A runners-up Greece and, despite his bad press, he was performing well on the pitch, too. Henry may have only scored two goals in the group stages, but he had had seventeen attempts on goal, which was more than any other player. However, in 2004, Greece surprised everybody.

The Greeks had a great start to the tournament in Portugal when they upset the hosts 2-1 in the opening game. But even with that fine result, no one gave them a hope against the European champions. Greece were a well-organised team built on a sturdy defence and a good spirit, and they had the better of the first-half against *les Bleus*. However, when France came out after the break and started playing much better, the Greeks hit them with a goal on the counter-attack – and once they were in front, they became even more resolute at the back and held on for a famous victory.

France were out of the tournament – the defence of another trophy had ended in disappointment – and Henry wasn't happy. 'It's true we didn't play well in the group phase, or in the first half against Greece,' he said. 'But in the second half the team rediscovered its direction. There was some good movement, but it was at that moment we were caught on the counter-attack and they knew how to take advantage of scoring that goal.

'I had a good chance at the end of the match,' Henry added. 'For once I headed the ball well, but it went just past the post. Fortune didn't smile on us and that makes our defeat all the more bitter.'

Greece went on to win the tournament, but that came as little comfort to Henry and his team-mates as they left Portugal for their summer holidays.

Many reasons were put forward for *les Bleus*' fall from grace: a combination of fatigue, differing game plans suiting various key players in the team, an old and creaking defence, and maybe even the fact that it was just the Greeks' year.

Wenger had his own ideas on the French failure, comparing them with the other fallen giants of international football, Germany, who were knocked out at the group stage. 'Germany are poor on personnel, yet France had almost the opposite problem,' the Arsenal manager said. 'They have many great players but, after not losing in qualification, they didn't question what was wrong in the team. The same happened after the group stage, when they were lucky to take seven points. I think that was a trap for the players and the manager. They thought that the good form would come because they were winning. But the France team had no real balance. They found out the truth against Greece.'

With France out of the tournament, Jacques Santini was free to take over in his new role as manager of Tottenham. He was reported to have made claims of a training ground bust-up between Henry and his Arsenal team-mate Robert Pires. Henry was livid at the allegation and even took time out from his holiday with his wife in Mexico to give his version of events.

'How can you imagine that I would have a fight with Robert?' Henry said to the *Evening Standard*. 'It just isn't true. You know what I am tired of? I am so tired of having to say that all this crap is wrong. Robert and myself are good friends and we had an argument that was finished as soon as it had started. No fight. Nothing like that.'

Henry is so passionate about his football he may have raised his voice to his colleague to get his point across, but certainly no blows were exchanged. 'It was the kind of thing that happens in every football team. It was just an exchange of words. Nothing more,' Henry added. 'We were so close to sharing a holiday – that is what good friends we are. But we missed each other by a couple of days. You want to see what a friendship we have? Look at the way we celebrated together after I had scored against Switzerland.'

With Arsenal's French contingent still great friends despite their Euro 2004 exit, Wenger was concerned as to how it would affect his men in the coming campaign. 'My problem in the new season will be that France did not get started at this tournament, so I will have to lift my French players,' Wenger told the *People* newspaper. 'I remember how hard it was when they came back from the last World Cup. They were down and disappointed and it was some weeks before that left them.

'I will talk to them, tell them it is history now and make sure they are focused on looking forward, not back,' the Arsenal manager continued. 'When France won the World Cup in 1998 and the European Championship in 2000, all the players came back on a high.

'Suddenly, we faced a tough game somewhere like Southampton and I was trying to motivate them, but I could tell in their eyes they were thinking they'd played a truly big game just a few weeks earlier.'

The way in which Henry goes about his game, it is hard to believe that he ever needs motivating, but Monsieur Wenger knows best.

Whether Henry was suffering a post-European Championship depression or not, it seemed from his words that he and his mentor would be together in north London for some time to come. 'Arsène believed in me and I cannot forget that,' Henry said in the *Sunday Times*. 'That is why I want to do it at this club and nowhere else. This is why I want to dedicate my whole career to Arsenal. People say, "You could play for Real Madrid." But I don't want to play for Real Madrid. I want to give back to Arsenal what they gave me.'

With Henry still improving, coupled with the amazing spirit in the team, everything was moving in the right direction for the future. 'This season everyone is fighting for each other,' the striker said. 'There is a commitment in the team now and that took a while, and we aren't taking it for granted. This is our moment. If you want to destroy something, it takes half a second, but if you want to build something, it takes time.'

With such impressive building materials as the unbeaten Arsenal squad of 2003–04 and with the new season looming large, there was still plenty of room for improvement. Looking ahead to the 2004–05 campaign, Henry knew what Arsenal's 'Invincibles' had to do to be considered as a great team. 'I will agree with what people say that now we have to do something in Europe,' Henry said. 'Things don't happen just like that; it took time for us to become the main threat to Man United in the league, so now we will try to do it in the Champions League.'

Even after scoring thirty Premiership goals and thirty-eight in all competitions, Henry refused to predict how many he would get in the new season. 'I never set myself any targets, I just go with the flow,' the prolific Frenchman said. 'People maybe find that a bit strange or won't believe me, but that's just the way I am. When I go out there on the pitch I just try to do my best – sometimes it's not enough, sometimes it is. I just want to be available for my team and make sure that I can help them, that's the most important thing for me. Then, afterwards, if people like what I'm doing that's a plus for me. As long as my team-mates and my fans and the people who really care about me are happy, that's the most important thing to me.'

After five fantastic years at Highbury and with more than 150 goals, the fans were more than happy with Henry's contribution... And there was plenty more to come.

Chapter twelve
Cup Consolation

Obviously, missing the FA Cup final is not what I would have wanted. Yes, I could have said to Arsène Wenger to put me on the bench, so that I could possibly get a medal and earn some glory. But that would be unfair on my team-mates. Incredibly selfish, in fact. Maybe I'd come on at Cardiff, but I would have been able to give only 15 percent. What use is that?'

Putting the team first once again, Henry told the *Evening Standard* that he was going to miss the climax to what had been a disappointing season.

'I have had to make some big decisions in my career, but this one was easy,' he went on. 'I just could not play. I am in too much pain. When I start to run, it hurts. If I go out to the shops, I can also feel it. I have played a lot this season and I like to think I've given my all. It is a problem for me, but hopefully I will be fine for the start of next season. I am sure I will be fine.

'After Euro 2004, I had a few weeks' rest, but had only three days' training before my first game, the Community Shield. The problem has been with me since then, even though it has been playable. Now it is not. Every morning I have got out of bed and have had to see whether or not I could train.'

It was a sad end to the season for Arsenal's talismanic striker, but it had started in much more promising circumstances as the 'Invincibles' continued their unbeaten streak into the 2004-05 campaign. Despite their amazing season, Wenger had once again strengthened the squad with Robin van Persie joining from Feyenoord Rotterdam, goalkeeper Manuel Almunia from Celta Vigo and Mathieu Flamini signing from Marseille. As well as recruiting, Wenger had let some old favourites go, as Ray Parlour, Giovanni van Bronckhorst, Martin Keown, Kanu and Sylvain Wiltord all moved on to pastures new.

After another quiet summer in the transfer market, at least on the buying side, with only £3.5m spent, few people thought that Arsenal could hold on to their title. Sure, they may have completed the previous season unbeaten, scoring more goals and conceding fewer than any other team in the league, but with the rise of the Russian superpower – Roman Abramovich's Chelsea – public opinion was divided before the start of the new campaign.

'Yes, English football is tough and it takes something special to defend a championship,' Henry said. 'But we love this challenge. We do not mind it at all if people write off our chances. We just play and show people season after season how determined we really are.' One thing everyone could agree on, though, was how important Henry was to the Arsenal cause.

Henry had scored thirty of the Gunners' seventy-three league goals in the 2003–04 season, and if they wanted that success to continue, they would need to be less reliant on the French striker. With half a season of Premiership football under his belt, it was hoped that Jose Antonio Reyes would be able to lighten the load, but the two attackers appeared ill-suited to playing together upfront, as they both preferred to run the same inside-left channel.

But the young Spaniard quickly dismissed talk rubbishing their fledgling partnership. 'We both like to score and that is what the game is all about,' Reyes told the *News of the World*. 'It is a dream of mine to play alongside Henry and if I am given the chance I will not ruin that dream.

'I have been brought in to score goals and I feel I can do that anywhere in the world. Of course, it is not easy to just enter a country and have a big, big impact. You have to adjust. But I truly feel I can form a partnership with Henry, or whoever I play with at Arsenal. I want to prove to Arsenal fans that I am worthy of becoming someone they respect. I like to think my game is not just about goals, but I can learn so much from playing alongside great players at Arsenal and Henry's example can only get the best out of me.'

With the addition of van Persie, the continued excellence of Dennis Bergkamp upfront, and Ljungberg and Pires contributing from midfield, there were still plenty of goals in the Arsenal team despite the departure of Wiltord and Kanu. And so it proved as Henry made his first appearance in the red and white of Arsenal since the 2–1 win over Leicester that had completed the unbeaten season.

Playing once again at the Millennium Stadium, Wenger's team beat the FA Cup holders 3–1 to win the Community Shield. With goals from Gilberto, Reyes and an own goal from Mikaël Silvestre, it was a fairly comprehensive win against a Manchester United side that had one eye on their Champions League qualifier the following Wednesday. Henry only played the first half, having done just three days' training since France's unceremonious exit from Euro 2004, but the striker was happy with his forty-five-minute workout. 'The most important thing for me was to go through the first half without feeling my Achilles tendon,' he said. 'I felt it at the beginning of the match, but at the end of the first half I was fine. I'll be ready for Everton.'

But the real story in Cardiff was the performance of Cesc Fabregas, as the seventeen-year-old Spaniard announced his first-team arrival with an impressive performance at the heart of the Arsenal midfield. Showing great poise and fine distribution while in possession, it was the way the youngster broke up opposition play that really caught the eye, as he failed to be intimidated by either the occasion or Roy Keane.

It was the perfect time for a midfielder to impress at Arsenal, as the annual uncertainty over Patrick Vieira's future was at an all-time high. A £23m bid had come in from Real Madrid for Henry's long-time friend and team-mate, and the club appeared to be considering it. In previous summers, the manager had done everything in his power to stop the colossal midfield warrior from moving on, but now it seemed as though Wenger was tired of standing in the way of the man he had helped mould into a world-class footballing superstar.

'If Patrick is focused to leave there will be an open door,' Wenger told the press after the game. 'We have been disrupted in our preparations by this talk. We respect what he has done and, until now, he has given eight years to the club. We want him to be focused on the club, not half in and half out. Everyone wants him to stay and he can make a difference.'

Vieira was set a deadline before the first game of the season to make up his mind and, after much to-ing and fro-ing, he decided to stay at Highbury due to the 'strength and potential of this Arsenal team'.

'If we had lost Pat I don't see how we could have carried on with the ambition of winning,' Henry later revealed in the *Sun*. 'We'd have lost one of the best defensive midfielders in the world and what do we do after that? I would have respected his opinion, but I'm happy he listened to me before taking his final decision. I believe we spoke with each other at the right moment and I told him what I thought about it.

'I'd have missed him as much on the playing side as in my feelings and I would surely have asked myself questions. I'd have asked why the club persuades me it is building something but lets one of the cornerstones go, one of the bases that holds up the building.'

It was the perfect fillip for the Gunners heading into the

first game of the season, against Everton away. Playing the kind of football that had thrilled football fans up and down the country and that had taken them unbeaten to the title, Arsenal continued where they had left off in May, as they extended their unbeaten league run to forty-one games, beating Everton 4–1.

But even more impressive than the demolition of the Toffees was the spirit the Gunners showed to win 5–3 in the first home game of the season. Arsenal got off to a good start as Henry opened the scoring, and his account for the season, after twenty-six minutes – racing on to Reyes' long pass and lifting the ball over Mark Schwarzer in the Middlesbrough goal.

Just eight minutes into the second half, however, Arsenal were 3–1 down and staring down the barrel of a first league defeat in more than fifteen months. With Vieira and Campbell both out injured the Gunners were susceptible defensively, but they were in no mood to surrender their incredible run at home to Boro. Bergkamp rifled home from 20 yards within a minute and, another ten minutes later, he combined with Henry to create the equaliser for Pires, fresh off the bench.

While the crowd were still celebrating the comeback, Reyes seized on a loose pass, drove into the box and put Arsenal into the lead. 'We are unbeatable,' sang the fans, and it got even better in the final minute as Henry put the finishing touch to more good work from Pires and Bergkamp.

The comeback showed the mental strength of the players, who were willing to give everything for each other, and it served to remind Vieira, watching from the stands, that he had made the right decision to stay. As Henry said: 'There are so many players who are linked with other teams but, at the end, they all stay here. It's difficult to leave Arsenal. The boss said that not so many players who have left Arsenal did great afterwards. You know what you're losing, but you never know what you're going to find.'

It is true that Manu Petit, Marc Overmars, Silvinho and Nicolas Anelka had all struggled to recreate their Arsenal form at their new clubs, but what is it that makes the club so special? 'It's difficult for me to talk about as I've always made it clear that I'm happy here,' Henry added. 'Our win against Middlesbrough was something amazing that it's difficult to walk away from.'

Asked if he had ever played in quite so dramatic a comeback, the fleet-footed Frenchman admitted: 'Only in my neighbourhood when I was growing up, when you're 8–0 down but still win 10–8! It was unbelievable; it was the first time I'd heard Highbury like that. It was just mad!'

It was a truly amazing comeback thanks to a fine display from the ageing Dutch master, and Henry was quick to praise his strike partner. 'At 3–1 down, we were thinking it was not good,' Henry said. 'But thank God Dennis plays like he is twenty, not thirty-five. He was amazing – what can you say about a guy like that?'

The win took Arsenal's unbeaten run to forty-two matches, equalling the record set by Brian Clough's great Nottingham Forest team from 1977 to 1978, and it was hard to see where or when the run would come to an end. 'Everyone knows that one day it's going to happen, but we're trying to make it last,' Henry said. 'We don't realise what we are doing at the moment. For me it's the beginning of the season, it doesn't mean anything if you break the record and you don't have anything at the end. But at the end of the day, it's something good to have. It is not a matter of losing or not losing – when you are on the pitch, you want to win.'

And they did just that in the next game to claim the record outright. 'It was good to get the record playing the Arsenal way,' Henry told the *Daily Star*. 'We keep on passing the ball along the ground. In the first half we tried, but it wasn't really working. However, in the second half, we didn't get frustrated, we carried on playing along the ground. We got what we deserved.'

Blackburn were the victims at Highbury as Henry scored one and created the other two for Fabregas and Reyes in a 3–0 win. The form of his two young Spanish team-mates impressed Henry and reminded everyone of Wenger's talent-spotting ability. 'You have to give credit to Arsène,' Henry told the assembled media. 'He pulled Kolo out of his magic hat last year and now he has pulled out Cesc – I don't know what to say about him. It's not just the way that he plays, but he looks so mature for his age. He looks like he is controlling the game. He plays like he's been in the team for many years.

'I remember when he bought Jose,' the former Juve man went on. 'Everyone was wondering whether it was too much money but, although it's early to say it, I think everyone can now say it was well worth it.' Reyes was showing great form as he scored in each of Arsenal's opening four games. The Spanish winger made it five from five away to Norwich City, and Henry also scored at Carrow Road, heading home a Ljungberg cross as the Gunners continued their incredible form with a 4–1 win.

Of the four Arsenal goals, Henry scored one and created two more; it was another display indicative of his early season form, as he had scored four and had had six assists in the Gunners' sixteen Premiership goals. 'We always try to set up the guy who is in the best position,' Henry said. 'So many times some people could have been greedy, but we just tried to make sure that we scored the goal.'

With the double PFA Player and FWA Footballer of the Year award-winning striker continuing the form that had seen him receive so much acclaim in England, it was time for Henry to join up with his international colleagues once again. France faced Israel in Paris in their first match since Euro 2004, for the opening game of their World Cup qualifying campaign and, ahead of the game, Henry made a startling revelation about his international career.

'I thought about leaving,' the Arsenal striker told the press. 'But it didn't last very long and I brushed aside the idea. It was my duty towards the young players to be here. There are very gifted ones. It's now up to them to gain experience and to improve themselves. But it comes to us, the old ones, to help them out. It's the way it happened for me when I came here for the first time.'

Following the European Championship, Zinedine Zidane, Marcel Desailly, Bixente Lizarazu and Lilian Thuram had all retired from international football, and *les Bleus* had a new coach in Raymond Domenech following

Jacques Santini's move to Tottenham. There may have been many changes to the France set-up, but the fans were very glad they still had Henry whose experience, with twenty-seven goals from sixty-four appearances, would now be more important than ever. 'There is a new generation coming up and there is a new squad to build up,' Henry continued. 'I want to be part of this story. France need to get back to winning ways and the sooner the better. We badly need a string of wins now.'

With Vieira named as captain by the new coach, Arsenal's French contingent was going to be vital in the new squad. 'There are players within the team who are on top of the pile, who are maybe more important than others,' Henry was quoted in the *Liverpool Echo*. 'The objective for us is to put France back on the winning track. There are a lot of things to re-build, and we, the experienced players, will help the young players alongside the new staff.'

But neither Henry nor any of his team-mates could breach the Israeli defence and the visitors held on bravely for a well-deserved point. Chances were few and far between and the fans booed the team off the pitch at the Stade de France; it wasn't just the supporters who were upset with the 0–0 scoreline. 'No one was happy with the result, far from it,' Henry told the *Agence France-Presse*. 'We should have scored, but we couldn't get the win. Tactically we have to adjust to the 3-5-2 system; not many of us play with this system at club level. It doesn't just come like that. But the problem is we don't have the time – we've already lost two points.'

Les Bleus had continued where they had left off in

Portugal, but the media still jumped on the recently retired greats and their missing influence in the team. 'It's true they're missed, but we have to start again and go forward,' Henry continued. 'One generation has passed – people have to get that into their heads. Now there are players who need to take a step up the ladder to gain promotion. It's not easy – I had to do that. But we can't talk about the retired players each time – if we do that we'd still be saying that we missed [Michel] Platini, too.'

Henry's absent friends were less missed the following Wednesday as France beat the Faroe Islands 2–0 to go joint top of Group Four alongside the Republic of Ireland and Switzerland, with all three teams on four points.

Back in London, Henry helped Arsenal to a fifth straight league victory, with a 3–0 win away at Fulham, and the scary thing was that the Frenchman wasn't even running at 100 percent. 'At the moment, I'm not doing what I can do on the pitch,' he told the *Observer*. 'I can't make the runs. I'm not match fit. I'm just concentrating on my passing and being available for the team.'

Even below his best, Henry was still making a valuable contribution to the team's success and, in the next game, he helped them to a 1–0 Champions League victory over PSV Eindhoven to get their bid for European glory underway. It was a hard-fought game and Henry created the only goal of the game as Rodrigo Alex guided the Arsenal striker's hard, low cross into his own net.

The Dutch side defended from the outset and space was at a premium, limiting the Gunners' fluent attacking style, but it was only the result that mattered to Henry. 'We like to go forward, but you cannot always do that,' he said in the *Evening Standard*. 'We know we can score, but we need the ball to do that. We could have done better last night, but we had to be careful because they were trying to hit us on the break. Sometimes you just have to win this type of game. You can't always win easily and play the game you want to play. We managed to get the 1–0 win and that was important for the team.'

With potentially tricky away trips to Panathinaikos and Rosenborg Trondheim ahead in Group E, it was vital that Wenger's team got three points on the board to head off on their European travels full of confidence.

After their stuttering win over PSV, Arsenal dropped their first league points of the season as Bolton came from behind twice to draw 2–2 at Highbury. Henry scored the opener and Pires restored Arsenal's lead, but the Trotters weren't to be denied their point. The early season élan had been replaced by some more workmanlike performances and the Gunners dug in again to hold on for a hard-fought 1–0 win away to Manchester City. Wenger's side were also below par in Norway, where they dropped two points against Rosenborg, drawing 1–1.

'We were a bit disappointed not to have won, considering the possession we had,' Henry told the *Sun*. 'But a point away is still a good result. We still consider we played well. I can remember not so long ago when we'd play away in the Champions League and not create any chances at all. We scored early and thought it was going to be our night, but Rosenborg came back strongly and you have to give them some credit.'

Although obviously frustrated with the result, it left Arsenal on top of the group with four points from the first two games, which was a great improvement on the previous year. 'We are in a much better position than we were at the same stage of last season,' he added. 'So we cannot be too upset. But we know our next game, away to Panathinaikos, will be very tough. They have amazing fans who get behind their team.'

But it would be another three weeks until the trip to Athens and Henry first had to help his team-mates keep their domestic season on track. With rumours of a post-match scuffle between Lauren and Vieira on the team bus in Norway, the press were trying to undermine the spirit of the Arsenal team, but the players appeared as close as ever as they bounced back from their European setback with a 4–0 win over Charlton at Highbury, illuminated by yet another piece of footballing genius from Arsenal's No. 14.

Three minutes into the second half, with Arsenal 1–0 up, Henry received the ball with his back to goal. On the corner of the six-yard box with Jonathan Fortune in close attendance, the French maestro simply back-heeled the ball with pace and precision into the far corner of the net. 'I just wanted to keep the ball away from Fortune,' Henry said in typically understated fashion. 'In training you try some strange stunts, but I just tried it today and it went in.'

Having set up Ljungberg for the opener, Henry also added Arsenal's third and Reyes got the fourth to take the Gunners five points clear at the top of the table. All the talk after the game, though, was of Henry's wonder goal. 'I have scored a lot of goals for Arsenal and some good ones, but

I'm still not certain how I scored this one,' he told the *People*. 'I will have to watch it a lot of times on television for it to sink in. I can't remember what was going through my mind; I just knew I had to react quickly.

'The defender had stopped me from turning, so I just thought to myself do something quickly. I've tried this sort of thing before in training, sometimes it works sometimes it doesn't, but what's important is that you have the confidence to do it in a game. I am very happy with it, but happier that it helped Arsenal win again. A lot has been said about events off the pitch this week and I just wanted to show people that it's what we do on it that truly counts.'

And with the nominations for FIFA World Player of the Year imminent, his manager was certain about who deserved the gong. 'I believe Thierry is the best player in the world and I've thought that for the past two seasons,' Wenger said. 'His was a superb goal today, not because it was technically difficult, but because of the swiftness of the response to the situation and the way he analysed what was going on. There has been a lot written about our unity this week, but we have shown by what we do on the pitch that there is absolutely nothing wrong with the spirit, it's as strong as ever.'

Wenger was happy to speak about Henry and, in an *Evening Standard* interview, he compared his young prodigy to France's most recent superstar. 'Henry's twenty-seven now and between twenty-seven and thirty-two you make your name,' the Arsenal manager said. 'I've seen Zidane at twenty-seven and I think Henry is in advance of Zidane. At twenty-seven people said Zidane is a good player, a fantastic player, he will be a world-class player and he became one. Thierry is already fantastic and his best years are in front of him. He has all you want. It's always difficult to compare but I feel he is just amazing. He has all the ingredients.'

Ever willing to lay on a pass or an accolade to his more dynamic team-mate, Bergkamp told the *Evening Standard*: 'Thierry Henry? He can get even better, even stronger. It is difficult to find a weakness in his game. If anyone asked me, "What is his bad side?" I couldn't come up with anything.'

It wasn't just the current Arsenal players who were impressed by Henry's skills, as Alan Smith, who scored the Gunners' winning goal in the 1994 European Cup-Winners' Cup final told the *Observer*: 'I saw him play against Liverpool about three seasons ago and he terrorised them. Afterwards, I spoke to a number of pros and they all said they hadn't seen anything like it. On his day, he has become unplayable and more and more since then it has been his day. I have to say I haven't seen a player like him. He's an athlete with great technical ability and a tremendous desire to be the best.'

Henry was on top of his game and all the praise was well deserved, but as the Arsenal team broke up once more for international duty, one man found time to say something much less pleasant about the talented Frenchman. As Reyes joined up with the Spanish squad, his international manager tried to motivate him by allegedly telling him that he was better than that 'black shit' Henry.

The man in question was Luis Aragones, and was reported saying: 'I consider myself a citizen of the world and I have many black friends. I don't think anyone takes these comments seriously because I never intended to insult or disrespect anyone. I think I made a comment to Reyes to motivate him.'

Henry refused to get drawn into an argument, though, and it was not the first time he had been called names because of the colour of his skin. 'I won't let myself down for someone who has not developed themselves or may not want to accept me,' Henry said. 'Even when I was young, growing up at times was hard. Sometimes, when I played in cities where they were not used to seeing black, Arabian or other different races, you do hear things. Sometimes people follow and say things and they don't know what they are saying. They seem to do what others are doing.

'The worst thing is when I see kids saying racist things and they don't even know what they are saying. They don't know what life is all about and you see their father sitting next to them not saying anything. That is when it becomes a danger. When you see a nine-year-old saying something about your colour and the dad and family are just laughing. That is when I think we are in trouble.'

But speaking to promote Kick It Out's Anti-Racism Week, Henry spoke of how football could help bring down racial divides and fondly remembered the way his country's World Cup win had helped bring together a multi-cultural France. 'I love sport. In my opinion there is little or nothing else that can bring such joy,' he went on. 'When I won the World Cup in 1998 with France, I will never forget the pictures of everyone cheering on the Champs Elysées in Paris.

'And it was everyone. White, Caribbean, Arabian. They

were jumping up and down kissing each other. I know it only lasts for five minutes, but it was five really important minutes. This illustrated the power of sport. The key for me is education. If you are hearing every day that Asians and black people are not good, then it is inevitable that youngsters will believe this. My parents educated me in a way that, thankfully, I do not have this prejudice. I am as open-minded as everyone.'

Fortunately, Henry did not have to wait long to get back to football, as *les Bleus* entertained the Republic of Ireland at the Stade de France. But he failed to recreate his club form and France stumbled on to another 0–0 draw, a result that left both teams at the top of the group on five points from three games, along with Israel and Switzerland. 'We are trying to rebuild a team,' Henry said. 'We have played just three games and, if you look at the squads, they were not all the same for each of them. You need to know your team-mates to play well. You can sense that in the Ireland squad.

'Sometimes they play as though they have been together for a long time. We are slowly trying to get there. At the end of the day, although we are going through a process of change, we did not lose the game. I am sure Ireland will think that they can win the group. Why not?

'Everyone can think that. I think Israel may have thought that when they drew in Paris. I don't know what will happen. So many strange things can happen in football. I remember in our first season in the Champions League that people said that we were out because we had taken just one point from three games, but we finished on top of the group. Things happen in football that you can never predict. That is why we all like football. If it was always predictable, it would be boring.'

The Gunners' star struggled to explain why he couldn't carry his Premiership form onto the international stage, but thought that, with all the changes, the new players were just getting used to each other. 'You need to know your team-mates really well to play well and you can sense that we maybe don't at the moment,' he said. 'I am not frustrated that I didn't score because I know I will be back to my best with Arsenal. I say that without joking because that's how I feel.'

Henry and his international colleagues managed to relieve some of the pressure on their shoulders with a 2–0 win in Cyprus, and Henry even managed to get on the scoresheet with a typical finish, running onto a throughball and slotting it past the 'keeper on the angle in the second half. But his international goal drought hadn't caused him any concern. 'My lack of goals has worried you more than me,' Henry said. 'It hasn't prevented me from sleeping. This team is in the process of creating something and we will continue to work towards that end.'

Back in England, Arsenal's prolific striker continued to cause possible sleepless nights for defenders as he led them a merry dance home and away. Facing Aston Villa at Highbury, Henry scored one as the Midlanders were beaten 3–1. After the game, he turned his attentions once again to Europe, and Henry was adamant that the Gunners could transfer their dominant domestic form to their continental excursions. 'We have to be the team people are afraid of when they come to play us in European games and we're not at that stage yet,' Henry said. 'Games are obviously not easy in the Champions League. We didn't play that well in our first game this time, but 1–0 against PSV was enough to give us three points. When they see what we do in the league, people cannot understand why we cannot do it in the Champions League, but we can beat any team in Europe when we play like this.'

But the Gunners couldn't reproduce the destructive form they had displayed in the Villa match against Panathinaikos and the game ended 2–2. Arsenal took the lead first through Ljungberg and later through Henry, but two mistakes from Jens Lehmann meant that the points were shared. To make matter worse, Henry also picked up an injury. 'I twisted my ankle at the end of the first half, but I wanted to carry on,' he said after captaining the side in the absence of Vieira and Bergkamp. 'It's OK now and hopefully it will be that way tomorrow. We are confident about the game at Old Trafford on Sunday. Matches between Arsenal and Man United are always tough, but it's better to go there having not lost here.'

With Vieira and Gilberto definitely out, and Edu and Pires doubtful, it was imperative that Henry recovered for the trip to Manchester. 'I will be fine. I will be there,' he said. 'It is going to be a special game. We will go out there and see what we can take from it. I respect United a lot. All the time people try to write them off, but they are always around at the end. And it is only the tenth game of the season, so it is still very early. I know it is all exciting, but it is early.'

Ferguson's side were floundering eleven points behind

Arsenal and, with a run of forty-nine league matches unbeaten behind them heading North, the game gave the Gunners the chance to extend their incredible record to fifty. 'Everyone is now talking about this game,' Henry said. 'We know that it will be special, but we will just try to go there and take what we can take. If it's a draw, it's a draw.'

That was just the wrong attitude to take into what was a must-win game for the home side, but it was misfortune rather than complacency that brought Arsenal's unbeaten run to an end. The Gunners were on the receiving end of a couple of debatable refereeing decisions at Old Trafford that saw the game swing away from them, and they returned to London with the confidence that their 'invincibility' had brought about replaced by a sense of disappointment and simmering outrage. Freddie Ljungberg looked to have been fouled by Rio Ferdinand midway through the first half and Mike Riley didn't even give a free-kick where some officials might have given a red card.

His error was compounded by the fact that Ferdinand was head and shoulders above his team-mates as their best player on the day, and when Riley awarded his eighth penalty in eight matches to Ferguson's side, in the seventy-third minute, it was clearly not Arsenal's day. Wayne Rooney took a tumble in the Arsenal area, despite no apparent contact from Sol Campbell, and Ruud van Nistelrooy, himself perhaps lucky to be on the pitch after clattering into Ashley Cole at knee height, put away the spot kick with his usual aplomb.

Rooney added a second in injury time and, after the game, it was reported that one Arsenal player highlighted the fury in the side by allegedly throwing food at the opposition manager. Bringing the long unbeaten run to an end, the result proved a turning point in the season – the Gunners won only one of their next five league games.

Henry was in fine form scoring in each of the subsequent four games, but even his goals couldn't stop the rot. After a 2–2 draw with Southampton at Highbury, Henry addressed the press. 'People are saying we're not playing as well as we can,' he said. 'But after going 2–1 down against Southampton, it was all about commitment and desire. We did not play that well against Bolton, Middlesbrough or Manchester City this season, but we still won. It wasn't there a lot of times. It wasn't there against Southampton, but we didn't lose. I don't want to look at any other teams. The important thing was that even though we were trailing with four minutes to go, we did not lose.'

With Arsenal struggling domestically, it was of little surprise that they continued their run of draws in Europe. Henry claimed the Gunners' only goal from the spot as the home game with Panathinaikos ended 1–1, but he contributed little else to the team and the media were quick to criticise the Frenchman. Wenger immediately leapt to his leading man's defence. 'I feel the criticism of Thierry is completely undeserved and amazing,' the Arsenal manager said. 'Don't forget, this guy is top scorer and provider in the league, and top scorer in the Champions League for us. Look at his record. He's won championships in England and France, cups in England, the World Cup and the European Championship with France, but he still has to justify himself.

'Who can you compare him with? Nobody. You cannot compare him with Ruud van Nistelrooy. Thierry is a goal-scorer and a provider, while van Nistelrooy is a goal-getter in the box. Nobody else up front can repeat, week in and week out, the quality of what he is achieving. You cannot do it in every game. Andriy Shevchenko doesn't do it, Ronaldo doesn't do it – nobody does it. You have to accept that a man is not a machine. But Thierry has still done it in big games. He's scored eight goals against Manchester United, a hat-trick away to Roma and two against Inter last season.

'Thierry responds well to criticism, but in this case it's a bit overboard. When you're a striker, you have to accept that you will miss chances, or you would commit suicide. I don't think that it is playing on his mind. He was a world champion at twenty. Do I think he's the best striker in the world? Of course I do.'

Henry scored a sumptuous volley in the next match against Crystal Palace, but the Eagles hit straight back and came close to winning the game at Selhurst Park. In the end it finished 1–1 and although the Gunners were pleased to avoid defeat, Henry knew it wasn't good enough. 'Everyone is expecting us to do better all the time and, while we have not lost our past three games, we know we can do better.'

With the first North London derby of the season looming large, the Gunners *had* to do better, and the majestic Frenchman knew exactly how much the game meant to the fans. 'My first professional game for Monaco was a derby against Nice,' Henry told the *Sun*. 'That match had a special atmosphere, but the north London derby is also an incredibly special match. When I first arrived, everyone said that was *the* game. And they were right. It is really good.

'You can be sure it will be an unpredictable match. But when has an Arsenal v Tottenham game not been unpredictable? Never. Look at the results over the years. They are all tight games, full of last-minute goals. There is never a side totally on top, totally outplaying the other.'

Never was that sentiment truer than in the 5–4 thriller that followed at White Hart Lane. Henry scored Arsenal's equaliser and each of the nine goals was scored by a different player, in a match that showcased some truly woeful defending. 'All that mattered was three points,' Henry said.

But it was the only maximum Arsenal achieved for some time, as Wenger's team struggled with confidence and form. The real problem was in defence, where Sol Campbell was sorely missed after having picked up an injury in the defeat against Manchester United. Without the England centre-back's organisational skills and experience in the back line, sloppy goals were conceded on a regular basis. It was no coincidence when his return brought about a first clean sheet for fourteen games in all competitions and three valuable points in the league.

Arsenal beat Birmingham 3–0 at Highbury with the former Tottenham captain in the side, and Henry scored two more goals, taking his total to sixteen for the season. It wasn't only Campbell that had been missing for the Gunners, as Gilberto was still sidelined by a back injury and Edu was also out with a broken toe; combined with the knock to the team's confidence from actually losing a game, these absences in key positions had brought about Arsenal's worst run of form for some time, as they took just six points from six league games.

'People need to remember we are not machines,' Henry said in the *Sunday Mirror*: 'Every team in the world goes through bad moments. You have to remind people about previous seasons. Even last season we drew a lot of games we perhaps should have won in November. The year before we lost four games in a row, but that didn't stop us having a year unbeaten after that. I'm sure, or let's say I hope, that if we do something good at the end of the season, nobody will remember what went on in November.'

The Gunners' poor form had helped them continue their sequence of draws in Europe and they headed into their match day six showdown with Rosenborg knowing that only a win would be enough to ensure their qualification for the knock-out stages. 'If the team doesn't win against Rosenborg I know I will be criticised no matter how I play,' Henry said at a press conference. 'If we are out of the competition, like it or not, it's going to be my fault and that's the way it is. But trust me, I will still sleep at night. I will never change my place for anything. That's why I wanted to play football. When things are bad you have to accept it, dig in, get your head up and try to come back.'

With Vieira and Lauren both out suspended and Gilberto and Edu still injured, the youngsters stood up to be counted for Arsenal. Justin Hoyte came in at full-back and Fabregas and Flamini dominated in the middle of the park as the Gunners ran out 5–1 winners to top Group E. Henry scored the second and won a penalty as Wenger's men recorded back-to-back wins for the first time since early October. 'Cesc and Mathieu showed that they didn't hide,' Henry said. 'They played their part out there against Rosenborg and tried to help us. Cesc has been showing he is a talent and has quality.

'People have been saying that we don't have as large a squad as some of the teams in the Premiership, but we do have some young players, not just Cesc and Mathieu, but also Justin Hoyte and others. You never know when a dip in form is going to come. We can only try to rectify that on the pitch and that is what we are doing.'

It was vital that the players renewed their confidence ahead of a top-of-the-table clash with Chelsea, who had continued unabated while their London rivals had faltered and now had a five-point lead over Arsenal in the Premiership.

'Usually when we play Chelsea we are in front of them,' Henry said. 'For the first time in years they are going to be in front of us. You have to give them credit. Everyone was giving them stick for defensive football, but now they are in front of us. We have to make sure we can change that. We have to do it the hard way.'

Henry opened the scoring at Highbury with a spectacular strike early on after linking well with Reyes and he restored the lead on the half hour with a quickly taken free-kick following John Terry's equaliser. But without their most experienced midfielders the Gunners couldn't dominate the game as they would have liked and it finished 2–2 thanks to Eidur Gudjohnsen's header early in the second half. Unfortunately for Arsenal, Chelski never looked back –

under the impressive leadership of their new Portuguese manager, Jose Mourinho, the Blues were a different proposition from previous years and they remained at the top of the table for the rest of the season.

Yet, despite taking a point at the home of their closest rivals, Mourinho and his players were livid with Arsenal's second goal; it was a contentious decision that angered the visitors, but Henry claimed that was well within his rights. 'He [the referee Graham Poll] asked me, "Do you want to wait for the whistle and for the players to go back 10 yards?" He said, "You can have a go" and I was just waiting for Eidur Gudjohnsen to move out of the way. I thought it would be enough for us to win, but once again we conceded two goals from set-pieces.'

The Gunners were coming back to form though, and they won four in a row after their derby draw. Henry only scored once in those four wins, but the goal against Fulham took him level with Ian Wright's total of 128 league goals for Arsenal. However, the Frenchman still had some work to do to beat Cliff Bastin's record of 150 league goals for the Gunners.

As 2005 approached there was a lot of talk about Henry, who was a strong candidate for both the World and European Player of the Year awards. But Henry wasn't interested in personal glory. 'The most important thing for me is to win things with the team,' he said. 'You can't play alone on the pitch. Without them I can't express myself.'

His manager was more forthright with his opinion. 'It would be a scandal if Thierry did not win one,' Wenger said. 'If it was down to me I would give him both. For me it's the players around Thierry who have to justify they are as good as he is. If you look at statistics, no one played more games than Thierry. If you look at what he's done in the last year it's incredible. No one scores more goals, no one has more assists.'

The praise was coming from all corners as even Manchester United's players wanted to praise the Arsenal star. 'As a football fan I enjoy watching Henry,' Ryan Giggs said in the *Mirror*. 'And some of the goals he scored last year were frightening. He's one of those players where you know what he's going to do, but you just can't stop it. He's so quick, so confident and so strong. It feels like every game he's going to score a goal.'

On the shortlist for the FIFA World Player of the Year award along with Henry were Brazilian midfielder Ronaldinho and AC Milan striker Andriy Shevchenko. The Barcelona ace was full of praise for his rival as he told the *Sun*: 'Henry is a great player and I admire him a lot. I hope he keeps playing well because he is one of the best in the world. I like Arsenal's style and everyone involved in football gets joy from watching him. But I think every top player in the world thinks about being the best and winning these awards.'

And Shevchenko was also full of praise for his rivals. 'It has been a great year for me,' the Ukrainian said. 'I feel very honoured to be here with these great champions by my side.'

The FIFA president, Sepp Blatter, pinned his name to the Henry cause as he felt the Frenchman was the most deserving of the award, as he said: 'Henry, for me, is the personality on the field. He is the man who can run and organise the game.'

But once again Henry missed out as Shevchenko won the Ballon d'Or and Ronaldinho took the FIFA award. But second again in the vote for World Player of the Year, Henry was as magnanimous as ever in defeat. 'If you do not win you cannot say you are happy, but the other two are tremendous players,' said the imperious goal-scorer. 'When you see what Shevchenko is doing in Serie A and Ronaldinho in Spain, they are the kind of players who make you jump off your seat. It's amazing to be around this kind of player. To be here two years in a row means I have been consistent for a long time and that really pleases me.'

Speaking at the gala dinner, Henry, wearing a black and white wristband – the symbol of his 'Stand Up, Speak Up' campaign – took the opportunity to highlight his intention to kick racism out of football. 'Players cannot do very much when they are on the pitch, but this [wristband] is a symbol of how we feel, it is part of a campaign,' he said. 'Perhaps we can help to make the public do something. I know it is difficult, but if we can stop it for an hour and a half at every match, if we can get fans to stand up and speak out, that is something good. That can be a victory.'

Arsenal entered the New Year second in the table, but Henry refused to give up on the title, despite Chelsea's incredible consistency. 'If we didn't believe we could catch Chelsea, we might as well give up and go home right now,' Henry said in the *Mirror*. 'We have to believe in that and we do. The most important thing is to concentrate on what we do, not on Chelsea. I don't care about what they do. I didn't go into the dressing room to ask about Chelsea's result because we need to do what we have to do.'

No one could accuse Henry of giving up, and there were other trophies on the striker's mind as the season marched on. 'It would be good to win the Champions League with Arsenal,' he said in the *Sun*. 'That would represent real success in my eyes. It would have been so easy for me to win it with Real or with a European mega club. It would also be a first for Arsenal and that has no price. My feeling of belonging to a club that is growing since the arrival of Arsène Wenger as manager is so strong.'

Arsenal's second game of 2005 saw them fall further behind Chelsea in the title race, as they drew 1–1 with Manchester City, but the next game was in the FA Cup against Stoke City and it gave Wenger the chance to give Henry a well-earned break. Despite having carried an Achilles injury since the European Championships, the Parisian had started every one of Arsenal's Premiership and Champions League games and had only been substituted once during that time.

Barring the last eight minutes of the 4–0 win over Charlton in October Henry had been an ever-present (except in the League Cup). 'Sometimes people rely on me to play, but against Manchester City I was a bit tired,' Henry said. 'For a long time they were better than us. We looked tired and were not as fresh as we can be.'

The top scorer was not missed as the Gunners managed to beat a competitive Stoke team 2–1, in a match that saw Emmanuel Eboue make his Arsenal debut following his move from Beveren. Henry's break did little to freshen his play as he failed to score against Bolton the following week as Arsenal lost 1–0 at the Reebok Stadium.

'We are going through a bad spell right now,' Henry told the *Sun*. 'I know that. You have to be honest. When you are on a high, things go for you. You get into a rhythm. At the moment, Chelsea are on a high. When you have had a few bad results, things are more difficult. Teams get more confident against you, which is what probably applies to us at the moment. All we can do is try and win our games. We can't do any more. Every game this season has been a must-win game and nothing has changed as we go into the Newcastle match.'

Arsenal managed to beat the Geordies 1–0 at Highbury thanks to a Bergkamp goal and Henry was keen to see him keep going for another season. 'He fancies playing another year; I also fancy him playing for another year,' Henry said after the game. 'Without saying anything bad about anyone, when Dennis plays, I only concentrate on going behind the defence. When he is not there, I have to drop back. I have played with a lot of great players and he is amazing. He always has a great desire when he is on the pitch and you can never complain about him. At his age, to be doing what he is doing, it is unbelievable. I don't know if I will still be playing at his age. He is a great guy.'

Henry is also a great guy and he took time out of his footballing schedule to officially launch his 'Stand Up, Speak Up' campaign. 'After the recent problems, especially the one with Aragones and the monkey chants heard during Spain versus England match, I wanted to react,' he said. 'Lots of players, like Ronaldinho, have been shocked by those stories. Something needed to be done. It won't perhaps change anything, but doing nothing won't change anything either. Things can change. When someone told me [about Aragones' comments], I thought it was a joke, but then I heard it on the TV. I reckon he should have been punished more severely by the authorities. There is a proverb I like: I forgive but I never forget.'

Back on the pitch, the Gunners won an FA Cup tie with Wolves 2–0 and Henry even made a rare start in the fourth round of the competition, but he still couldn't find the back of the net as he completed a sixth game without a goal. The prolific Frenchman was continuing to create chances for his team-mates, but his barren spell was now his longest since the one he suffered at the start of his Arsenal career. Sadly for Arsenal that run stretched to seven games, as their title aspirations were dealt a heavy blow three days later when they lost 4–2 to Manchester United at Highbury.

'The Champions League is a priority for everyone, but a bit more for us after Tuesday night,' Henry told the *Sun* after the Gunners failed to close the ten-point gap separating them from Chelsea. 'Maybe we'll concentrate more on that now and see where we can go in the FA Cup as well. It is crucial we go to Villa and deliver a good performance. The next few weeks are so important. Our confidence is low, but it is up to us to get on with it. We must go back to basics – and we will.'

Arsenal showed their mettle at Villa Park and within half an hour they were 3–0 up. Ljungberg opened the scoring with ten minutes on the clock and Henry ended his goal-drought just four minutes later, racing on to a Vieira throughball and hammering the ball past Thomas Sorensen to register his first goal in eight games. Henry also created the third for Cole after twenty-eight minutes as the Gunners bounced back quickly from their dismal performance against their fierce rivals.

Ahead of a Valentine's Day fixture against Crystal Palace, Henry once again went on record to declare his love for Arsenal. 'I would like to stay here, but it's up to the people involved,' Henry told the press. 'If it was only up to me then it's no problem, but we all know how it is in if you stop scoring goals: someone young can come along and kick you out. No one would have thought that when Ian Wright stopped, someone else would come in and do something. Nicolas Anelka came for two or three years and when he stopped everyone said, "Who are we going to have?" Then suddenly I arrived. It's going to be the same with me and that's the way it is. I'm just realistic. When I stop, Arsenal will always be Arsenal, whether I'm in the team or not.'

Henry was in fine form against the Eagles, scoring two and making one more as Arsenal won 5–1. Wenger made more history against Palace, though, when he named the first overseas squad for a Premiership match; after Cole's withdrawal through illness, none of the sixteen players involved on the pitch and the bench were English.

One of those foreigners was singled out for praise by Henry: Reyes had been the victim of a Spanish radio hoax that tricked him into admitting that he was unhappy in England and that he wanted to play for Real Madrid, but his strike partner stuck by him. 'He was tremendous against

Crystal Palace and the fans were tremendous with him as well,' Henry said to the assembled media. 'We all know what happened last week, but his reaction was just amazing. He hadn't scored for a long time in the league, so it was quite important for him and us, but the reaction of the fans goes without saying.

'It is difficult to settle in a foreign country. I've had it twice, in Italy and in England. Then when you have people trying to play tricks on you, it becomes even more difficult. Things are hard. You can have the language barrier and can sometimes miss your home country or what you are used to, but the guy has shown he has quality and he's a great player. He showed that with the goal he scored against Palace. That's what we want to see from him, what a great player he is. This was the right answer.'

But the answer from the Spanish FA following their international team manager's hearing was certainly not right in Henry's eyes. Having allegedly made his unsavoury racist comments, Aragones had been fined just £2,000. 'Clearly the punishment does not fit the crime,' Henry said to the *Sun*. 'Look at Lauren: he pushed Ruud van Nistelrooy last season and got a £40,000 fine. I am not trying to excuse Lauren because what he did was wrong. He deserved the fine for pushing van Nistelrooy. But are you telling me that Lauren's push was twenty times worse than what Aragones said? Don't make me laugh. At the very, very least, they should have had the same punishment. That, to me, is completely obvious. The fact that Aragones got one twentieth of the fine... maybe the Spanish FA were simply having a few problems with their maths.

'I can celebrate a real victory if all this rubbish disappears from people's mouths. In England, I am lucky. I have never had any racism against me and that is fantastic. As a sportsman, I owe an enormous amount to people like John Barnes and Cyrille Regis, who did not have it quite so easy when they played. Hopefully, countries like England and France can move on, but it seems as though other countries are not quite so ready to live in the twenty-first century.'

The off-pitch disappointment was soon matched on the pitch for Henry and his Arsenal team-mates, however, as they drew with Sheffield United in the FA Cup in the Frenchman's absence before he returned for the dismal 3–1 away defeat to Bayern Munich in the second round of the Champions League. In a typically muted European performance, the Gunners were trailing 3–0 in the Olympic Stadium until Kolo Toure grabbed a late goal, giving them a faint slither of hope for the return leg. But there were three domestic games before they could get any revenge over their German conquerors.

Arsenal dropped further points in the league at Southampton, drawing 1–1, and survived a penalty shoot-out, winning 4–2 after the match finished 0–0, to get past Sheffield United in the FA Cup, before Henry took his Arsenal total to 177 goals, scoring his sixth Gunners hat-trick in a 3–0 win over Portsmouth. The win and the goals gave Henry confidence ahead of the game against Bayern, but he knew that it would be tough.

'If we don't believe, we might as well ring them up and tell them to stay at home as they've won,' Henry said. 'But you have to be confident. It will be difficult, but we will try our best. Then again, football is about winning. I will be happy if we can turn things around, but I won't be over the moon. If we lose in the quarter-finals after beating Bayern Munich, that won't do anything for me. Maybe we saw the wrong Arsenal in the first leg, but hopefully we can see the good Arsenal this time.'

A lot of people said the Gunners' chances to turn it around rested entirely with Henry, and the same people were beginning to blame him for each and every Arsenal failure. The manager stood by his prodigy, though. 'Thierry is always under big pressure as people get used to him scoring goals for fun, so when he doesn't deliver, they ask what's wrong,' Wenger said. 'But you must always consider that what he does is exceptional and you get spoilt by what he does deliver. The Champions League level is more difficult, but his record in that is very good as well. And who can deliver three goals in every Champions League game?'

Not only was Henry to blame for every Arsenal defeat, he also needed to cheer up, according to the press. Accused of looking moody and unhappy on the pitch, the Frenchman decided to set the record straight. 'Sometimes I see people thinking I'm having a go at someone else. It has happened, but more often it's because I'm upset with myself,' Henry said at the pre-match press conference. 'Usually I don't talk before a Champions League game, but I thought it was important to explain, once and for all, about my attitude and body language. I know sometimes I can be a pain, I'm aware of it, but it's because I want to win. It's not because I'm not happy, it's just that sometimes it kills me when the game is not played how the game should be played. It does my head in. I always apologise to the guys when I go back in the dressing room. People who know me know that I'm never satisfied with myself. Always after a game, what I think about at home are the things that I didn't do well.'

It was the same attitude that had been instilled in a young Henry by his father when he was still a child. 'When I was eleven or twelve,' he went on. 'If I scored, my dad used to say that I didn't make any goals. When I used to set up some, he used to say that I didn't score. When I did both, he used to say that I should have given that ball or this ball. I've been educated in a hard way. I'm not trying to do the crying game, but I don't come from a nice area, so the only way for me to get out of it was for my parents to be really hard on me. I'm not there on the pitch to laugh, I'm there to play.'

Henry played his heart out against the Germans, but he could only score one at Highbury and the Germans won the tie 3–2 on aggregate. So yet another Champions League campaign had ended in failure and, to make matters worse, Henry also picked up a calf injury, one that sidelined him for three weeks. In his absence, the team managed a couple of 1–0 wins to beat Bolton in the FA Cup and Blackburn in the league.

After an international week, when an Henry-less France drew 0–0 with Switzerland in Paris and 1–1 with Israel in Tel-Aviv, Henry was fit to play for the Gunners and, with 178 Arsenal goals to his name, he needed only one more to go past Bastin and just seven more to go level with Wright as the Gunners all-time No. 1. 'I remember Mr Dein gave me a tape of Ian Wright when I first arrived here,' Henry said in the *Mirror*. 'He said to me: "That's what you have to do." I remember looking at the record and I just thought: "185 – that's a long way." First of all I just wanted to score one. Then I started to score and score and score and then I didn't really think about it. Then people started to ask me whether I was thinking about the record. I would be lying if I said I didn't think about it, but even though the record is right in front of me, people have to appreciate that the team is more important. If I was interested only in the record, then I would take penalties when I'm brought down or I wouldn't slide the ball to someone else when I'm in front of goal. That's something I'm more proud of.'

The *News of the World* interviewed Henry further on the subject: 'Beating Ian Wright's record of 185 – and being remembered by the fans for that landmark – is what I really want. It would be extraordinary for me to reach that total. It's the sign of real consistency. It's something which can make you a legend because, to do it, you have to possess a bit of everything. You have to keep your place in the team over a number of years and, ultimately, of course, you have to be good.

'I hope the Arsenal fans remember me for this. It's a reflection of my loyalty and longevity. You have to commit to one club to be able to do it. Wright did it over eight seasons and now I have my chance. But it's not just a record – it's the whole achievement. I want to leave my mark at Highbury. When you end your career, whether people liked you or not, you want them to remember you. You have to create something that lasts for that to happen.

'With the French national side, we have made our place in history and that's what I want at Arsenal. My stats are good in the France team – less good than at Arsenal, but that's because you have fewer games. You can't compare the two. A club is like a family: you see the guys every day and you learn to live and develop something together. In the national team you don't see people often enough. But I have won Premiership titles and now perhaps the scoring record and that is what it is all about – that's why I play football.'

Norwich were the visitors to Highbury as Henry made giant leaps towards his target, scoring another hat-trick as the relegation-destined Canaries were put to the sword 4–1. The win lifted Arsenal above Manchester United into second place and the manager was very happy with Henry's work. 'Thierry played with his brain because, physically, he was not fit,' Wenger revealed. 'So a hat-trick isn't bad! He was rested by France in midweek and the break has obviously helped. I'd be worried if I was Ian Wright now. I bet he hates Thierry!'

But Henry was keen to deflect attention from the record he was homing in on and played down the importance of his goal-chase. 'I'll only talk about beating Ian's record if I do it,' he revealed. 'I know that Cliff was a great player, like Ian, and for me to be up there with them is amazing. But it's a team game, it's not right to pick on an individual, and there would be no comparison between me breaking the record and the team going unbeaten in the Premiership all last season. That will stay in history forever.'

As he closed in on Wright's record, Henry told the *Sun* what he knew of the old Highbury hero. 'We did not get much English football when I was living in France, but we did see the 1990 FA Cup final when he scored two from the subs' bench to force a 3–3 draw with Manchester United,' he said. 'And I also saw him do well in some games against French teams in the Cup-Winners' Cup, particularly one match against Auxerre.

'The first time I met him was at our training ground a few years ago. He was loud, very loud. Clearly a great character. Also, he was a great player. In the same team though? Me and him? Boy, we would have some arguments. Certainly when you take into account we are quite similar characters. What a thought. We would have been at each other all through a game. We would have sent the manager crazy, I am sure.'

Henry's march towards the record was delayed a little as he failed to score at the Riverside Stadium for the first time in five years, but Arsenal still won 1–0 thanks to a Pires goal, and their faint hopes of defending their title were not yet vanquished.

'We always try to achieve a better result than Chelsea, but how can you do that when they keep on winning?' Henry said. 'Now it is all about finishing the season well and seeing what it brings. There is still some hope there for the title. We are going to try and grab what we can. Obviously to finish first would be more than amazing but, even if we don't, second is still important because psychologically it would help us. At the moment, we are not conceding many goals and we have won the last three away from home, but time is running out.'

Time had run out for Henry's season as he suffered an

injury in training, as his manager revealed ahead of the FA Cup semi-final against Blackburn. 'Henry is out with a groin problem and it is a massive blow,' Wenger told the press. 'It is an inflammation of his groin. We have to check it by scan to find out how long he will be out, it could be a few weeks or just a few days. It could be quite serious. We wanted to have Thierry with us, but we must now focus on the strengths we have.'

One of those strengths was Bergkamp, who helped the Gunners beat Blackburn 3–0 and later inspired Arsenal to a 7–0 win over Everton at Highbury, and Henry was overjoyed for his long-time team-mate. 'I was really happy for Dennis,' he said. 'I saw the way the fans were asking for another year, so it is the least you can do for a player like that. I've said it so many times – he makes things easy. You saw how many times he was involved in the goals, I lost count – it was amazing. He has been amazing throughout all the years that he has been here and, if it was down to me, I would give him another year.'

Happily for Henry, Bergkamp was given an extended contract and they hadn't played their last game together. Arsenal played out their matches without Henry, who suffered pain in both Achilles tendons after his groin inflammation calmed down, and finished the season second with eighty-three points, a total that only they had beaten twice since 2000 and a respectable title-winning haul in all but one of the previous five years. But in 2004–05 Mourinho's side had taken things to another level. Bankrolled by Abramovich's almost unlimited funds, the Blues racked up an incredible ninety-five points and were twelve points clear of the Gunners in the final standings.

Henry finished as the Premiership's leading scorer for the third time in four years, his twenty-five league goals saw him win the European Golden Boot for a second successive season and he also notched up fourteen assists in the league. His achievement was all the more impressive considering the fact that he missed the last six league games of the season through injury. Unfortunately for Arsenal he was also missing for the FA Cup final and, before that game, Henry reviewed Arsenal's season, certain that the end of the unbeaten run had been a turning point. 'That affected us badly, not so much because we lost, but because of the way we lost,' he said. 'That penalty they gave against us – I could spend all day talking about that penalty.

'It has been difficult. We can still win the FA Cup, but the thing is, when you play for teams such as Arsenal, it is not enough to win just the League Cup or the FA Cup.'

It may not have been a great season, but the FA Cup is always a nice consolation prize and Henry's absence wasn't too costly, as his team-mates gained revenge for two league defeats at the hands of Manchester United by beating their fierce rivals 5–4 on penalties after a drab goalless draw.

The celebrations continued for Henry, as he became a father for the first time the following week. His wife Nicole gave birth by caesarean section to a beautiful baby girl on 27 May 2005 and they named her Tea, not as homage to an English institution, but a traditional French name pronounced Tay-ah.

'People are telling me that becoming a father will be the most amazing thing that will happen to me.' Henry told the

Mirror. 'I have to admit that throughout this season it has been on my mind all the time, but my brother has four kids and I was an uncle at fifteen, so at least I know how to hold a baby. I hope my girl will grow up in England because I want to stay at Arsenal for as long as they want me.

'I am happy here. Madrid, Barça, Milan and Juventus were teams I dreamed about when I was young, but now it's a different story and I am happy in London.'

It was just what the Arsenal fans wanted to hear before heading off on their summer holidays: their talented talisman still had his heart at Highbury, despite having lost the Premiership crown to Chelsea and despite having suffered another failure in the Champions League. However, by the time the new season came around, things were looking less rosy in Wenger's garden.

Chapter thirteen
Final Countdown

'I'm more than proud,' he said of his team. 'We can say that against the best team in Europe we can play good football, even with ten men. It was a team who outplayed the other team and made them look just ordinary. I'm sorry, but tonight they looked, to me, really ordinary.'

Arsenal lost the Champions League final 2–1 after Barcelona snatched two late goals in Paris, but Thierry Henry was right to be proud of his team-mates. The Gunners battled valiantly despite playing, since the eighteenth minute, with one man less than Barça. In that time they had even taken the lead and held the Catalan side at bay until the final quarter of an hour, but it was Carles Puyol and not Henry who lifted the big trophy at the Stade de France.

Winning the European Cup would certainly have put the shine on what had been a very mixed season, but looking back on the 2005–06 campaign there were a lot of positives for both Henry and Arsenal. There was disappointment in the league certainly, but the new captain guided his fearless young team through a lot of tough games on the continent to get to the final, and the mercurial Frenchman enhanced his mighty reputation with commanding performances against some of Europe's biggest names. There may not have been any silverware to show for all his good work, but the experience gained during the long season will surely bring trophies in the future.

The last season at Highbury started among some massive transfer rumours. Barcelona had begun to re-establish themselves as the biggest club in Spain, winning their first *la Liga* title since 1999 and, under the young Dutch coach Frank Rijkaard, they were still looking to grow. To do that they had their eyes on the most talented players across the footballing world and that, obviously, included Arsenal's flying Frenchman. 'The player that interests me is Henry,' Rijkaard told the press.

The Barcelona club president, Joan Laporta, made no secret of his desire to bring the Highbury hero to the Nou Camp, but denied that he had made a bid. 'Barça have not made an offer for Henry,' Laporta said. 'It is true the coaching staff think he is a very good player, but we are happy with the squad we already have.'

Even if an offer did come Arsenal weren't interested, even for the £50m fee that was mentioned in the press. 'I haven't planned to buy too many and if we did it would mean we were under tremendous stress to sell players, which we don't want to do,' Wenger said. 'When you watch our team play, we don't really need anyone. We have to keep faith with the young players we already have.'

The club weren't interested in losing their most valuable asset and he didn't want to leave. 'If Arsenal still want me, and we can come to an agreement when my contract runs out in June 2007, I will be happy to remain until the end of my career,' Henry said in Italian paper *Gazzetta Dello Sport*. 'Now I have an English family, and I believe it shows I'm happy in London. The fans and the club have always treated me really well. In football you never know if you will be happy where you go, but here I feel really great. The Champions League has never been won here at Arsenal, and that is the only thing missing on my CV. But there is plenty of time yet.'

But if Henry was going to win the Champions League at Arsenal it would be without Patrick Vieira, as the club captain was sold to Juventus for £13.7m. The previous summer Wenger had entertained Real Madrid's advances for the imposing midfielder, but his skipper decided to stay. In 2005, Arsenal accepted the bid from the Italian champions and Vieira was on his way to Turin after nine years in north London.

Many people questioned Wenger's judgement in letting arguably the world's finest defensive midfielder leave the club, but Henry kept faith in his manager. 'Of course, it is a blow to lose Patrick, you cannot hide from that,' the former Juve winger told the press. 'But as we saw last season, alongside Patrick there are lots of able youngsters. They showed a lot of quality and are getting better.

'More importantly, you have to trust Arsène Wenger. How can you not trust a man who has won four FA Cups and three league titles? He has proved he has a fantastic eye for a player. No one had heard of Patrick Vieira when he signed. I am sure Arsène has a few things up his sleeve. There is no doubt that he will sign some more players that few people have heard of, but they will go on to become great players.'

Wenger was busy trying to work his magic in the transfer market once again, but he was scuppered in a number of deals by the vast wealth of Chelsea and the allure of Real Madrid. So, entering the new season, the manager's confidence in the young players would undoubtedly be put to the test. Alexander Hleb was the most notable acquisition as he joined from VfB Stuttgart for a fee believed to be in the region of £10m, and Wenger also picked up the youngster Alexandre Song, just shy of his eighteenth birthday, on a season-long loan from Bastia. The two new midfielders would be needed to fill the void created by the departure of not only Vieira but also of Edu, who had joined Valencia on a free transfer.

Henry was made club captain, clearly a move by Wenger to appease his protégé after the sale of Vieira and the speculation over his future. The decision was greeted with scepticism in some parts, because although the prolific Frenchman was clearly seen as an influential and gifted individual, he was not considered by many as the type of player most suited for the role. Certain people consider strikers to be in no position to lead any team.

Certainly an attacker can score goals and can lead by example, but a defender can see the whole game ahead of him and can instruct accordingly, and a midfielder can dominate a match by controlling the centre of the park, but Henry was Arsenal's best player and he welcomed the decision. 'This is a new beginning for me,' he revealed to the *Evening Standard*. 'I know I will have to lead by example. If anything, there will be more work off the pitch than on it. I will also have to represent the players away from a match situation. I'm looking forward to it. It helps we have a great bunch of lads here.'

Henry had never captained Monaco or Juventus and as a kid he had never even captained the junior clubs he played for in Paris. He had only stood in as captain for Arsenal on three occasions, twice against Norwich and once against Panathinaikos, but the French star did have some captaincy experience from leading his country's youth teams at Under-16 through to Under-21 level.

Fortunately, Henry had plenty of team-mates who he could rely on for help. 'On the pitch, we already have lots of other captains,' he added. 'Dennis Bergkamp communicates as though he is a captain. Ashley Cole is a captain. So too are Sol Campbell and Jens Lehmann. It is important for a big team to have lots of big characters. Hopefully, we can all pull together and take Arsenal on. The last two captains of the club have been Tony Adams and Vieira and they are a couple of big acts to follow.'

But with his determination and dedication, Henry would certainly give it his best. The new captain was straight into action in the pre-season friendlies. Unlike the previous season, where he had just three days' training before the Community Shield, Henry was present from the first of Arsenal's matches in July. He scored a penalty as they beat Barnet 4–1, and plenty more goals followed for the Frenchman as he enjoyed Arsenal's Austrian training camp.

As the new season approached, Henry had still not signed an extension to his contract and, with only two years left on his existing deal, the rumours about a move to Spain continued to grow. He allayed the fans' fears in a press conference. 'I am really happy here,' he said. 'Things are going well for me and I've just been named skipper. Like I've said so many times – as long as they want me here, I will stay here. The talks are on and I just hope we can find an agreement.

'People keep questioning my desire and commitment for the club, but every time I step on the pitch I try to do my best. I'm doing something I love. Even if I wasn't playing for Arsenal and I had to play in my friend's back garden I'd play the same way. I'd still argue like I do now and still be trying some stuff. I'd still be unhappy or happy because I lost or because I won. I'm not demanding anything except to play and to try to lead the team to some silverware.'

Trophies would always be important to someone as competitive as Henry, but cash certainly was not. 'I didn't come into this game to win money,' he continued. 'I came into football first of all to make my dad proud because he was the most important influence on me at the time and I just wanted to make him happy.'

Arsenal headed into the Community Shield on the back of six friendly wins, but Chelsea were a different proposition from the other sides the Gunners had faced and they lost 2–1, thanks to the Blues' stout defence and two Didier Drogba goals on the counter-attack. Henry refused to believe that the defeat signalled another season of Chelsea dominance, though. 'If you look at all the Community Shield results before, it didn't really affect the way the season went,' the new skipper said. 'Last season we won 3–1 against Manchester United and it didn't stop us losing two times against them home and away. You can't take anything from this into the season. The English season is really long and really difficult, so it's going to be another story.'

One of the key facts in the Arsenal story was that the 2005–06 season was to be the last at Highbury and the club had reverted to a redcurrant strip to commemorate ninety-three years at the old ground. 'I think the kit is great,' Henry said. 'I like the fact that it's exactly how it was at the beginning of Highbury. I'm sure people will appreciate that.'

The kit was christened with an opening-day win for Arsenal as they beat Newcastle 2–0 at Highbury to get their Premiership campaign off to a good start. Henry once again scored Arsenal's first league goal of the season and he celebrated by making a 'T' with his fingers and kissing them in a tribute to his baby, Tea. 'I made a little sign for my daughter,' he revealed. 'It was the first time that she had been in the stadium, so it was a special day for me – the first time that she came to see her dad play.'

The penalty, ten minutes from time, was also Henry's 182nd goal for Arsenal and, as he edged closer to Ian Wright's record, the inevitable questions followed. 'A lot of people have been asking me about the chance that I have of breaking the goal-scoring record at the club,' Henry said. 'But to be honest, I'd rather that others spoke about it and I just got on with my football.

'What I will say is that it will be more than amazing if I could achieve the record, especially when you consider what a special season this is for the club, being the last at

Highbury. My dream is to break the record at Highbury – to do it here would be the cherry on top of the cake. I don't think it would be quite the same to do it in an away game.'

Before Henry could get any closer to the Arsenal record, however, he joined up with his French team-mates for a friendly against Kolo Toure's Ivory Coast. Due to Vieira's sale and Robert Pires' bust-up with Raymond Domenech, Henry was now the only Arsenal player in the France squad, where so recently there had been four. He was, however, looking forward to meeting up with some other old team-mates, such as Zinedine Zidane, who had come out of international retirement to help his country qualify for the World Cup, and the Real Madrid star had also talked Claude Makelele and Lilian Thuram into making the same decision.

The Arsenal man was delighted to have them back. 'The group is so tight that one win against one of the big four teams is likely to swing the qualification,' Henry explained. 'With players like Zidane, Makelele and Thuram, we have a better chance of getting that win. It's obvious. They've got great experience and just seeing them on the pitch will be reassuring. They are guys who thrive in big games and, right now, that's what we need.'

France were three points behind top spot with only four games left to play and they had a vital showdown in Dublin against Group Four leaders Ireland looming large in September; the return of the big guns was very welcome. *Les Bleus* beat 'The Elephants' 3–0 in the first international of the season and Henry grabbed the third goal as France were revitalised by the return of the old guard. And, four days later, Henry was hoping to get another one over the

Ivory Coast skipper Drogba as Arsenal faced Chelsea at Stamford Bridge.

Looking back at the Community Shield defeat, Henry refused to be scared by the champions. 'What did Chelsea do that day?' the Arsenal skipper asked in the *Sun*. 'Only defend. Besides, they defend each time they play us, whereas it's different with other rivals. The way Chelsea played against us the other day is, to me, like a form of respect. So they fear us.'

The Chelsea players certainly respected Henry, as Frank Lampard revealed in the *Evening Standard*. 'Henry is a great man, I really like him,' the England midfielder said. 'He is a great professional and I think he will be a great captain for them. He has been the outstanding player in the Premiership for the last three or four years.'

As talented a player as Henry is, though, he could find no way past Petr Cech in the Chelsea goal and Drogba's lucky late goal won the game for the Blues 1–0. Arsenal failed to perform at Stamford Bridge and Henry was criticised for not motivating his team as well as John Terry had done with the Blues. 'Before, when we used to lose, it was always mine or Patrick's fault anyway, so I don't feel any extra pressure by being captain,' he told the *Sun*. 'I enjoy it. It makes no difference to me – it is always my job to try and get us out of trouble if necessary and that hasn't changed. A lot of people have asked if it would affect me, but it won't. Perhaps I have to work on not showing my frustration so much if things are going wrong, as it is up to me to inspire the team, but it won't change my game. If the team is not playing well, I have to give them belief.'

Henry did exactly that in the next game as his two goals helped Arsenal come from behind to beat Fulham 4–1 at Highbury. The brace took him to 184 goals for the Gunners, just one away from the record. 'For me, Ian Wright was a legend and still is a legend, so to beat his record would be something really amazing,' Henry told the assembled press. 'But I don't want to speak too soon because things in football can happen really quickly, so I just want to concentrate and keep scoring goals for my team.

'Of course I care about the record, but I don't really think about it when I step out on to the pitch. I will maybe go over the moon when it happens, but that's not the case yet. When it happens, no one will talk about it any more, so that will be another good thing.'

His goals also helped Arsenal to three points – which were crucial after losing to Chelsea as they needed to get back to winning ways as soon as possible and they didn't have another game for two-and-a-half weeks, due to Liverpool's involvement in the European Super Cup and an international break.

In that international break, France faced two must-win World Cup Qualifiers and Henry was again under fire for his less-than-prolific form for *les Bleus*. With twenty-nine goals in seventy-one games his record was nothing to be embarrassed about, but he had only scored twice in his last nine outings for his country. Still, the ever-unflappable striker took all the criticism in his elegant stride. 'Before Euro '96, Alan Shearer went ten games without scoring for England, but he came good,' Henry reminded the *Sun*. 'Everyone has their droughts and I had mine. The important thing is to come back stronger. There is pressure and criticism, but I can deal with that. Even last season, when I finished as top scorer, people still criticised me. What do people want?'

It wasn't the first time that Henry's performances for *les Bleus* had failed to meet expectation. 'After the 1998 World Cup, I was sent to play with the Under-21s again,' he went on. 'I was not happy, but I got on with things. One time, I played for the Under-21s against Belgium in front of just 200 people and then sat in the stand when the senior team played the following night. That was difficult, but I came through it.'

France beat the Faroe Islands 3–0 in Lens to put them joint top of the group with Switzerland and Ireland and set them up perfectly for the game in Dublin, but Henry was substituted after missing a handful of chances and he definitely wasn't happy. 'I was annoyed,' the Arsenal man said. 'Not because I hadn't scored, but because I don't like being taken off. I like playing.'

Henry was taken off again at Lansdowne Road, but only after he had decided the game with a piece of typical Henry brilliance. In the sixty-eighth minute, he extracted the ball from a mass of legs outside the Ireland area, strode forward and curled the ball past a despairing Shay Given and into the top corner of the net. Henry left the pitch soon after and the match finished 1–0 to put France in command of their World Cup destiny.

'I didn't get a look-in tonight and so I thought I should try something a bit different,' Henry said of his goal. 'It is good we got three points, but let's not get carried away.

'The result is good, but I don't think we won prettily. Ireland did not deserve to lose. Nothing is done yet. It is a strange group and I think it is the first time one of the top teams has beaten the other. I had to battle, as it is difficult up front on your own. We shouldn't be over the moon as there is still a long way to go.'

The three points meant that the French had made giant strides towards automatic qualification, but it came at a cost both for France and Arsenal as Henry suffered a groin injury. At first it was thought that he would only miss one match, but he didn't play again until mid-October and missed nine games in total, seven for Arsenal and two for France. 'I have been suffering with pain in my left groin for some while,' Henry revealed in the *Evening Standard*. 'Right back to March, and I need to rest. It is a disappointment, but I have no choice.

'The injury has come and gone since last season. When we were playing one match a week right at the start of the season, it was not so bad. But now it is a game at the weekend and a game in the week. I have noticed the difference and the groin has become more painful. I knew my body wasn't right and I just have to rest. I don't want to copy what I did last season when I played on with an injury.'

Les Bleus coped much more admirably with the striker's absence than Arsenal, as they drew 1–1 with Switzerland and beat Cyprus 4–0 to guarantee their place at Germany 2006. Wenger's squad was already struggling to come to terms with Vieira's departure and, with Henry out, injured they were a shadow of their former selves.

Arsenal missed the midfield powerhouse more in the

dressing room than on the pitch, and Henry summarised how everyone felt. 'When Patrick left I was shocked,' he revealed to the *Sun*. 'I admit that. I did not want to see him go. None of us at Arsenal wanted him to leave, but, sometimes, big players go to other big clubs. That is the way things work out. Arsenal have not only lost one of their best players, they have also lost a fantastic person from the group. He is a great man, a great team-mate and a great person. I feel privileged to have played with such a great player. We will miss him and, let's be honest, so will the team. But you have to look forward and Arsenal will move on.'

But with their two most influential players from previous years out of the picture, the Gunners were struggling. They lost away to Middlesbrough and West Bromwich Albion and drew with West Ham before Henry regained fitness. At least his team-mates managed without him in Europe, where wins at home to FC Thun and away to Ajax had put them in control of Group B.

Henry's enforced absence would have been the perfect time to sort out his contract, but the striker decided to wait until the end of the season before signing a new deal, adding fuel to the flames of his 'supposed' move to Barcelona. Everyone at Arsenal wanted him to stay and the sooner he resolved the situation the better, but whenever a deal was struck it would certainly be very sweet financially. Arsenal chairman Peter Hill-Wood told the *Daily Star*: 'We have not talked about the offer yet, but it is fair to say that he would become the highest paid player in Arsenal's history – and deservedly so. We would also have liked to talk before the end of the season, but it is Thierry's right to leave it until then. It is his life, but we want him to stay and he knows that.'

When Henry did return to the side, he put in an inspirational performance that left everyone in agreement about the skipper's value and importance to the Arsenal cause. Replacing Jose Antonio Reyes after quarter of an hour in Prague, Henry chose the perfect time to score his 185th goal for the Gunners. Kolo Toure sent a long ball forward and the French striker controlled it brilliantly, instantly creating enough space to curl the ball inside the far post from 18 yards. It was a memorable strike to equal Ian Wright's Arsenal goal-scoring record and, after seventy-four minutes, Henry made the title his own, slotting the ball past the Sparta 'keeper from Robert Pires' fine throughball.

'It sounds great to hear "Thierry Henry, record goal-scorer for Arsenal",' Henry said after the game. 'Wrighty was a great player and will always be a legend at Arsenal; it's tremendous to beat his record. I really wanted to do it at Highbury, but if I get the chance to score I'll take it.'

Still only twenty-eight, with plenty of football ahead of him, the question was, 'How many goals Henry could score for the Gunners?' and talk inevitably turned to his still un-extended contract. 'It's really important to concentrate on this season and see what happens. I will discuss it at the end of the season,' Henry added. 'I've seen a lot of speculation, but whenever I step on to the pitch I give it all my heart and play 100 percent. You can never doubt my commitment on the pitch and, hopefully, people will respect that.'

Even with his future in doubt Henry's return was still crucial, as Arsenal were enduring their worst injury-crisis since Wenger took control of the club. Cole, Campbell, Ljungberg, Hleb and now Reyes were all out and even Henry wasn't fully fit.

'I wasn't meant to travel and I wasn't meant to play,' he told the *Evening Standard*. 'But when Jose Reyes was injured the boss said to me, "You can't have five minutes to warm up. Keep on running on the pitch." That's what I did. I thought about pacing myself, but I sprinted straightaway.

'I just wanted to help the team because that is why I am there and I just wanted to show my desire. I watched the game at West Bromwich last Saturday and I was biting my nails. Even at Highbury when I was watching games it was painful. I wanted to be out there, helping the team. Sometimes you see the opportunity to put the ball in the back of the net and you're not able to do it. It is so frustrating. Did I feel ready to come back? To be honest, no. But sometimes you feel ready and it doesn't happen. Last night, I just said to myself, "Hang on a minute, you have to step on to the pitch and try to do your best, fit or not fit."'

Having finally broken the record, Henry's manager was one of the first to champion his champion's achievement. 'He'll not only have a place in the history of Arsenal, but in the history of football,' Wenger told the assembled media. 'He's not even a typical goal-scorer. He's an all round player, not a guy who lurks in the box.'

And Wright wasn't far behind. 'I am a predatory striker,' said Wright. 'That is why people say they would have liked to see us playing together. He does what he does outside the box and I would be inside waiting to get bits and that would have been good to see.'

Wright phoned Henry straight after the game to congratulate him and the Frenchman was flattered by the call. 'My only regret of my career is that we never played with each other,' Arsenal's new record goal-scorer told *Arsenal.com*. 'Maybe at times we would have been upset with each other on the pitch, but that's the way it is. He is a great guy. To lose the record and still call to congratulate me is really respectful.

'I would have liked to have played with Ian Wright and Nicolas Anelka to see what we could have done together. But it's a curiosity a lot of Arsenal players must have, to see what we could have done. With Nicolas, I know what we could have done together. I could have played on the wing or behind those two. It's a shame I never played with both of them.'

Any combination of the three strikers would surely have resulted in plenty of goals, but Henry's two against Sparta Prague had done enough to secure a 2–0 win that further strengthened Arsenal's position at the top of Group B, which was in stark contrast to their Premiership placing. In England they were in eighth place, a massive fourteen points behind Chelsea. Henry's return helped Arsenal win their next match, against Manchester City, but that game will be best remembered for a botched penalty attempt.

With the Gunners 1–0 up at Highbury, thanks to a Pires penalty, following David James' foul on Henry, the home side won another spot-kick. Trying to emulate a famous Johann Cruyff penalty from 1982, when the Dutch legend exchanged passes with Ajax team-mate Jesper Olsen before rolling the ball into the empty net, Pires was to roll the ball sideways for an onrushing Henry to wallop home. Unfortunately, Pires' touch let him down and the ball barely moved off the spot before his captain ran past and the referee gave a free-kick to City. Luckily, Arsenal held on to their 1–0 lead and no points were lost, but it was an embarrassing situation for everyone involved.

'We practised it in training a few days ago and it went very well,' Pires said. 'It was Henry's idea, though, and I didn't really want to do it because I didn't think it was the right kind of game, it was too tight. I regret it. I apologise to the fans and to the manager and I won't do it again unless it's Henry who passes the ball to me.'

Although the trick did not come off, it highlighted Henry's intention to entertain and create something memorable every time he walks on to a football pitch, and the captain took full responsibility for the farcical outcome. 'I take the blame, it's all my fault,' Henry said. 'But it's not my fault that Robert got a numb leg. I will, however, be taking the penalties from now on.'

Unbowed, Henry insisted it would work next time. 'I will try it again – but next time I will push the ball off the penalty spot for someone else,' he revealed in the *Sun*. 'The main problem will be finding someone to do it with me, especially after Saturday.

'I have been trying to do something like this ever since I was in my early teens, but I never found anyone who had the guts to do it with me. Robert did – but then he missed the ball. It's nothing to do with being brave, it's about getting it right.'

Fortunately Pires had his leg working again for the next

game as his goal rescued a point from a trip to White Hart Lane. Henry missed the derby through injury, but he returned four days later and showed he hadn't lost his scoring touch as Arsenal secured their progress to the knock-out stages of the Champions League with a 3–0 home win over Sparta Prague. Arsenal's leading goal-scorer grabbed the first against the Czech side and made it three in two games with the Gunners' second and third goals in their 3–1 win over Sunderland.

After beating the Black Cats, Henry joined up with France for a charity match against Costa Rica, in Martinique. 'The game is being played to raise money for a plane crash which occurred in Venezuela in August,' Henry told the press. 'And the people of Martinique, itself a French *département*, have been waiting for the national team to play on their island for a long, long time. My mother is also from Martinique and so I look forward to playing there.'

Wenger was not particularly enthralled with the travel involved, but understood that the cause was close to Henry's heart and released him for the game. Costa Rica took a 2–0 lead into half-time but Henry helped France win 3–2, creating the first for Anelka and scoring the winner himself – back-heeling Jerome Rothen's corner into the net. 'What a pleasure that was!' Henry said afterwards. 'We couldn't come here for the families of the victims and lose.'

And the always-gracious striker went on to thank his manager for allowing him to play in the match: 'Arsène has always had a lot of respect for West Indian sportsmen, but he is defending his club. His argument was with the date, but he would never have stopped me from coming. I came here with his blessing. I could not imagine myself missing this.'

Three days later, Henry played another forty-five minutes for France as he came off at half-time during a 0–0 draw with Germany at the Stade de France. The international break failed to disrupt Henry's Arsenal form, though, and he grabbed two more goals as the Gunners struggled to a 3–2 win away to Wigan Athletic.

But the rumours about a move to Barcelona wouldn't stop. 'I think today you saw why I play,' he said of his commitment to Arsenal. 'People talk more about it [my future] than they talk about *Eastenders*. They should talk more about the game – we finally won away from home. I am starting to get sick of seeing my face in the papers.'

Wenger saw a lot of promise in the many young players filling the Arsenal shirts, and hoped that his bright prospects would help keep Henry at the club. 'Our potential will certainly be one of the things that can convince Thierry to stay,' Arsenal's manager admitted. 'We have a young side and, if we manage to do well, it can make him think this team has a future. It's one of the ingredients that will help.'

Arsenal continued to dominate their weak group in Europe and beat FC Thun 1–0 away before facing Blackburn in the league. Henry claimed another milestone against Rovers as he scored the second goal in a 3–0 win: it was his 100th league goal at Highbury and made him the first player to score 100 Premiership goals at any one ground. 'I would love this place to be my garden!' Henry said. 'This place for me is just tremendous. The fans love Highbury and it's not just me who's going to miss it. It's special and there's something about it that is difficult to describe. When you arrive, you hardly see the stadium as it's between two blocks of flats, but you feel that you are somewhere special.'

Just when everything seemed to be going right for the Gunners, they entered December and fell apart. First they travelled to Bolton and lost 2–0; they then drew 0–0 with Ajax – with Henry putting a penalty wide of the post – which didn't really matter as they had already won the group, but two games without scoring soon became three and then four as Arsenal lost 1–0 away to Newcastle and 2–0 at home to Chelsea to fall twenty points behind Mourinho's men.

Having lost three league games in a row, the captain knew how important the next game was. 'What we need to do is to keep going and put the team back on track,' Henry said in the *Evening Standard*. 'The next game, at Charlton on Boxing Day, is going to be crucial. They are not doing well in the league and neither are we. It is a derby game and it is vital to get three points.

'The most important thing is to look in front of us. What has happened is already done. We need everyone back to their best. This season, I don't think we have been outplayed. We have to keep going and make sure it doesn't affect us.'

Arsenal beat the Addicks 1–0 to move up to seventh in the league and Henry was happy with his team: 'We put the hard work in today. The lads didn't give up and, hopefully, now we will see the Arsenal of old.'

And in the last home game of 2005, Henry scored twice to claim his first goals for a month as the Gunners beat Portsmouth 4–0 at Highbury. The captain also created a goal for Reyes in front of Patrick Vieira, who was on his midwinter break with Juventus. As the year drew to a close, Henry was once again named French Player of the Year and revealed that his ankle problem was ongoing. 'I have been playing for the past two years with some problems on my Achilles,' he told the press. 'A lot of people have been talking about me, but I have to play. That's just me. I went to the hospital just for a simple check. I have said so many times I always try to do my best. I go on to the pitch to try to help the team, that's what I am there for. You need your skipper to be out there to help the team.'

Wenger's captain tried to explain the poor first half of the campaign, which had left Arsenal fighting solely for cup success. 'It hasn't been easy because of the injuries,' Henry said. 'I was missing at the beginning, which was, I think, important, so was Sol Campbell, Ashley Cole, Gael Clichy and Alex Hleb. And Patrick left. Then we lost games and things were not going our way, but that is how it is sometimes and you have to dig in and show your character. It takes time for it to come back, but it did come back, so let's now try to see what we can do at Aston Villa on Saturday.'

The Gunners failed to make it three wins in a row at Villa Park, but they did keep another clean sheet in the 0–0 draw and repeated the scoreline three days later against Manchester United. The point against the Red Devils lifted Arsenal into fifth place in the league, twenty-four points behind Chelsea and eleven points behind Ferguson's team. With such a gulf to overcome, thoughts were no longer of the title, but of securing a top-four finish and a place in the Champions League for next season.

With the league now the priority, Wenger took the

opportunity to rest Henry for the FA Cup third round match against Cardiff City. But even constrained to the sidelines, Henry couldn't keep out of the headlines. As Arsenal fell further and further behind the league leaders, the transfer speculation continued to grow and it intensified as a former Highbury hero spoke out about the situation – it was the last thing the fans wanted to hear.

'If I was Thierry Henry I'd have to seriously consider quitting Arsenal,' Ian Wright told the *Sun*. 'My gut feeling is Thierry is going to leave. If I was in the same position as him, I would. For Arsenal to get into a situation where Thierry Henry is even thinking of not signing a new deal is not good.

'When I was an Arsenal player, it never crossed my mind to leave, but I was never the world star that Thierry is, so I was quite happy to be at a club of such stature. I could also see that the team was getting ready to take off. You were looking at a team back then that could dominate, as it did for a while, but I can't see that now. When Patrick Vieira left I was shocked and now I think Thierry might have done as much as he can do at Arsenal.'

Wright spent seven years at Highbury in the 1990s and had developed a good friendship with Henry since the young forward arrived from Juventus, so for Arsenal fans to read his words was just another disappointment in what was rapidly becoming a season to forget. Fortunately, for everyone involved with the club, Wright's words only served to bring out Henry's declaration to stay – it was music to the ears of his adoring fans.

'I love this club and I've made up my mind to stay. There

was a lot of ridiculous speculation, but this will put an end to all the stories and we can move on,' Henry told the *Sun*. 'I'm still only twenty-eight. I did think about moving, but when I see the fans and the way they talk to me, it helped make my decision. They didn't boo me or make life difficult for me on the pitch.

'Obviously I did think about leaving Arsenal. It's a big decision because I thought if I did commit to this club then it could be for life. I can say to all my fans and the people who care about me that I want to lead the team out in the new stadium. I will talk to Arsène Wenger, to David Dein, and to the board and I will talk of the future.

'My mind is to stay and we have to sort this out. They said the ball was in my court. Now the ball is in their court. There was a lot of ridiculous speculation, but the truth is this: I never spoke with or met with a single person from any other club at any time. We need to move on now. I'm staying here to build one of the best teams in Europe. We need to be competitive. The club said it was up to me and now it's up to them. I've made my decision and I can't say more than that.'

Henry has always been a man of integrity – a breath of fresh air in the days of players kissing the club badge one day and putting in a transfer request the next – and it was difficult to imagine him going back on these pledges. With his English wife and his young daughter it seemed as though Henry was happy in London and happy at Arsenal.

The announcement lifted everyone involved with the club and they managed to beat Cardiff 2–1 in the FA Cup without Henry thanks to a Pires brace. The captain was rested again for the League Cup semi-final first leg three days later, and Arsenal lost 1–0 to Wigan at the JJB Stadium. Henry's first game back in a redcurrant shirt since his promise to stay was against Middlesbrough and Steve McLaren's team were in the wrong place at the wrong time as the Gunners turned on the style.

Henry scored a hat-trick in the 7–0 demolition of Middlesbrough to equal Cliff Bastin's record of 150 league goals for Arsenal, and there could quite easily have been more. There were soon more reasons to cheer as Wenger made a hat-trick of January signings to strengthen the squad. Midfielder Vassiriki Abou Diaby joined from Auxerre, Togolese striker Emmanuel 'Sheyi' Adebayor signed from Monaco and, most exciting of all, sixteen-year-old forward Theo Walcott was recruited from Southampton.

Walcott was described as a lightning-fast striker who was equally comfortable on either wing or up front and the comparisons with Henry were obvious. What's more, the new signing described the Frenchman as his idol. 'People say there are similarities between us and it's good to hear what he said about me,' Arsenal's skipper said. 'I first saw him play in the Youth Cup and I saw him as a player with great pace and a lot of tricks. I've also seen him play this year. I can't even remember what I was like as a player when I was that age, so it's difficult to say if we are alike. But he's a young player with a lot of desire and skills who obviously loves to play football.'

But even in the euphoria of the new signings and off the back of the incredible Boro rout, the Gunners were still struggling on the road and lost 1–0 away to Everton. One week later, and Arsenal were out of both domestic cups with only the Champions League to aim for.

Henry started his first League Cup tie for six years in the semi-final second leg and even scored a header to level the aggregate scores and force extra-time. Robin van Persie put the home side ahead in the 108th minute with an unstoppable free-kick, but a late strike from Jason Roberts put Wigan through to the final on away goals.

Arsenal were then knocked out of the FA Cup by Bolton, as an Henry-less side were beaten 1–0 at the Reebok Stadium. The season was rapidly falling apart and things got even worse as West Ham came to Highbury and made off with all three points after winning 3–2. Henry grabbed his 151st league goal for Arsenal to bring it back to 2–1, but two defensive errors from Sol Campbell had given the Gunners a mountain to climb. Bergkamp added a late second after going 3–1 down, but there wasn't time to claim the equaliser Arsenal arguably deserved.

A 2–0 away win at Birmingham was a rare good result as the absence of Kolo Toure was felt deeply in Arsenal's defence. The Ivorian was on African Nations Cup duty along with Eboue and their absence, combined with injuries, left the Gunners very short at the back. However, the young deputies – Mathieu Flamini, Philippe Senderos, Johan Djourou and Sebastian Larsson – did brilliantly to keep Emile Heskey and Chris Sutton at bay, and the two Ivorians would soon be back to strengthen the defence.

Adebayor's Togo had been knocked out of the tournament in the group stages and he opened his goal account for Arsenal when he put them ahead at St Andrew's before

Henry grabbed his 200th for the Gunners to make the game safe. Coincidentally, he had scored his 100th Arsenal goal at the same ground three years previously.

Wenger's side were still miserably inconsistent, though, and they went on to drop two points in a 1–1 draw at home to Bolton before losing 1–0 at Anfield. Despite Henry's pledge to stay, he still hadn't signed a contract and the Barcelona rumours were more frequent than ever. Indeed, he was soon on his way to Spain, but this time only to play for Arsenal.

The north London side had been drawn against Real Madrid for the first knock-out round of the Champions League and nobody gave the Gunners a hope against the *Galacticos*. Wenger, however, was confident that his star pupil would deliver in the big match. 'I have a feeling it will be a good day for Henry,' the Arsenal boss said at a press conference. 'Although it will be a difficult game, the best players rise to the occasion for important matches and he's one of the best players in the world.'

Henry undoubtedly rose to the occasion, as his goal in the forty-seventh minute separated the two teams on the night. Arsenal defended solidly throughout the game, passed the ball fluidly and accurately across a five-man midfield and ran themselves into the ground to completely dominate the middle of the park, but it was Henry's goal that turned a good result into a great result.

Fabregas seized the ball from Ronaldo and fed it to his captain, the Frenchman breezed past a faltering Ronaldo, surged past Guti and left Alvaro Mejia trailing in his wake before holding off Sergio Ramos and slipping the ball beyond Iker Casillas.

After holding on for a memorable win, Henry told the press: 'It's been a long time since you've seen an Arsenal team play like that. We were brilliant defensively and we were not scared to play. And when we are not scared, we can play superb football. And that is what we have been a bit afraid of recently away from home.'

Wenger was understandably delighted with his players. 'I hope the quality our young team has shown tonight will persuade Thierry to stay,' the coach said. 'It is important that the leader stays with these young players and it would be a setback if a player of such importance left. But it should convince him he should stay when these young players perform like that.

'I told you Thierry would produce tonight, but it wasn't just Thierry. There was nobody who didn't have an outstanding game tonight.'

But the tie was far from over and it was just a shame that Henry and his team-mates hadn't added to the 1–0 scoreline. Henry for one was refusing to write off Real.

'It was a great night, but the first thing I would like to say is that we need to keep our feet on the ground and not get carried away with the result,' he said. 'It is a great result to start the game at Highbury, but we need to stay calm. We all know they have a great team and that they can turn things around.'

Arsenal's performance in the Estadio Santiago Bernabeu had impressed the whole footballing world and the Madrid defenders were still in awe of Henry once the dust had settled. 'We did everything to try and stop Henry,' Alvaro Mejia, the defender, revealed in Spanish sports paper *Diaro*

AS. 'We tried to push him, pull him and we tried to kick him, but nothing worked – he was unstoppable. I've never seen anything like it. The only thing Arsenal did was organise themselves at the back and link up with Henry, who is their main man and one of the greats of Europe.

'We tried to stop him by kicking him, but he just came away carrying the ball. First Ronaldo tried to get him, but didn't,' he went on, describing the goal. 'That helped us to unbalance him. Then I tried to tackle him, but he went over the top of me. Guti was next and he tried to take him down, but Henry rode the challenge and kept his feet. He is so strong.'

Strength, skill, pace and deadly finishing put Henry in demand and the Gunners needed to finish in the top four of the Premiership to keep him happy and provide him with a chance of Champions League football the following season. Those aims were disrupted by a 1–0 loss to Blackburn the following weekend, though, as Arsenal's domestic away form continued to disappoint.

However, the Gunners did manage an away win the next Saturday, as Henry scored two to help beat Fulham 4–0 at Craven Cottage. 'We did what we had to,' Henry said at the post-match press conference. 'We put the ball in the net and the most important thing was that we played as a team. Everyone will be watching us against Madrid at Highbury. I hope we can go through, and it's better to prepare with a victory like this, but even if we had lost, we always have the quality to turn things around.'

In the return leg against Real Madrid at Highbury, Arsenal passed the ultimate test of nerve with a display of dogged resilience to keep the *Galacticos* at bay. Jens Lehmann was superb throughout and his flick around the post from Raul's shot while running back towards his goal was particularly impressive. The whole team could be proud of themselves, as the 0–0 in north London sent the Gunners through to the quarter-finals, courtesy of Henry's goal in Madrid. But the captain was keen for everyone to share in the plaudits after a display of real teamwork.

'We didn't concede a goal in two games against Real Madrid, which was a great achievement,' Henry said. 'We know we can do good things, but the most important thing is that, like at Fulham, we defend as a team. It's always good to knock out a great team, but we have to stay focused.

'It is amazing we're through to the quarter-finals again. We have shown great belief and commitment. We can achieve a lot. It was a proper Champions League game, which had everything. It wasn't a boring 0–0 draw. There was so much suspense at the end, but now we know we can do some great stuff.'

The Arsenal players and fans were beginning to believe that they could emulate Liverpool's achievement by winning the Champions League despite a poor showing in domestic football. 'Liverpool, Porto and Monaco have shown that when you play with character and desire you can do some stuff against any team in the world,' Henry said of the competition's recent winners. 'Liverpool showed that to the whole world last season. When Liverpool reached the final against Milan I had some friends who left the house at half-time to get something to eat and came back from the restaurant and saw Steven Gerrard lifting the trophy. When you have desire, commitment and togetherness, you can achieve anything. That's what they showed last year. It was a great example. But we're not there yet.'

Arsenal were still four games away from the final, and they had a long way to go if they were going to finish in the top four of the Premiership. Barely four weeks after a dismal showing at Anfield the Gunners showed how much the win over Madrid had revived the club in the return fixture against the Merseysiders at Highbury. Henry opened the scoring after running onto a superb throughball by Fabregas and only some poor finishing stopped the game from being sewn up by half-time. With quarter of an hour left to play, Luis Garcia equalised to give the visitors hope of a barely deserved point, but then Steven Gerrard's back-pass went straight to Henry, who rounded the 'keeper and restored the lead.

It was a strange sense of déjà vu for Gerrard, who had done a similar thing playing for England against France at Euro 2004. That time David James brought down the French striker and Zidane scored the resulting spot-kick, but both times Gerrard had passed to Henry and the ball had ended up in the back of the net. Henry tried to divert some of the blame from his opponent, but to little avail. 'To do it once every two years isn't too bad considering what he does for Liverpool and how he helps them win,' the Frenchman said. 'He is an amazing player. It [proved to be] the winning goal, but he is a brilliant player, one of the best out there at the moment.'

The win took Arsenal back into fifth place – within two points of Tottenham – and there was even hope of overtaking Liverpool to finish third. The Gunners' league ambitions were given a further boost with a comfortable 3–0 over Charlton, before attention turned once again to Europe and a quarter-final showdown with Patrick Vieira's Juventus. Henry was excited to be facing both his old team – and his old team-mate – and was looking forward to the game. 'I'm sure it will be really strange for him,' Henry said at the pre-match press conference. 'You can imagine when he steps out onto the pitch how the place will go crazy, but he was more than a great servant for this club. It's going to be a special game and I'm sure if he has to put his foot in then he will put his foot in. I spoke to him on Friday after the draw and that [our conversation] will stay between us, but it will be a special game for him.

'People might fancy Juventus because of their history and the fact that they are top of their league and have not lost for a long time, but we've shown that, when you play, it's down to what you do on the night. We respect Juve, but we will see who wants it the most on the night.'

With Fabregas in sparkling form in the Arsenal midfield, the match was billed as a battle between Fabregas and Vieira – the young apprentice against the old master – and on the night it was the Spaniard who took both the plaudits and the spoils. Henry set up Fabregas for the first goal and the teenager returned the favour after the break as Arsenal won 2–0.

The first came after forty minutes, as Pires caught Vieira in possession and passed to Henry, who surged forward and fed Fabregas on the edge of the box. The young Spaniard opened his body feigning to put the ball into the right-hand side of the goal, but then rolled it into the other corner, with Gianluigi Buffon caught flat-footed.

After seventy minutes it was 2–0, as Hleb put Fabregas in on goal with a slide-rule pass, and with Buffon running out to close him down, the eighteen-year-old midfielder laid the ball square for Henry to finish. The ball was a little bit behind the Frenchman, but he finished it as skilfully as you would expect from such a talented player.

The Gunners were worth more than a two-goal advantage after dominating the game from start to finish and Wenger was disappointed that they didn't make more of their superiority on the night.

But at least they wouldn't have to face Vieira in Turin, as the former Gunner picked up a booking that ruled him out of the return leg. Mauro Camoranesi and Jonathan Zebina would also miss the game at the Stadio Delle Alpi as they were both sent off in the closing minutes after losing their composure. For once Henry wasn't the subject of all the post-match questions, as the performance of Fabregas had everyone's tongues wagging. 'Cesc did brilliantly and it was not just Patrick Vieira he was up against,' Henry said. 'There was Emerson, Mutu, Camoranesi – a great team in front of us. We did what we had to and it was vital that we did not concede a goal, but I know how difficult Juventus can still make it for us.'

The manager, though, was confident that his team would complete the victory in Italy. 'My players are not inhibited and I find that a great quality,' Wenger said. 'At the start of the season we needed to readjust. You never lose a tremendous player like Vieira without suffering a bit, but another team was born and we have grown. I believe we can go through now, I believe we will finish the job in Turin.'

Arsenal prepared for the away leg with a simple 5–0 win over a woeful Aston Villa team. Henry scored two as the Gunners made it four wins in a row, extending their new unbeaten run to six games in all competitions and having only conceded one goal in the process. 'I think the team now is right back on track,' Henry said in the *Mirror*. 'Sometimes things are easy, you go out on to the pitch, the game becomes easy and you just know that you will not lose. When everyone is willing to pass the ball, you will do it without even thinking. That's just how it is. It's like breathing – you don't even notice you're doing it. That win at Real Madrid did give us a lot of belief and now everyone is confident.'

Knocking the world's most famous club out of Europe's most prestigious competition had given the Gunners a lift; it had revived the players' confidence in themselves and each other. Playing the kind of football that Wenger's team play, the men involved need to believe that they can win the game. Their one- and two-touch passing requires a lack of fear, because the moment you are afraid to lose, you are more likely to take an extra touch, or hit long balls forward. With Arsenal's pace and quality throughout the side, it is their ability to break from deep at speed that allows them to carve through the opposition seemingly at will. They had demonstrated it to perfection against Villa.

But even with Arsenal coming back into form Henry couldn't say for sure that he would be at the club the following season. 'At the end of the season we are going to have to take a decision,' Henry told *Arsenal.com*, in response to yet another question about his unsigned contract extension. 'It will be done before the World Cup, that's for sure. My main concern right now is to finish in the top four, because it's vital for the club and anything that is going to happen at the club next, and to concentrate on winning the Champions League. That is where my focus is right now.'

Henry's new statement came in brutal contrast to his pledge to stay only a couple of months before and, with the captain's future once again in the balance, it was jubilant news when Arsenal's manager reaffirmed *his* loyalty and dedication to the club. 'If I left I would feel like a deserter – like the guy who walks away from the army once there is a war,' Wenger told the *Evening Standard*. 'I am highly committed to this club. I love what I do here and I love the spirit of the team.'

It was the Arsenal spirit that saw them through in Turin, as Juventus made a much better fist of things in the city that had been Henry's home for seven months. The home side started well, but Arsenal then began to impose themselves on the game. At half-time the Gunners still hadn't found the extra goal to kill off the tie and Juve came out after the break determined to get back into it. Arsenal were forced back increasingly in the second half and it seemed only a matter of time before the 'Old Lady' made a breakthrough. All that changed, however, when Pavel Nedved was shown a second yellow card fifteen minutes from time.

Having lost their deadliest player Juve finally looked beaten and the game finished 0–0 as Arsenal qualified for their first Champions League semi-final, where they would face unfancied Spanish side Villareal.

Following the midweek exertions, Henry started on the

bench for Arsenal's trip to Old Trafford. The Gunners started brightly, but failed to take advantage of their early chances and, as the game wore on, Manchester United took control of the game, eventually winning 2–0, despite Henry's introduction as sub in the seventieth minute.

Wenger refused to accept that the game was lost the moment he had named Henry among the substitutes. 'Thierry had not recovered from Wednesday,' said the Arsenal manager. 'He has played more games than the other players and he has just played on his own up front against Juventus twice. But we did not concede the first goal because he was on the bench. Manchester United won the game because, overall, they were sharper than us.

'Thierry will be back on Wednesday,' Wenger went on, looking forward to the match against Portsmouth. 'You know the problem with Thierry. If you lose the game and don't play him then it's the wrong decision, but what if he'd played, we'd lost and he'd picked up an injury? That would've been the wrong decision, too. Whenever you lose a game you are wrong. I just felt he needed the breather.'

After his rest Henry returned recuperated for the game at Fratton Park but, with plenty of other players missing through injury, Arsenal could only draw 1–1 with the relegation battlers, despite Henry's exquisite opener. After dropping five points in two games, Arsenal's race for fourth place was looking increasingly tricky.

They helped their cause with a 3–1 win over West Bromwich Albion in what was christened 'Dennis Bergkamp Day' at Highbury. In homage to the Dutchman's eleven years at Arsenal, thousands of fans had come to the ground dressed in orange and the former Ajax and Inter Milan striker did not disappoint. Bergkamp created the second goal for Pires and scored the third himself, curling it home from outside the area in what can best be described as 'Bergkamp fashion'.

'It was a typical Dennis Bergkamp goal and what an end to the game,' said Henry, eulogising his long-time strike partner. 'I have always said Dennis Bergkamp will remain the best partner I have ever had. He is a dream for a striker. He is not greedy – you saw that on the second goal. He could have just gone for glory because it was Dennis Bergkamp Day – but no. He dummied the goalkeeper and cut the ball back for Robert Pires, who put it in the back of the net. If you are in the game, on the bench or watching on TV and you want to learn, then just watch Dennis Bergkamp, with the way he can kill a team with one pass. He is just amazing. He will sometimes do things out of nowhere.'

Bergkamp's chances to impress were growing few and far between, however, as his age and a change in formation limited his appearances. Adebayor and van Persie had both seemingly climbed above the Dutch master in the pecking order and Henry continued to plough a lone furrow up front in European matches.

In front of the five-man midfield and the increasingly assured back four, the Arsenal captain took the game to Villareal at Highbury in the Champions League semi-final first leg. After keeping a record-breaking eight consecutive clean sheets in Europe, the back four of Eboue, Toure, Senderos and Flamini had received plenty of praise, but many claimed that Arsenal were just Henry plus ten others.

Manuel Pellegrini was not one of them. 'I would not define Arsenal as just Thierry Henry and a good defence,' the Villareal coach said. 'They deserve to be here and have eliminated good teams like Real Madrid and Juventus. There are many coaches who try and stop Henry – but that is why he is Henry, he can invent amazing things on the pitch.'

Heading into a European match as favourites for the first time since the group stages, Arsenal failed to perform as brilliantly as they had done against Real Madrid and Juventus, but still managed to secure a 1–0 win thanks to Toure's first-half goal in the last ever European game at Highbury. Arsenal were lucky not to concede a penalty when Gilberto brought down Jose Mari, but they also had one Henry goal wrongly disallowed for off side and deserved the win overall. With a solitary goal in it, the tie was on a knife-edge as Arsenal headed into a week that could make or break their season. Before the return leg in six days, they faced a vital north London derby.

After having spent another tough ninety minutes alone up front, Henry would again be on the bench for the game against Tottenham. He knew that with so much resting on the result, it would be the biggest derby for years. 'It will be war at Highbury,' Henry said in *L'Equipe*. 'An Arsenal v Tottenham match is a London derby; it's traditionally one of the more important games of the season. This time, the match will be even more important. Fourth place and qualification for next season's Champions League are at stake. We must win.'

Arsenal went 1–0 down soon after Henry entered the fray and his sublime goal helped level the scores, but there were no further goals and the game finished 1–1. There was controversy about the Tottenham goal, as they had played on while two Arsenal players were down injured. The Frenchman's strike, however, was a thing of beauty that deserved to win any game. The pass came into the area from Adebayor and as Henry ghosted into the box his first touch brought the ball down and before it could reach the ground he flicked it past the onrushing Paul Robinson and into the back of the net. His goal once again underlined both his ability and importance to the team but, more significantly, it kept alive the Gunners' slim hopes of a fourth-place finish.

Four points behind Martin Jol's side with three games left to play, including a game in hand, Arsenal had to win all three and hope that their rivals dropped points. But even with their chances of qualifying for the next season's Champions League diminishing, there were many reasons to be confident about the future as the young Guns continued to impress. 'They can be as good as they believe they can be and as good as they want to be,' Henry told the *Sunday Mirror*. 'Being young and confident is better than being old with experience.

'I can tell you when you start to get older you think a bit more and then sometimes you think too much about things. Before we were talking about them not being ready because they had this block in their mind, but once you pass it when you're young, you will only play well. When you are young, you are not scared of anything. It's only when you grow up you realise that if you do something wrong it may come back at you. You realise if you miss a penalty you're dead! But not when you are young.

'I am only twenty-eight, but I feel my age around some of them. There is such a big gap between us; it's amazing. Sometimes I speak to them about the World Cup in 1986 and they just look at me completely clueless. So I ask them when were they born and they tell me 1986.'

Eboue, van Persie and Reyes were all born in 1983 and Senderos, Fabregas, Flamini, Diaby, Clichy and Adebayor are even younger, but they continued to impress Henry and everyone else who watched them play, and they secured their place in the Champions League final with a 0–0 stalemate in the return leg against Villareal. It was possibly Arsenal's least convincing European performance of the season, as they failed to impose themselves on the game due to an over-cautious approach.

It was not the manager's intention to sit back, but the midfield seemed reluctant to support Henry in any real numbers and possession was surrendered far too easily throughout the match. Despite their inhibited display the Gunners still got through, though, with much credit going to Lehmann as he saved a last-minute penalty from Juan Roman Riquelme, after Jose Mari had collapsed in the area after appearing to be barely touched by Clichy. 'Today was about desire and commitment,' Henry told *ITV*. 'You didn't see much of me up front, but we worked hard.'

The manager also praised his team's hard work. 'We didn't manage to play tonight and I don't really know why,' Wenger said to *ITV*. 'We never came into our fluent game, but you need a bit of luck and resilience and we had both tonight and I'm very proud of the character in that young team and of the more experienced players.'

Lehmann's experience was vital in goal, and his spot-kick save was incredible. It didn't, however, owe anything to his skipper's advice. 'I know that when Riquelme's under pressure he always likes to shoot down the middle,' Henry revealed to *Sky Sports*. 'So I told Jens that when the penalty is important he likes to put it down the middle. What I wanted to do was to put a little bit of doubt in his [Riquelme's] mind. When he saw me going to speak to Jens I wanted him to maybe think about changing his mind. I've seen him a couple of times in the Champions League and even in la Liga taking a penalty right in the middle. But, fortunately for us, Jens didn't listen to me and Riquelme changed his mind.

'To be honest, at that time I thought he was going to save it. I don't know if I was dreaming or if I was thinking it, but that was in my mind. On the other side, Jens now has a great reputation for saving penalties. The first year that he was here he saved from Ruud van Nistelrooy in the Community Shield, and he's saved some others in the league. But that was definitely the moment to save one.'

With the other semi-final yet to be completed, Arsenal knew they would face either AC Milan or Barcelona in Paris. Henry wasn't bothered who the opposition would be, he just wanted to win. 'Milan and Barcelona for me are two great teams,' he continued. 'Milan have won more Champions League titles, but whoever goes through will be favourites.

'But it doesn't matter for me who it is. It will be a difficult game. Because we knocked out Real Madrid and Juventus, some people probably thought yesterday's game against Villareal would be an easy game. But yesterday it showed that even if your name doesn't ring a great bell in the history of football, you can still make it a difficult game for your opponents, so you never know what's going to happen. I don't have a choice, but whichever team is in the final it will be a difficult game. It will be amazing to lead the team out in Paris, where I'm from, but it would be even more amazing to leave the stadium with the trophy.'

Days later, Henry's impressive season got even better as he was named FWA Footballer of the Year for an unprecedented third time. Sir Stanley Matthews, Kenny Dalglish, John Barnes and Gary Lineker had all won the award twice, but Henry was the first man in the fifty-nine-year history of the award to claim a hat-trick, and it showed the extent to which the Frenchman is respected and appreciated by the nation's press. 'As I always say, in football it's all about the team and, without my team-mates, I would not have won this award,' Henry said in his acceptance speech.

'What I'm especially proud of, though, is that I'm the first person to win the Footballer of the Year trophy three times. It's always pleasing to be the first to achieve something – it's a little piece of history. My hope now is that the team go on to create our own piece of history by becoming the first ever Arsenal side to win the Champions League. I would just like to thank all the FWA members who voted for me. It's a real honour and I feel privileged to have won.'

Having claimed a place in the final, taking place ten days after the last Premiership match, Henry and his team-mates could focus on qualifying for the next season's competition. The Gunners knew that if they finished fifth in the league and then won the final they would still qualify to defend their title, but Arsenal wanted to finish fourth to take some of the pressure off the outcome of the final and to ensure that the ten-year run of finishing above their north London neighbours continued.

Arsenal did their utmost, securing back-to-back away wins, beating Sunderland 3–0 – with Henry grabbing the third – and Manchester City 3–1 to go into the last day of the season one point behind Tottenham. In an emotional last ever game at Highbury, the Gunners had the chance to reclaim fourth spot from their north London rivals and secure a place in the Champions League to ensure that the stadium closed on a high. 'Our final game will be against Wigan, but I have to say I don't even want to turn up for that day,' Henry revealed earlier in the season to the *News of the World*. 'I don't want to be there when we all have to accept it will be the last game at Highbury – that's why I want to have memories of a great Champions League night instead.

'We have the chance to create an everlasting memory by going on in this tournament,' which fortunately they did. 'I don't want to remember it for 'Black Sunday', the date of that final match. After that day, I will never be able to return and feel the shivers I get when I run out on to the pitch. It's going to be tough to get used to not hearing the name we are used to. I can't imagine it will be as good saying the Emirates Stadium at Ashburton Grove.

'We will all miss Highbury, that's for sure. It's sad, too, to think that I will never be able to come back and see it again and feel the sensations for one more time. The place will be gone and that means things will never be like they were. I think we're all just going to have to get used to it.'

Henry gave Highbury the perfect send-off though, as his hat-trick brought Arsenal back from 2–1 down to win 4–2 and, with Tottenham losing 2–1 at Upton Park, the Gunners finished fourth. It was fitting that Arsenal's greatest ever goal-scorer should claim the last three goals to be scored in competitive games at the famous old ground. His third goal was a penalty and, after sending the ball home, Henry got down on his knees and kissed the turf in a farewell salute to the place he had described as 'his garden'.

'That was the perfect send-off,' Henry said after the game. 'We are fourth in the league and the table does not lie after thirty-eight games, so we deserve to be in this position. We've missed so many players this season and we did it the hard way. It's not normally what we do, finishing fourth, but we will take that this season. However, we still have to play qualifying games, so we are not quite in the Champions League yet.'

The striker went on to say. 'When I kissed the ground after my third, I was saying goodbye to this stadium.'

After the game there was a closing ceremony and Henry stayed out on the pitch until the very end, along with Ashley Cole and Robert Pires, both of whose futures were also in doubt, and the speculation continued as to whether they were simply soaking up the last seconds in a stadium that had become like a second home to them, or if they were enjoying their last moments at the club.

Henry, though, spoke passionately about Arsenal after snatching fourth spot from Tottenham, who had a number of players struck down by illness on the day of the game. 'I know there is going to be a lot of talk about who deserved it or not,' the twenty-eight-year-old told *Arsenal.com*. 'At the end of the day, the table does not lie. I heard they [Tottenham] had people with food poisoning, but the only thing I can say is did anyone bother when we had nine players out? No. They were saying, "Arsenal are not playing well," "Arsenal are not the team they used to be."

'But that is how it is in the game – sometimes you do have people who are ill, or turn up with a headache and are not on the team sheet. That is the way it is. Nobody had any sympathy for us when Ashley was missing, when Sol was missing – we had to deal with it and play.

'You have to give the lads credit for what they have turned around. I heard so many people saying: "What a shame, if they win the Champions League, then maybe Tottenham can appeal." I was always saying to myself at home: "But they are not fourth yet. The league has not finished. They do not need to change anything because Tottenham are not there." I said to the lads you only sing at the end – and we were singing at the end today.'

But ever the professional, Henry revealed that his celebrations at finishing fourth were over. 'Party? No. I'm going to go home, to chill – and now I'm definitely starting to think about the Champions League final.'

Everybody was looking forward to the biggest spectacle of the club season that would be contested by the two best footballing sides in Europe. Arsenal against Barcelona in Henry's home town, the club where he had grown into a world-class star and possibly the club of his future meeting a matter of miles from where he grew up. 'We are all proud, of course I am proud to have finally reached the Champions

League final with Arsenal for the first time in their history, and for me to lead the team out in Paris will be a special moment,' Henry said.

But it was all about winning for the Frenchman. He wasn't travelling for the experience or to enjoy it – he was only going for the cup. 'There is a difference between being happy and satisfied,' Henry told *Arsenal.com*. 'If we win the cup I will be happy, but when you are satisfied you relax, and I want to carry on. I keep my trophies but no, I don't cherish them. What I cherish is the respect of the game, just to play football. You can never reach perfection and I am trying to do it, that's the only way you can try to get better. We know that in the game nobody is perfect, we know everybody will miss something, so trying to reach perfection will keep you on your toes. I'm trying to do that.'

And the manager hoped his star would be close to perfection at the Stade de France. 'Of course, the big players like him and Ronaldinho or Eto'o will be under pressure to perform,' Wenger said. 'What happens in this sort of game is that people will always compare, but I do not want too much pressure on Thierry. If we play well as a team, which I'm convinced we will, Thierry will automatically be very good. If we do not play well as a team, Thierry will suffer – and we have seen that against Villarreal away from home, where the team refused to play and where we suffered offensively. So my main concern is that the team plays its game, then I am not worried about Thierry.'

But Barcelona captain Carles Puyol was concerned with Henry, and also with some of his own countrymen. 'We cannot simply obsess on Henry because, although everyone talks about him, Arsenal have other great quality players,' the Spaniard said. 'Cesc Fabregas or Jose Antonio Reyes can turn around the game. We have to work defensively as a team to make sure we stop Henry and the rest of them.'

Puyol was right to be wary, but Barcelona got lucky in Paris and it was he and not Henry who held aloft the massive trophy after the game. Lehmann was sent off after eighteen minutes for bringing down Samuel Eto'o and, although it was a clear prevention of a goal-scoring chance, Ludovic Giuly rolled the ball into the net after the foul. The referee, Terje Hauge, could have allowed Giuly's goal to stand and merely booked Lehmann, but the German 'keeper was shown the red card and Arsenal would have to play the remainder of the game with ten men.

The Gunners had started the game at breakneck speed and after a ten-day rest they looked sharp and hungry for the win. If they had continued in that form, they would surely have had a good chance of overcoming Giuly's goal with eleven men, but the Norwegian referee's decision robbed football of what could surely have been one of the all-time great finals.

Henry had two chances to open the scoring in the first three minutes. With two-and-a-half minutes on the clock, the French striker controlled Eboue's cross brilliantly to get away from his marker Rafael Marquez, but the ball didn't drop quickly enough for Henry and Victor Valdes had time to rush out and block his attempt.

From the ensuing corner, the Arsenal captain exchanged passes with Fabregas before unleashing a venomous shot from the corner of the box, but he was again denied by

Valdes. After the sending-off, Wenger removed Pires to bring on the replacement goalkeeper and, without the five-man midfield, which had looked so commanding throughout the European campaign and in the opening exchanges of the final, Arsenal lost control of the game. Barcelona started to exert some pressure, but it was the English side that took the lead.

Eboue drove once more into the opposition half and, although he fell somewhat theatrically under Puyol's challenge, he managed to win a free-kick on the right-hand side of the area. Henry curled a delightful cross in and Campbell met the ball with a thumping header to put Arsenal ahead. The Gunners held on until half-time, thanks to a great save by Manuel Almunia, who turned Eto'o's shot onto the post late in the half.

The second forty-five minutes continued the same way, as Arsenal were starved of possession and relied on individual forays into the Barça half to relieve the pressure. Henry made countless runs forward with or without the ball and, in the sixty-ninth minute, he had a chance to win the game. Hleb picked him out with a wonderful throughball in the inside-right channel, and Arsenal's No. 14 raced away from Marquez, but then failed to beat the 'keeper, as he shot too close to Valdes. After the match, he revealed that, because he had done so much running, he was just too tired to finish as he normally would. It was disappointing, but to be expected.

Unfortunately one goal was unlikely to be enough to beat Barcelona and, in the seventy-sixth minute, they were level. Substitute Henrik Larsson laid off Andres Iniesta's throughball to Eto'o and the Cameroon striker beat Almunia at the near post. There was debate as to whether Eto'o was marginally offside, but the goal was allowed to stand; it brought Arsenal to their knees. Worse was to follow four minutes later as another fine pass from Larsson put Juliano Belletti in on goal and he shot through Almunia's legs to make it 2–1.

Barcelona played plenty of keep-ball in the last ten minutes and held on to win the European Cup. Speaking immediately after the game, with the pain of defeat still burning, Henry was nowhere near his usually magnanimous self. 'We haven't got anything out of the final, despite all our hard work,' Henry told *BBC Sport*. 'I was kicked all over the place. I expected the referee to do his job. I don't think he did. I'm not usually a troublemaker, but I've just seen the television replay and Eto'o's goal was offside.

'It was always going to be difficult to play Barcelona. But with ten men that is almost impossible. Jens probably deserved to be sent off – there is nothing to be said about that. But in the first half, Rafael Marquez and Carles Puyol went right through me and they didn't even get a yellow. Then I got the ball in front of the bench and Mark van Bommel kicks me and I end up getting a yellow.'

There were many decisions the referee made which left Henry fuming, but none more so than allowing the equaliser to stand. 'When you see Eto'o is offside it kills you,' he went on. 'It kills you because you've been defending and running. I was dead after an hour. I was trying to do some stuff when Alex Hleb gave me that amazing ball. I tried to go as far as I could and hit the ball, but I just couldn't. It's just sad. You can lose, but to lose like that. I tried to do what I could and try and defend and try and bring the ball back and help the team, but if they allow an offside goal it is going to be even more difficult.'

After all the pre-match hype about Henry and Ronaldinho, the Frenchman was keen to praise the player who had made the biggest impact on the night, Swedish striker Larsson. 'Everyone was talking about Ronaldinho before the game,' Henry added. 'I didn't see him today and I didn't see Eto'o. Henrik Larsson made the difference by setting up two goals. That was the key. We can be proud, we can be more than proud, but, I'm sorry, some of the refereeing today was horrendous.'

Despite the defeat, Henry was right to be proud of his team, and himself. After another long season, he had scored thirty-three goals in all competitions, twenty-seven of which came in the Premiership, to add yet another Golden Boot to his collection. It was the third consecutive season he had finished as top scorer in England and the fourth in five years. He was also named Barclays Premiership Player of the Season.

The goals and the awards helped acknowledge the fact that Henry had long since become a world-class striker who was able to play for any club he wanted and, before the start of the World Cup, he ended months of speculation by announcing that that club was Arsenal.

Chapter fourteen
Arsenal for Ever

'What I've seen over past few months was enough to make me believe there's a lot of potential here,' he told the press. 'It was not about the economic question – it was not about money. People want to give you a label as a footballer where it's all money, money, money, but there's love, there's emotion, real emotion, real love. It's not always about money, whether you stay or leave. For me it was my family, my love for the club and this passion in England that I don't think I'll find elsewhere.'

Thierry Henry was staying at Arsenal. Just two days after the Champions League final he signed a new four-year extension to his contract and finally put an end to twelve months of speculation. The striker had long been the subject of Barcelona's attention and his position at Highbury had been questioned, with good reason.

Massive changes were afoot at Arsenal. As well as saying

goodbye to Highbury, the Gunners had seen the last of Dennis Bergkamp after ten fine years of service. And Henry wasn't the only one of Wenger's players whose future was in doubt. Speculation was rife regarding Robert Pires, while Ashley Cole, Sol Campbell and Lauren appeared to have lost their status as first-team regulars – the core of the team that Henry had helped to two titles was suddenly a thing of the past.

Where once the Arsenal team had been built on the 'Four Musketeers' of Henry, Pires, Patrick Vieira and Sylvain Wiltord, now there was only Henry. And whether his friendship with those players had made his time at Arsenal more enjoyable or not is pure conjecture, but in their prime they had made up the spine of the finest team in England. In 2005–06, however, the Gunners had been fortunate to finish fourth.

Wenger had recruited many talented young players in Cesc Fabregas, Mathieu Flamini, Philippe Senderos, Emmanuel Eboue, Gael Clichy, Robin van Persie, Jose Antonio Reyes and Theo Walcott – making Arsenal's Ashburton Grove future very bright, but for a man so determined to leave his mark on football's history, Henry knows that players are remembered by their trophies.

Even with Wenger's shrewd eye for young stars, coupled with the increased revenue of a 60,000-seater stadium, how can any team realistically hope to challenge a Chelsea team bankrolled at a £200m-a-year loss by one of the world's richest men. Not content with successive Premiership titles, Roman Abramovich has okayed the reputed £130k-a-week wage bill of Germany captain

Michael Ballack, and that capture was reinforced by the £30m-plus signing of former FIFA World Player of the Year Andriy Shevchenko from AC Milan.

One of Henry's international team-mates has even grown weary of the almost-guaranteed success at Stamford Bridge. William Gallas handed in a written transfer request as he sought fresh challenges but, unsurprisingly, the Chelsea hierarchy were unwilling to listen to offers for one of football's finest defenders. Didier Drogba was also reported to be unhappy and seeking pastures new and, for competition's sake, it had to be hoped that squad disharmony would undermine Chelsea's attempts to make it three Premier League titles in a row.

In the face of such powerful opposition, Henry had to believe within himself that this new Arsenal team was capable of challenging Chelski before he could put pen to paper and stay at the club he so often said he loves.

Fortunately for Arsenal and the Premiership, he was given that belief by his team's performance against Barcelona in the Stade de France. 'I won't lie, I thought about it,' Henry said about the possibility of moving on. 'When this kind of team [Barcelona] wants you, you have to think about it, but my heart belongs here. The team showed me on Wednesday that we would have done anything to beat Barcelona. They can be so proud about what they did and they reassured me in that performance how much they wanted it.

'With me in the team I'm even more confident we can win things. I go back to what the team has achieved over the past few months. The form they've shown recently is amazing, and I just wait to see what, with a little bit more experience, they can do. I was thinking if I do leave also, it would be more difficult for them to shine.

'This is my last contract. This is where I belong. It's where my heart is. That's what I was thinking about as it's my last big contract. It was about going somewhere or staying here, and you know the answer.'

It was fantastic news for the club and Wenger summed it up when he described Henry's decision as even more important than winning the European Cup. 'My target at the start of the week was to put everything right – to win the Champions League and keep Thierry,' the Arsenal manager, said. 'I managed only one, but for the future, it's certainly the best one.

'If we wanted to continue the progression, I knew we would rely on Thierry's decision. You cannot say this team will go much higher up when you lose your best player. For the progression of the team, it was vital to get this response. We would have had to cope with any decision, but it's an insurance for the future of the team. I was confident that, in the end, if the side showed they could compete with the best teams in Europe, he would stay.'

The Arsenal chairman David Dein was also delighted and described how valuable Henry when it comes to attracting new players to the club. 'When we signed Walcott, Diaby and Adebayor, the first question they asked us was: "Will we be training with Thierry?"' Dein said. 'So Thierry staying has a fantastic influence when it comes to signing players, and it shows our ambition. He has given the fans such excitement, such entertainment, and is an iconic figure. This is a momentous occasion, because we have kept Thierry Henry at Arsenal.'

The joy was not restricted to Arsenal, though, as the French striker has reached the stage where his talent has transcended club rivalries. The whole of the Premiership was delighted by Henry's decision to stay, and it was that kind of appreciation that helped keep him at Arsenal. He undoubtedly had the talent to ply his wonderful trade anywhere in the world, but it is hard to think of a league where he would have been more revered, especially in such a non-invasive way.

By remaining at Arsenal and leading them into the new era at Ashburton Grove, Henry will be able to add plenty more goals to his record of 214. But there are still some records that are likely to remain out of reach for the Frenchman. With only thirty-eight league games in a season, it would take something ethereal to beat Ted Drake's record of forty-two league goals in a season, but the overall season record of forty-four, which Drake got in that same 1934–45 season, could theoretically be attainable, if Arsenal were drawn against some minnows in Europe.

Cliff Bastin's record of twenty-six FA Cup goals remains a long way from Henry's total of six, and with his record of only three League Cup appearances in seven years, it would take a change in policy and some incredible performances for him to take his total of two League Cup goals past Ian Wright's record of twenty-nine. Far more achievable is the French goal-scoring record and, in the coming years, Henry can be expected to run David Trezeguet close in the chase for Michel Platini's forty-one goals.

The Arsenal striker has scored thirty-one from seventy-six games, while his former Clairefontaine team-mate has scored the same number of goals from just sixty games. Trezeguet has been more prolific for *les Bleus*, but Henry is higher up the pecking order and should break the record some time in 2007, injuries permitting.

After his record-chasing, title-winning, goal-scoring, crowd-pleasing playing days are over, Henry intends to remain in football, but in an as-yet-undecided capacity. Henry was named as FIFA Ambassador Against Racism in January 2005 and, at the time, he revealed his thoughts on the future. 'I don't believe there can be a future for me without football. I want to stay in this world,' he told Italian paper *Gazzetta Dello Sport*. 'I love this sport too much, even if I don't know yet what sort of role I will take up. Perhaps it will be as a FIFA ambassador against racism. I've just taken on that responsibility and I would love it if the problem of racism in stadiums ended before my career as a player, but I fear there will still be many years of work to do.'

Everyone at Arsenal hoped they would see him in the red and white shirt for many more years, and his manager believes there's still room for improvement. 'I think every team that plays against us is worried about him,' the Highbury headmaster said. 'He is physically extremely strong and recovers so well. Heading is certainly the main area where he can improve, as he can jump to the sky if he wants. It's just a decision that he has to make – do I want to be strong heading the ball?

'Once he has made that decision, he will achieve it, as he has the technique to do it. He's already frightening without it. With it, he will be even more so,' Wenger continued. 'What is important for Thierry is to keep improving, to try to have the right attitude and to keep humble. He plays in a great team; he knows that and his partners fight for him as well. That helps him to improve. He learned a lot from playing next to Dennis Bergkamp. He knows that and he will still improve.'

If Henry continues to improve, he will surely be voted FIFA World Player of the Year sometime soon, and Wenger thinks it would be good for many people to see Henry at the top of the tree. 'I would like him to become a real star because that would be an inspiration for the youth as well because there have been people in football who were not an inspiration for kids.' Wenger said. 'It is good that Zidane and Henry have become stars, because the lives they lead are good examples.'

When asked by GQ magazine about his heading ability, or supposed lack thereof, Henry replied by borrowing a joke from his Spanish team-mate, Jose Antonio Reyes. 'We were in training recently when the ball came across for a header and Jose did a bad volley instead. Someone said to him, "You should have used your head." And he replied, "The head is for thinking."'

The Frenchman certainly doesn't get much chance to practise his heading in matches, as the majority of Arsenal crosses come along the ground, and he takes most of the set pieces, so he never has the chance to get on the end of any of those, but if Arsenal were to change their gameplan and started to whip in old school crosses for a target man, Henry would no doubt be able to bring his heading up to speed pretty quickly, such is his versatility, ability and the gallant Frenchman's desire to work for his team.

'Some strikers like to stay in the box. Some always try to get the ball and play it back. I always turn and go, bending my run to bring danger to the other team.' Henry said to the *Daily Telegraph*. 'Sometimes I can be a pain because I play too quick and make mistakes. I am aware of defenders dropping deeper more against me.' Rightly wary of his explosive pace off the mark, it has become tantamount to football suicide to try and defend a high line against Henry and his team-mates.

Not all defenders drop deep against Henry now, though. Some just go straight through him, but it doesn't concern the striker now that he's a battle-hardened Premiership campaigner. 'If someone kicks me now, I don't stay down to get them booked.' Henry says. 'I stand up and get on with it, if I see that the guy has tried to play the ball. It is upsetting when the guy forgets about the ball and just comes through me. That happens a lot, a lot. But not just in English football. It happened when I was playing in my neighbourhood in Paris.'

Outside of the French capital, there are a few more law-abiding stoppers. 'Defenders at the top English clubs are tough, but not necessarily dirty. There is a respect.' Henry tells us. 'A player will come in for a fifty-fifty ball fairly; he will not put his foot over the ball. He will go in hard, use his arms and elbows, but not to hurt me, just to let me feel he is there.' By scoring and creating so many goals since his arrival in England, Henry could be sure that defenders would always know where he was.

'Coming to Arsenal is the best thing I've ever done. I am delighted to pledge my future to this great club.' Henry said.

'It is not a case of taking the money and just sticking around at Highbury. I want to do well for this club, both domestically and in Europe. I have enjoyed some good years at Arsenal and I want to give something back.'

Away from football, Henry leads the life of a model professional; he doesn't touch alcohol and shies away from the celebrity openings and screenings that seem to lure so many other high-profile sportsmen and women. He and Claire/Nicole 'lead a simple life, it is the way we are'. And Henry endeavours to save his energy as much as possible for the place where it does the most damage: the football pitch. Henry likes movies, hanging out with his friends and watching sport on TV.

'The only thing I won't watch is darts,' he told *GQ*. 'And I don't watch cricket. How can you like a game that requires you to take four days off work to follow a Test? And I don't really like golf. I know a lot of English footballers play, but I know that if I go with the club to play, sooner or later, I will end up trying to smash the ball with my foot.'

Henry also likes to dress well. 'Well, a little fashion doesn't hurt anyone. I don't really talk to other players about clothes, but we do have a laugh in the dressing room if someone turns up in something strange.' Surely not a dig at footballer/model Freddie Ljungberg? 'No, no, no. It can be me sometimes and the lads let you know when you are wearing something funny. I wore some army trousers once and, as soon as I walked in, they were rolling around the floor and making machine-gun noises. But that shows good team spirit.'

The easiest way to make Henry happy is to give him a ball

to play with. 'I always have a football handy at home and I'll play with it.' Henry says. 'Sometimes it'll get on my wife's nerves, but the moment I've got a ball at my feet, I'm happy'

There's plenty of room to kick a football around inside the Henry's home, a £6m house in Hampstead. A lot of his team-mates live locally and Henry is very happy with the leafy suburb. 'I like it here; it's like a village in the middle of the city. I go to the cinema or out for a meal. I feel at home.'

And it seems a nice place to bring up a family, as the elegant striker shared his thoughts on fatherhood with *Father's Quarterly* magazine. 'Nothing can compare,' Henry told *FQ*. 'I've won stuff in my life, but nothing can beat that. It's on another level. I just couldn't speak. I was speechless. We did that. That's us. Just looking at her.'

The couple had chosen the name 'Tea' for its uniqueness but realised that people would inevitably mispronounce it. 'We liked it because it was original, but I know people will call her "Tea",' he said, before outlining his ambitions as a father. 'Arsène is a great human being who is always willing to listen. That is something I'd like to offer Tea. She will get chances in life that I didn't have, but I'll make sure she knows you need to work hard to get what you want.'

Fatherhood hadn't changed Henry as he was already a very settled man and had long since given up partying. 'I got bored of clubbing when I was about twenty-one,' he went on, before talking about his relationship with other dads in the Arsenal team. 'We talk in the changing-room. Lauren's daughter is slightly older, so we talk about the stages they go through. He asks what Tea's doing and might give me some advice or tell me what to expect next. I need my sleep like everyone, but when you know it's for a good cause it's OK. I turn up to training feeling sleepy, but by eleven I'm OK.'

The interrupted sleep failed to affect Henry's performances on the pitch, but with significantly more injuries in the last two seasons, maybe his wife's pregnancy and the ensuing parenthood had a detrimental affect on his recovery time.

Someone who would have been very happy at Tea's birth would have been Henry's mother, Maryse, the only person in the world Arsenal's star striker is scared of. 'I don't have doubt on the pitch and when I play I have no fear of anybody or anything. There's nothing I'm scared of in football. The only thing I'm scared of is my mum.

'Anybody can be the tough guy on the streets or wherever, but when you go home you know who the queen is, and that's your mum. It doesn't matter what I do, she's my mum.'

It's nice to know there is someone out there who can control Thierry Henry and that he has his feet firmly on the ground. He may or may not be the best footballer on the planet, but one thing is certain: he will be doing his best over the next few years to make the most of his God-given abilities and score as many goals as possible. Defenders, beware...

Chronology

1977: born 17 August, Paris.

1990: joins the French National Football Institute at Clairefontaine, aged thirteen.

1994: 31 August – makes his First Division debut against Nice, two weeks after his seventeenth birthday. Monaco lost 2–0, under then manager Arsène Wenger.

1995: 29 April – scores first professional goals, grabbing a brace in Monaco's 6–0 victory over RC Lens.
12 September – European debut. Comes on as a substitute for the last twenty minutes of UEFA Cup tie at home to Leeds United, also his first taste of English football, Monaco lose 3–0.

1996: June – captains France to glory at the UEFA European Under-18 Championship in France, scoring the only goal in the final.

31 August – makes his first appearance for France U-21, in a 1–1 draw with Norway.

15 October – scores first European goal, in Monaco's 4–2 win against Borussia Monchengladbach in Germany.

12 December – signs pre-contract with Real Madrid, who approach player through agent not registered with FIFA. The world football body fines both the player and the Spanish club, and cancels their agreement.

December – voted French Young Player of the Year by *France Football* magazine.

1997: 13 January – signs first professional contract with Monaco on 13 January.

3 May – Monaco win French league championship.

May – is named player of the tournament as he captains the France Under-21 squad to victory at the Toulon tournament.

June – reaches quarter-finals of World Youth Championship with France in Malaysia.

1 October – Champions League debut. Henry masterminds a 4–0 win over Bayer Leverkusen in Monaco scoring two and creating the others.

11 October – wins first French cap in World Cup warm-up match against South Africa, played in le Stade Felix Bollaert, Lens.

1998: 18 March – part of the Monaco team that knocks Manchester United out of the European Cup at the quarter-final stage. Henry scores six goals to help Monaco ultimately reach the semi-finals.

June/July – plays in six of France's seven games in the World Cup finals, remaining on the bench for the 3–0 victory over Brazil in the final. He finishes as his country's leading goal-scorer with three first-round goals, including his first for France.

1999: 18 January – signs for Italian giants Juventus, for £12m.

17 April – he scores first goals in Serie A, claiming two in 3–1 win against league leaders SS Lazio.

3 August – two weeks before his twenty-second birthday he signs for Arsenal for £10.5m.

9 September – having been converted from a winger to a striker, he nets his first Arsenal goal after coming on as substitute in away victory at Southampton.

8 November – watches Ian Wright's runs, as the Arsenal legend plays in Lee Dixon's Testimonial.

2000: 23 March – controversially sent off in UEFA Cup quarter-final second leg, away to Werder Bremen.

17 May – Arsenal lose the UEFA Cup final to Galatasaray 0–0 (aet), 4–1 on penalties. Henry finishes his first season at Highbury as top scorer having scored seventeen Premiership goals in thirty-one appearances, twenty-six goals all competitions.

June/July – his country's top marksman as he scores three

times in five games in French Euro 2000 success, including the opener in semi-final clash with Portugal. Was named by the UEFA technical committee in the sixteen-man All-Star Team of the tournament.

December – named French Footballer of the year by *France Football* magazine.

26 December – scores first professional hat-trick in Arsenal's 6–1 Boxing Day demolition of Leicester.

2001: May – ends season with twenty-two goals – three behind Golden Boot winner Jimmy Floyd Hasselbaink.

June – misses France's Confederations Cup win in Japan and South Korea through injury.

19 September – sets new European goal-scoring record for Arsenal, grabbing a pair against Schalke 04 in the Champions League.

5 December – burgled, a robber makes off with £25,000 worth of jewellery and leather coats.

2002: 11 January – charged by FA for improper conduct towards referee Graham Poll following the Gunners' Premiership game against Newcastle on 18 December.

6 March – receives a three-game ban from the FA after being found guilty of improper conduct.

May – finishes the season with thirty-two goals, and the Premier League Golden Boot as Arsenal win the Premiership and FA Cup Double.

May – chosen as the new face of Renault Clio.

6 June – sent off for a dangerous tackle against Uruguay during France's disastrous World Cup campaign. Is forced

to watch from the stands as his country fails to get through to the knock-out stages.

10 September – after scoring against Manchester City, he lifts his shirt to reveal a message in honour of his friend Sharleen Spiteri's (lead singer of pop group Texas) new baby girl.

1 October – signs new five-year contract with Nike, reportedly worth £9m.

27 November – scores first European hat-trick as Arsenal beat AS Roma 3–1 in Italy in Champions League.

2003: 12 January – scores his 100th goal for Arsenal against Birmingham City.

27 April – voted PFA Player of the Year.

2 May – voted Football Writers' Association Footballer of the Year.

17 May – he is voted Man of the Match as he wins second successive FA Cup with Arsenal, against Southampton.

29 June – wins the FIFA Confederations Cup with France, scoring the only goal in the final against Cameroon. Is named player of the tournament where he is top scorer with four in five games.

5 July – marries English model Nicole Merry.

25 November – Henry makes two and scores two as Arsenal thrash Inter Milan 5–1 in the San Siro to revive their Champions League hopes.

15 December – comes second in the FIFA World Player of The Year vote, behind Zidane.

22 December – finishes second only to Pavel Nedved in the voting for *le Ballon d'Or*.

28 December – voted France's Sports Personality of the Year in a poll organised by *Ouest-France*, the country's largest newspaper.

30 December – named French Footballer of the Year by journalists of *France Football* and former award winners.

2004: 10 February – scores his 100th [and 101st] Premier League goal against Southampton.

28 March – scores 104th Premier League goal against Manchester United to draw level with Ian Wright.

16 April – notches up his 150th Arsenal goal, as he scores four against relegation-bound Leeds United at Highbury.

25 April – voted PFA Player of the Year.

10 May – becomes the first person to be voted Football Writers' Association Footballer of the Year in successive years.

15 May – wins a second English Premier League title and Premier League Golden Boot, finishing the season with thirty league goals.

24 October – forty-nine-match unbeaten league run comes to an end in 2–0 defeat at Old Trafford.

20 December – finishes second in the FIFA World Player of the Year vote, behind Ronaldinho.

26 December – scores 128th league goal for Arsenal in 2–0 win over Fulham, puts him level with Ian Wright, but behind Cliff Bastin's total of 150.

2005: 3 January – appointed Ambassador Against Racism by FIFA president Sepp Blatter.

14 February – 200th Premiership appearance for Arsenal in 5–1 win over Crystal Palace.

9 March – scores 178th Arsenal goal in 1–0 win over Bayern Munich to go level with Cliff Bastin as Arsenal's second highest goal-scorer of all time.

May – finishes the season with twenty-five Premiership goals to win both the domestic and the European Golden Boots. The third time in four seasons he had picked up the English award and the first time anyone had won the European title in successive seasons.

21 May – watches from the stands as Arsenal beat Manchester United 5–4 on penalties after a dour 0–0 draw in the FA Cup final.

27 May – celebrates the birth of his first child, a beautiful baby girl named Tea.

18 October – becomes Arsenal's all-time leading goal-scorer after bagging two against Sparta Prague in the Champions League.

26 November – scores his 100th Premiership goal at Highbury in 3–0 win over Blackburn Rovers.

27 December – once again named as French Player of the Year.

2006: 14 January – scores a hat-trick in 7–0 demolition of Middlesbrough to equal Cliff Bastin's record of 150 league goals for Arsenal.

1 February – scores his 151st league goal for Arsenal in the 3–2 loss to West Ham at Highbury to break Bastin's record.

4 February – becomes first man to score 200 goals for Arsenal as he bags the second in the 2–0 win away to Birmingham City.

21 February – scores only goal of the game as Arsenal beat Real Madrid 1–0 in the Bernabeu.

27 April – named FWA Footballer of the Year for an unprecedented third time.

7 May – scores a hat-trick in the last ever game at Highbury. His three goals are the last to be scored at the famous stadium.

May – wins the English Golden Boot again with twenty-seven Premiership goals.

17 May – captains Arsenal in their first-ever European Cup final as the Gunners lose 2–1.